Flying

Self-portrait drawn in the autograph book of a family friend while lecturing on aerodynamics in Santander and anticipating his planned balloon exploration to 20,000 meters, July 1936. Later in the month the Civil War broke out and the balloon was cut up for rain gear.

Flying
The Memoirs
of a Spanish Aeronaut

Emilio Herrera

Translated by Elizabeth Ladd
Edited by Thomas F. Glick

University of New Mexico Press
Albuquerque

Library of Congress Cataloging in Publication Data

Herrera, Emilio, 1879–1967.
  Flying: the memoirs of a Spanish aeronaut.

  Bibliography: p.
  1. Herrera, Emilio, 1879–1967   2. Balloonists—Spain
—Biography.   I. Title.
TL620.H47A34   1984   629.13'092'4 [B]   84-2334
ISBN 0-8263-0752-3
ISBN 0-8263-0753-1 (pbk.)

Design by Milenda Nan Ok Lee

Manufactured in the United States of America.
International Standard Book Number 0-8263-0752-3 (cloth)
                                  0-8263-0753-1 (paper)
Library of Congress Catalog Card Number 84-2334.
First edition.

Contents

Illustrations

Figures

Photographs

Part I

The Memoirs of
Emilio Herrera

According to the statistical tables, for every hundred babies that came into the world on February 13, 1879—the day I was born—only one is still living, and with a life expectancy of only two years. So, it is time to gather together the principal memories I retain of my long and hazardous existence, to record the impressions it has made on me, the conclusions it has suggested, and the work I was able to accomplish, if all this is not to be buried and forgotten.

From the heights of my advanced age I survey a vast horizon stretching before the eyes of my memory, bounding a landscape of recollections where one can see gently rolling meadows and craggy outcroppings—a varied and uneven terrain of dark melancholy valleys, sunny regions, and luminous peaks rising high above the general level. Gazing over this panorama of my history, dominated by those bright pinnacles, I note the curious fact that they are spaced regularly at a distance of nine years from each other, as if my life had been subjected to a rhythm or a cyclic periodicity by some mysterious agent who predestined its evolution. So, in presenting my memoirs, I will treat my life as divided into these nine-year periods, marked by the pinnacles, or milestones, through which I successively passed.

Milestone 0: 1878
Age, less than one year

This milestone, the most important, is situated on the edge of the horizon, invisible to the eye of memory, but visible to the eye of reason. It represents the beginning of my existence, the moment in which certain lively acids, not by chance, but in obedience to universal law, combined to form proteins; and these, in turn, formed the neurons capable of receiving a quantity of energy condensed into a psychic focus that gave rise to the existence of my being.

A few months later, on February 13, 1879, my living body was born into the loving care of my parents at No. 37 on the old street of San Isidro, in Granada. My mother, Rita Linares, was an artist whose fine paintings had been awarded many prizes. My father, Emilio Herrera, colonel of the Infantry Regiment of the Antilles, was a lover of the visual and performing arts, as well as of the physical and chemical sciences. He had a home laboratory stocked with all the latest scientific equipment of the time—cameras, electrical devices, phonographs, microscopes, early motion picture projectors, magic lanterns—and with all this I was to serve as his assistant. My older sister, Rosario, completed our family in that happy period of my life.

The house where I was born had an Andalusian patio, with columns, potted plants surrounding a central fountain and a pillar with a phrenological head as its capitol. From the patio one had access to rooms through doors with stained glass panes and iron gratings, which I used to climb to reach the balconies of the first story, where there was a garden with a greenhouse, a central fountain with a marble dolphin that spouted water, boxwood hedges, fruit trees and two great magnolias taller than the house. This main floor contained the dining room, kitchen, bedrooms, my father's office and library and two living rooms for music and receiving company. The second story housed the physics and chemistry laboratories, a planetarium and a large room in the form of a theater where my father gave demonstrations of pres- tidigitation, magic and disappearing acts. On the third story was the tower with views of the Alhambra, the fields and the Sierra Nevada. That house made such an indelible impression on my memory that even now it is the setting for most of my dreams. The only mischief I ever engaged in in those days was to get up secretly at two or three in the morning, wander around the house and go up to the tower at dawn to drink in the spectacle of the stars paling and disappearing and the white clouds brightening over the Sierra Nevada.

I always had a very emotional temperament, especially as a child. It was impossible for me to hide my feelings. There was a little girl my age, a niece of one of our neighbors, called Mariquilla, who used to sing that song, *"Cigarras y chulas, las de Madrid,"* which made me break out in goose bumps. It was enough for someone to mention her name in front of me and I would blush. This was a source of great amusement to my sister, who contrived to talk about Mariquilla at dinner just to make me turn red.

Music moved me to tears, especially when my sister played the finale of the opera *Hernani* on the piano, where the protagonist, about to kill himself, says farewell to his newlywed bride, Elvira.[1] Often, seeing my father happy and making jokes, I had to retreat to a corner to hide my tears, thinking that, because of his age, he must die soon.

During my childhood Granada suffered three disasters in three consecutive years: 1884–1886. The first was the great earthquake of December 25, 1884.[2] I was running, mounted on a stick-horse, when a violent tremor shook the house, cracking the walls, and at the same time there was a subterranean rumble accompanied by the clatter of a sideboard loaded with dishes crashing to the floor in the next house. My mother, trembling, tried to calm me by saying, "Don't be afraid, it's only a cart passing in the street." As there were repeated tremors, though less severe, in the following days, the people of Granada didn't dare sleep under roofs, and camps were set up in the city's plazas. My parents slept in the house but my sister and I tried to sleep in an army tent in the garden until, at midnight, we heard the night-watchman's chant and, reassured, abandoned the tent and went into the house to sleep with our parents.

The second disaster was the cholera epidemic of 1885 which claimed thousands of victims.[3] I remember the cart for the dead, painted yellow, which went about collecting corpses from the houses. When the epidemic was at its peak I woke up one night crying *"Mama caca,"* which alarmed my parents enormously for diarrhea was the symptom of the beginning of the terrible disease. They fed me bread and rice and kept me in bed, taking all the prescribed precautions. My father, though he was friends with many doctors, never called any of them in as he was on bad terms with official medical practice, in which he did not believe. He had a better microscope than the ones at the Faculty of Medicine, and he used to acquire his slides in Paris. When the cholera epidemic came, he prepared one of these himself, using a little brush dipped in bitumen, and presented it at a meeting with the Dean of the Faculty of Medicine. The latter declared that he saw very clearly the *bacillus virgula,* and my father replied, "Well, I painted this *bacillus virgula* myself!" All his life my father behaved this way, and never followed doctors' orders.

During the epidemic the people of Granada kept up their morale and sense of humor. They used to tell this story: when one of the carts was unloading its funereal cargo at the cemetery, one of the "corpses" began to shout, "I'm not dead!," and the grave-digger replied, "Shut up, the doctor says that you are dead; do you think you know better than he does?" and he threw him into the communal grave. A friend of ours, a physician, told us that he had been summoned by a cholera victim and had asked the patient's wife what he had eaten. She said a raw cucumber, and the indignant doctor reprimanded her for giving him something that was absolutely prohibited during the epidemic. He prescribed medicines for the next day and when the wife asked what she should feed the patient, he said sarcastically, "Well, you can give him another cucumber." The next day the patient was much better. His wife had given him another cucumber, thinking the doctor had spoken in earnest. This was the only patient saved by the services of that doctor. The day after I got sick, a neighbor came to visit, and when he found out I was ill, he fled the house in a hurry. I was saved, but that gentleman died the following night along with most of the neighbors on the side of the street where he lived, opposite our house.

The third disaster was the flood produced by a rainstorm that caused the Darro River to rise so high that it ran through the city in a torrent, washing away the tiles from the roofs of the houses. I was standing on a balcony of our house when I saw a rush of water and mud coming from above and sweeping away tables, chairs, booths and other objects from the market in the Puerta Real. At the same time, another torrent was coming from below, the two colliding in front of our house. The pedestrians caught between the two had to climb up the iron grilles on the windows of the houses, a policeman was carrying a priest on his shoulders, and we were worried by the absence of my father. Finally, when it was already night, the doorbell rang and my sister pulled the cord that opens the door with such force that it broke, so she dashed downstairs to open it, forgetting that the ground floor was covered with a meter and half of water, and she fell into it, arriving at the door practically swimming to let my father in. In the coating of slime that covered the whole ground floor and walls of the house for days we saw the trails of snakes that had been washed down by the current.

But these three calamities were not what made the greatest impression on me in those happy days as a tranquil and obedient child. Another situation that terrorized me even more was created by the Nuño girls, twins of my age, Laura and Clara, daughters of a friend of my father. They were two real little devils, for whom I was a puppet of flesh and bone, victim of their pranks in the house and especially if they ran into me on the street. One day they grabbed me, each by a corner of my coat, and began to run, dragging me, one on either side, until they made me crash into a gentleman who was walking in the opposite direction, who defended himself from the collision with his walking stick. Another time, I was wearing a brand-new hat that I was very pleased with, and the girls snatched it and threw it into a ditch full of water, where it was carried away by the current.

Milestone 2: 1887
Age, 8 years

My parents had taught me reading and writing and some arithmetic without sending me to school, but when I reached the age of eight they decided to have a teacher give me lessons at home, to complete my primary education. This teacher, whose name was Don Rafael Giménez Herrera, gave me a preliminary examination, to determine the level of my knowledge and aptitudes, and after several questions and arithmetic calculations which I solved without difficulty, he posed the following problem, the first of its kind I ever had to solve in my life: "A flock of doves encounters a sparrow hawk, who asks how many of them there are. One of them answers: with these here, plus another flock the same size, plus half of those plus a quarter of these, plus you, sparrow hawk, we would number 100."

After a little mental calculation, I found the solution, thirty-six. This enthused the teacher, who went to tell my father that I was some kind of child prodigy who could solve first level equations without knowing algebra. My father, a great fan of mathematics, told of my prowess to all his friends, very proud to have a son who was a budding mathematician.

Don Rafael taught me until I was eleven years old, when I began secondary school at the Colegio de San Pablo. Since I had never been to school and had never been separated from my mother, my classmates regarded me as a dull child who didn't know how to play. The teachers, on the other hand, thought I was a model student, number one in every class with grades of A in every subject and honors in several.

In dealing with my classmates at school I developed one of my inherent character traits—loyal friendship to all, but without letting them dominate me or influence me by their decisions. This made me reject all suggestions that I smoke, though they put pressure on me by telling me it was a sign of manhood. Since I saw no advantage or pleasure in sucking on a cigarette, I was not even mildly tempted to follow their example; on the contrary, I felt satisfaction in realizing that I was able to act on my own will and not follow like a sheep. In fact, I have never smoked in all my life.

I received my diploma with outstanding marks in science, but with a miserable "satisfactory" in letters, because I had neglected those courses. So it was decided that I should pursue studies in architecture, like my ancestor Juan de Herrera, builder of the Escorial, given my aptitude for mathematics and drawing. In 1894 I entered the University of Granada to take courses in physics and chemistry, in preparation for my chosen career.

The professor of chemistry, Sr. Alonso, was a real fiend, the terror of all his students because of his rigid examinations. With him I experienced the first conflict of my life, due to another of my character traits—intolerance of injustice, whatever might be the consequences of this intransigence.

This professor gave us a problem in which he asked us to calculate the quantity of common salt that can be obtained from a given weight of chlorine. I wrote down the data for the problem but forgot to make note of the atomic weight of chlorine, a datum which I took from my chemistry book (35.5), and I solved the problem. When I arrived at the University I found that my answer differed from that of the rest of my classmates, and I saw that the difference was due to the fact that they had used 37 as the atomic weight of chlorine—the value given by the professor when he presented the problem. Accordingly, I attached a note to my work explaining that I had used 35.5 instead of 37 as the atomic weight of chlorine.

This note seemed to have stung the professor like a barb, and on the following day at the start of class he said, "There is a student who, having no confidence in the data I gave, has given a wrong answer because he used the wrong atomic weight for chlorine."

So I went to the library and consulted all the chemistry books it had. In every one the atomic weight of chlorine appeared as 35.5, the same as in all my books, including the *Annuaire du Bureau des Longitudes* for that year. I pointed this out in another note to the professor, and this brought his indignation to a head. He told the class: "If this student believes he knows more chemistry than I, let him prove it in his examination." All the students were terrorized, seeing that I had gambled with my career and probably lost it with my argumentativeness, and my father decided I had better change direction, abandoning architecture to pursue military engineering, like my grandfather, General José Herrera Garcia, one of the bright lights of the military engineering corps.

And so, the question of whether chlorine has an atomic weight of 35.5 or not decided the direction and development of the rest of my life.

Milestone 2: 1896
Age, 17 years

I left the University of Granada because of this incident at the end of 1895, and my father looked for a preparatory school where I could complete the studies required to enter the Army Engineering Academy at Guadalajara as quickly as possible. At the school in Granada directed by Colonel Gómez Tortosa, of the Engineering Corps, he was informed that the next examinations were in May of that year, but that my preparation could not be completed in less than two years.

Under these conditions I began my studies with three other students who already had two years of preparation—I envied them because their knowledge would permit them to enter the Academy in three months. These students were my age: Dávila, Peña and Cienfuegos. Together we pursued the preparatory course and when May arrived and they were preparing for the trip to Guadalajara, I decided I would like to go with them. I proposed to my father that I also present myself at the examination, not with the intent of passing, but to have some practice for the following year and become familiar with how the examinations were conducted. My father consulted with the headmaster, who was opposed to the idea because he was sure the other three would pass and to have a failure (mine) would reflect discredit on his school. But I persisted and the director, sure of my lack of preparation and sure I would fail, finally gave in on condition that there be as little talk as possible of my going.

So the four of us went, the others hopeful and sure of succeeding, and I certain of failure but wanting the experience. The exam consisted of three sections: one in algebra, one in geometry and one in French and drawing.

The first to be examined was Dávila, who was eliminated in the first exercise with his first error. The next day it was Peña's turn, who, already demoralized by what had happened to Dávila, did not answer any of the questions asked and was dismissed. Cienfuegos went next with the same fatal outcome. The following day I went, but my certaintly of not passing put me in a state of mind of absolute tranquility—I fully expected to return to Granada the next day with the others.

The exam began at nine in the morning. I looked at the first question and saw with surprise that I could answer it well enough. The professor deluged me with tricky questions which I answered in total calmness, and so he continued his attack and I my defense until seven at night, with a half-hour break for cookies and a glass of sherry. On one question I made a small error which I was able to correct hastily just as he was about to utter the fatal words, "You may be excused"; but as this did not happen again, he told me to come back the next day and the examination continued until seven at night, with no errors on my part, and I passed with the minimum score of 7.

The next day I took the second exam, answering all the questions correctly, and passed with a score of 9. The third exam, French and drawing, I passed without difficulty and received a score of 10. So it happened that, contrary to all expectations, the three candidates who were sure of being admitted failed, and I, who was sure of failing, and only went for the experience, succeeded.

This episode caused such a sensation at the preparatory school that they published announcements citing me as "accepted with only three months of preparation." My parents were delighted with my success. I proudly displayed my student uniform from the Engineering Academy. Nuño's daughters, grown up into splendid young ladies, stopped infuriating me with their pranks, impressed by my uniform and my sword.

In September I left for Guadalajara to begin my life as a student at the Academy. Like all my new classmates, I was taught reverence for the silver castles, the then glorious emblem of the Army Engineering Corps, the only military branch in Spain that had never revolted against the legally constituted government. We were also indoctrinated with the sentiment of military honor as it had been defined by General Almirante of our corps—we were convinced that a word of honor given obliged us to fulfil it even if it cost us our lives.

The hazing the new students were subjected to by the upperclassmen before we were granted the privilege of addressing them familiarly was short and, although annoying, not dangerous. We had to blow on a light bulb in the ballroom during a dance until it went out; brush yellow oil paint on one freshman's nose and blue on another and make them rub their noses together until both were green; make two blindfolded freshmen feed toast dunked in hot chocolate to each other. We pushed the smallest and most boyish looking of the freshmen through the revolving door at the orphanage. One tearful and frightened freshman with a Basque name was made to sing, between tears and sobs, "The Tree of Guernica." Another, named Barutell, sixteen years old and never separated from his mother before, was obliged to present himself one afternoon at the house of an upperclassman to receive orders. Barutell showed up punctually at the hour specified and was received by some young ladies he thought were the upperclassman's sisters, but when he entered they shouted at him, "What are you doing here? You're at the wrong address. Don't you know where you are? This is a whorehouse!" Poor Barutell crossed himself and fled to a corner trembling and praying until he was able to escape from this "den of iniquity." His father had a good laugh the following Sunday when he heard about his son's adventure.

My own hazing ordeal was very inoffensive. An upperclassman, on finding out I was from Granada, ordered me so say *culebra* [snake]. I said *"culebra"* and he asked me, "Aren't you Andalusian? Then say: *'culebra, culebra.'"* I said *"culebra, culebra, culebra."* He didn't know that the superstition about the word did not exist in Granada, but in Seville, where one must not say the word and must substitute *bicha* or *señora*, saying at the same time *"lagarto, lagarto"* (this means lizard but is used superstitiously as an expletive to ward off bad luck), and making a circular motion of the right hand with the index and little fingers extended.

After a couple of months of hazing we were "promoted" and were allowed to call all the upperclassmen by their first names—

the bonds of fellowship were cemented between them and the freshmen.

We were also soon included in the social life of the town, invited to dances at "La Peña," the Casino or in private homes of resident families of Guadalajara. In this group a little blond girl stood out from the rest whom we called "The Little Calf" (*El Ternerillo*). She was the daughter of Ricardo Aguilera, the Chief Engineer of Public Works in Guadalajara, and we students regarded her as our mascot. She amused us with her deviltry, playing with boys and climbing trees like one of them. We gave her coins for ice cream cones so she would sing, with a younger sister, songs from *El rey que rabió* [The Mad King],[4] and she entertained us with her aspiration to become a boy—she even said novenas to the Virgin asking for this miracle. Once at a masked ball for children where she was disguised as a little old lady she beat up a little boy her age who had the audacity to ask her to dance.

A few months into this period of my life I experienced my first great sorrow. Christmas vacation arrived and with it the pleasure of being able to spend the holiday with my parents in Granada, but my father died a few days before. My mother asked a family friend in Guadalajara to tell me the sad news, but she, on seeing how happy I was about my trip home, could not bring herself to do it, and entrusted the message to a friend who was traveling most of the way with me. This friend also found himself unable to tell me and I arrived in Granada without knowing about the tragedy. A cousin was waiting at the station who thought I knew everything, and when I asked him how my family was he replied "Everyone is well but I have not seen them since the day of the funeral." "What funeral?" I asked. Learning of the event so suddenly and seeing my mother and sister in those circumstances with no preparation was a blow which radically changed my conduct for the rest of the time I attended the Academy. My mother found herself in a difficult situation with regard to paying the costs of my education, and she had to part with some of her jewelry. She did this gladly, saying she was following the example of Queen Isabella, who sold her jewels so Columbus could make his voyage.

As for me, I changed from a conscientious and subservient student into one who was rebellious and unruly. A group of us used to dress up as peasants and go about at night stealing doorknockers and street signs, taking apart the clocks outside jewelry stores, and picking fights with night watchmen. Once we walled up the door of the priest who said mass at the Academy with bricks. These pranks resulted in my being arrested several times and failing two courses.

Once I had the opportunity to taste the champagne produced by the Widow of Cliquot, and it was so agreeable that I decided to write a passionate letter to that lady, enclosing a photograph of myself and proposing marriage on the condition that she give me one bottle of her champagne every weekday and two on Sundays and holidays. In a few days I received a reply from the house of Ponsardin Successeurs, in Rheims, which began, "Dear Sir: We have received your interesting letter . . ." and went on to state their regret that they could not communicate my proposal to the Widow of Cliquot because she had passed away eighty years before.[5]

I remember with amusement the answers given in class by Llombart, a student with a resonant voice who, in military arts class—in which he was an absolute dunce—was asked what honors had to be accorded to the Prince of Asturias when he arrived at a fortified town. He answered, "They fire a cannon at him twenty-one times." Another time he was asked what must be done with the dead on the battlefield before burial; not knowing how to answer, he looked around the class for help, and one student, passing his hand over his face, tried to indicate that the bodies had to be identified. But Llombart misunderstood and answered, "You have to give them a shave."

Another student named Padial—the only one who was married—had spent a bad night because the baby had not let him sleep. By the time the professor had called some students to the blackboard to review the lesson, he had fallen asleep at his desk. While they were writing, a student sitting next to Padial let out an explosive fart, breaking the silence of the class. The indignant professor shouted, "Whoever committed this outrage, stand up!" The guilty party nudged the sleeping Padial, who awoke and jumped to his feet, and, believing that the professor was angry because he had fallen asleep, apologized by saying, "Excuse me, Captain, but I couldn't help it—it's just that I had such a bad night—since we had a double assignment I didn't get a wink of sleep." The incident provoked laughter on the part of everyone except poor Padial, who had to suffer eight days of detention for something he didn't do.

The professor of drawing, Captain Calvo, lavished the most detentions on me. One day he became indignant because in the margin of my drawing—among other fanciful sketches I had traced—there was a bust of the goddess Venus. This was enough for him to impose eight days of detention without telling me why. When I reported to Colonel Casamitjana, Director of the Academy, having completed the detention, he asked me what the reason was. I told him I didn't know; looking at my list of punishments, he grew pale and angry and, his long white beard quivering, said: "I can't believe my eyes reading the shameful thing you have done. Get out of my sight!" I left confused and frightened, wondering what reason Captain Calvo had put on my list of punishments. When I asked to see it to inform myself, I read the motive he had given for my detention: "Committing indecent acts in drawing class."

In spite of the fact that I was a good draftsman—some of my drawings were even kept as examples in the Academy's collecton, including a view of Granada fortified with the system of "Tajamadas" designed by my grandfather, General Herrera García (a collection that was later destroyed, along with my grandfather's portrait, in a fire at the Academy),[6] the professor continued to pile on detentions and even suspended me twice from drawing.

I finally passed the third course of studies and was named Student Second Lieutenant. Proud of my stars, I hoped that the professors would have to treat me in a way appropriate to any officer. But the drawing professor singled me out with his incessant persecutions and, as I did not progress rapidly enough in completing the drawing he had assigned me (the interior of a cathedral), he ordered me to come every day so that he could see I was making sufficient progress. The first day I drew a fat curate in the middle of the cathedral, explaining that I believed it was a good idea to include this figure to liven up the picture. The professor made a disagreeable face but did not reprimand me. The following day I drew another, fatter curate beside the first one. At this the professor blew his top and sentenced me to indefinite detention until I finished the drawing. I, now an officer, entered the detention room and was indignant at having a soldier lock me up and take the key. I considered this an affront to my dignity, believing that any officer could stay under arrest on his word of honor not to escape, to the point of burning to death if there was a fire, before betraying his word by breaking arrest. But the actual situation—being locked up by a soldier—provoked me to escape however I could. I asked to go to the lavatory, and from a window twenty meters above the ground, I lowered myself down to the courtyard by bracing my elbows and knees against two walls that formed a narrow angle. The students who found out about my escape admired my prowess, but the academic consequences were very serious. In front of the entire Academy assembled in the courtyard they made an example of me by reading my punishment aloud. It said, "Having committed an offense that makes you un-worthy of wearing the honorable uniform of the Engineering Corps, you are served with a warning of expulsion and all its consequences." The consequences would be the end of my career and the necessity of finding a niche in civilian life, as the military would be closed to me.

At the order to break ranks after my harsh sentence had been read, the students burst out with cheers of *"Viva Herrera"* and, hoisting me on their shoulders, paraded around the courtyard. These displays of camaraderie which I always received from the rest of the students did not prevent me from refusing to give in to influences they wanted to exert on me. Just as I had refused to smoke when the students at the preparatory school wanted to introduce me to it against my will, I refused at the Academy to participate in decisions made by others with which I did not agree. For example, all the students decided to buy a whole sheet of lottery tickets and share the winnings—only I refused to play unless I was betting against all the others, and I was the only one to win.

My education completed, the traditional party for professors and students was held, marred by some unfriendly words due to the bad relations I had with some of the professors. We all pledged not to accept promotions for honors gained in war. I was promoted to Lieutenant and assigned to the Zapadores [Sappers] Regiment in Seville, where I applied my artistic sensibilities to painting post-cards which I sent to the most popular girls in Sevillian society, who corresponded with me most amicably. During this period I attended the 1900 Universal Exposition in Paris, living for one week in that aura of the Belle Epoque and signing my name in the guest book on the third floor of the Eiffel Tower, as was then the custom for those who performed the feat of climbing the 300 meters.

The memories I have of my life in Seville contain some anecdotes which typify the character of its people. One such episode occurred in a restaurant where two fellow officers (Benjumea and Alvarez) and I were eating fried fish. In the next room, separated from us by a partition that did not reach the ceiling, was a noisy group of men and women singing and playing the guitar. As we applied ourselves to the anchovies and *manzanilla*,[7] an olive pit, thrown from the direction of this neighboring room, landed on our table. We were commenting on this when another landed and then Benjumea, who was very short-tempered, picked up a chair and threw it over the partition. There was a tremendous clatter of breaking bottles and glasses and a loud thrum on the guitar. An instant later our door was thrown open and a man with a forbidding face appeared and said, "I'd like to know who the guy who threw the chair is," to which Benjumea answered: "Me! So what?" And the man said, "Well, it happens that you are a couple of good guys and now we invite you to come drink a few glasses of wine with us." We had no choice but to accept the offer of these boisterious merry-makers, who ended up becoming very good friends, after such an unpromising beginning.

After a year in Seville I was sent to the camp at Gibraltar with orders to build a battery on top of the Sierra Carbonara—an extremely important strategic position that, at a height of 300 meters, dominated the entire settlement and port of Gibraltar which lay at its feet.

Although I had heard that the English government considered the addition of even one soldier to the Spanish forces at Gibraltar an insult to the British Empire, I thought the construction of our battery on the Sierra Carbonara had been ordered by the Spanish government with the knowledge of the British, so I proceeded openly in choosing its location and orientation. One day an English officer arrived at the site on horseback, and I received him in a friendly manner, showing him my work and inviting him to have a glass of sherry. The officer went back to Gibraltar very pleased and must have reported what he found to the British Military Governor, who passed it on to his government, who in turn passed it on to ours in the form of a protest. The result was that a few days later I received a telegram from the Engineering section of the Ministry of War ordering me to halt construction immediately and return to Seville.

Soon after, I was sent to the Engineering Command at Melilla, where I was appalled at the disgraceful state our garrison was in. The officers could not leave the confines of the camp or even look through binoculars at the Moroccan residents without risking arrest by the commanding general, if some Moroccan accused them of having committed an infraction of this kind. On the other hand, the Moroccans were at liberty to come and go in the camp, to fire at the fortified border at night, and come into the plaza the next day selling eggs, chickens, and roosters.

In 1903 I attended the Practical School of Aerostatics in Guadalajara, receiving my "baptism by air" in several ascents in captive balloons and in a free balloon piloted by Pío Fernández Mulero.[8] We landed in a bull pasture near Soria, where we were invited by the mayor to attend a festival that was in progress.

Some of the officers at the Melilla garrison had formed a club, which we called the Apaches, led by Manuel Fernández Silvestre of the cavalry (later promoted to general, he was reported missing in the disaster at Annual in 1921).[9] There were three military physicans (Mariano Gómez Ulla, Sánchez and Jurado), one military judge (García Otemin), two artillerymen (José Barbeta and Felipe Zúñiga), two military engineers (Eusebio Redondo and myself), and a dog named Capona.

The parties we held in the military casino in honor of Yastasituntanneh, the god of the Apaches, were so noisy that they provoked protest on the part of all the peace-loving members. The Navy officers in charge of the warships at Melilla rivalled us in wildness, and the dinners we threw for each other, in the casino or on board some ship, always ended catastrophically with dishes and gear thrown from the balconies or overboard. This was especially true if someone had ordered a soufflé flamed with rum, as, upon seeing the flaming dish, all the rest of the diners, shouting "Fire! Fire!" proceeded to help put it out with bottles, glasses and syphons of wine and water until the poor soufflé ended up on the floor floating in a huge puddle of all the liquids from the table.

Our leader Silvestre, a man with a great sense of humor, had one shortcoming that caused him a lot of embarrassment: when something struck him as funny and he tried to contain his laughter, he would end up bursting into an uncontrollable fit of thunderous guffaws, to the alarm and consternation of all present. Twice in front of us Silvestre fell victim to one of these explosive outbursts of laughter. Once was at the circus in Melilla, where the Apaches were sitting in the first row of ring-side seats, and two clowns were performing a pantomime that Silvestre thought was very funny. One clown was sitting in a chair in the middle of the ring, playing an ocarina, while the other advanced stealthily on tip-toe behind him, preparing to whack him with a big stick. The audience was silent, but when the attacking clown was on the point of delivering the blow, Silvestre could not contain himself and burst into an explosion of laughter that alarmed everyone, including the two performers, who turned their startled faces to see what had happened, spoiling the comic effect of the skit. Another time, at an erudite lecture given by a military judge in the military casino, where the Apaches were again seated in the first row, Redondo told Silvestre a joke. The latter stifled his laughter for a few seconds but finally exploded; the offended speaker left the room refusing to listen to the pleas, excuses, and explanations of the despairing Silvestre.

One night, after a ceremony for Yastasituntanneh in the Casino, the Apaches decided to break into a house of prostitution that had denied us entry. Since the door was locked, we forced open a window and entered, first the dog, then the rest of us. The madam had locked herself in one of the rooms with her girls around her, and we stormed through all the others. In one of them was a woman lying in bed with the sheets pulled up to her chin; furious, she heaped insults on us and commanded us to leave. Just as we were about to do so, we noticed a suspicious bulge under the covers and, yanking them off, we uncovered a gentleman in his underwear who shouted irately, "This is no way to come into a decent house." This incident, which the madam reported to the police, had some consequences for me when I was assigned to the Air Station in Guadalajara, which I will tell about later.

The commanding officer of Melilla, General Segura, died that year, and was replaced by General José Marina Vega, whom I accompanied from Madrid to Melilla. This gave me a chance to tell him about the situation we officers found ourselves in there, completely ignorant of what was going on on the other side of

Mt. Gurugu because of the prohibition on going outside the camp limits, and I proposed that he authorize a few officers, including myself, to organize an expedition to the Moroccan camp. He approved, and artillery Lieutenant Barbeta and I got in touch with a Frenchman, M. Debrel, of the court of al-Roghi, which was then installed in Alcazaba de Zeluán, asking if we could pay a visit. The sultan, a rebel against the sultan of Fez, authorized the visit on condition that we come dressed as Moroccans, and accordingly we were supplied with horses and *askaris* to accompany us.[10]

We made the journey, singing as we passed through the villages, *"Allah in sha* [God be willing]—Muley Mohamed," so people would not mistake us for partisans of Abd al-Aziz, the sultan of Fez, Roghi's rival and brother. At the same time I was making a rough map of the territory we were crossing. We carried a cage of homing pigeons to communicate with Melilla during our stay in Zeluán.

Arriving at Alcazaba, we approached in a roundabout way so Roghi's chieftains wouldn't see us, but some noticed our arrival and warned the sultan that we were carrying a cage of pigeons, of which they immediately relieved us, giving them for safekeeping to the ladies of the harem.

We were shown to a tent and the next day Roghi received us in his tent surrounded by his ministers. Sitting on the ground, we answered Roghi's questions, with M. Debrel acting as interpreter, while I, with one hand in a pocket of my robe supplied with pencil and paper, tried to draw as faithful a portrait as possible of this curious personage. He was one-eyed, very dark-skinned and had a full black beard. Over his turban he had wound around his head a white lace mantilla, like the ones Spanish women wear to the bullfight. The first question he asked was if we were satisfied with General Marina, because if not he would send him the curse of Allah so he would die, as he had done to General Segura on finding out he had arrested an officer who was a friend of his. (This was, in fact, Lieutenant Barbeta, who was present, and who had been punished for looking at some Moroccan village women through binoculars.) We said General Marina was a very good man, and urged him to spare him forever from the curse of Allah.

After the interview we asked permission to return to Melilla, but he refused, saying we had to stay in Zeluán indefinitely until he decided otherwise. Our visit lasted seven days, during which time Roghi sent us couscous to eat, made with rancid lamb-fat.

The only thing we could not do was bathe, due to a total lack of water; instead of washing, we scrubbed our faces with a white stone. During our stay we witnessed this drama. One of Roghi's horses got into a fight with a horse belonging to one of his ministers. The minister tried to separate them by swinging a stick, and unfortunately hit Roghi's horse. Roghi then ordered that the minister be beaten, and one of the blows to his head knocked out one of his eyes. In that condition he was thrown to the bottom of a dry well where his family threw him crusts of bread to eat.

At the end of a week, the Minister of the Treasury, a very tall black man, came to visit us with a big straw basket full of *duros*, saying that on behalf of Roghi, who thanked us for the gift we had brought (a Browning pistol) and because he knew that Spanish officers were badly paid, he was presenting us each with twenty duros.[11] We told him we were very well paid and would not accept any gift of money, whereupon he said if we disdained the sultan's gift he would order our heads cut off. In view of this threat we decided not to reject the the sultan's gift, but the Minister told us it was the custom to tip the members of the government, so we were each left with only one of the twenty duros.

Authorized to return to Melilla, we went back by the way of the Mar Chica and the Restinga and told General Marina about our expedition and how we had saved his life.[12] We sent Roghi a tapestry embroidered in gold from the Chinese shops, with a letter saying that with the duros he had given us and a little more, we sent him this gift and thanked him for the fine welcome he had extended to us. He wrote back saying he was sending us a horse as a gift, but it never arrived.

With the sketches I had made in the countryside I was able to draw a map of Melilla's surroundings, which were until then unknown. This map was sent to the Minister of War, and I received an honorarium for it. I also sent the portrait of Roghi that I had drawn in my pocket during the audience. It was evidently a fair likeness, because when it was shown to a Moroccan he exclaimed, "Es Sidi!" raising his hand with the index finger pointing up.

During my assignment in Melilla I had to go to El Peñón de Vélez in Gomara to do some work on military buildings. When the boat arrived at El Peñón we could not dock. In total darkness except for the rotating beam of the lighthouse, a little boat appeared to pick me up with the strangest crew imaginable: a priest with a guitar, a man in a *chambergo* hat with a large feather, and two or three sailors with macabre faces, all singing and drinking wine.[13] I debarked with these people at El Peñón and saw that the one with the *chambergo* was the lieutenant quartermaster assigned there. He told me that because all his life he had wanted to wear a hat like those of the Flanders Regiment, he had asked to be assigned to El Peñón where he could satisfy his whim. The sailors were prisoners from the penitentiary there, one an old bandit from the Sierra Moreno. In El Peñón I met the artillery lieutenant who commanded the battery and who had been a classmate of mine at the Engineering Academy from which, failing his courses, he had transferred to the artillery. This lieutenant was such an alcoholic that he never spoke to anyone and dedicated himself solely to the study of the geometry of n dimensions. Only on this topic, which began to interest me, could I talk with him, to the astonishment of the rest of the inhabitants of El Peñón. That was how my interest in hypergeometry and hypermechanics was born, sciences to which I have dedicated myself all my life.

Because of a Mediterranean storm that made it impossible for me to return for many days, I had to spend Christmas in El Peñón, attending midnight mass said by the priest. After the mass, the priest went to the libatory festivities which lasted until dawn, and when it was time to say mass again he couldn't stand up. We all advised him to go to bed but he insisted on saying mass, which he tried to do but couldn't finish. Unfortunately, this incident was reported to the Bishop of Málaga, who defrocked the priest. A similar misfortune befell the artillery lieutenant soon after. He celebrated his saint's day (San Justino) by drinking more than usual, and in an excess of enthusiasm, ordered a 21–gun salute. The noise of the cannon alarmed the commanding general of Melilla—he thought the Moroccans were attacking. When he learned the source of the shots, he ordered the officer responsible for the false alarm arrested.

Above left: Emilio Herrera at age two in 1881.

Above right: Herrera (left) with his father in the garden of their house in Granada.

Left: Herrera as a young cadet.

Herrera (second row, third from left) at the Academy of Army Engineers. Pedro Vives is seated in the first row, third from right.

Spanish military observation balloons, Júpiter, Marte and Urano, at Burgos to observe the solar eclipse of 1905.

Above: Balloon ascent in Spain in 1905.

Below: Herrera (center) and Jesús Fernández Duro (right) preparing for an ascent.

Above left: A rough landing in which Herrera is pitched from the gondola.

Above right: War duty in Melilla, North Africa, in 1909.

Above: Herrera with his oldest son Petere, about 1912.

Left: Pedro Vives, Alfredo Kindelán, and Herrera (standing, left to right) with Emilio Jiménez Millás (seated right) in the basket of the dirigible *España,* about 1913.

Above: Dining with Princess Isabel (third from left), King Alfonso XIII's aunt.

Below: Herrera (center) in Lima, Peru, with Gen. Wilhelm von Faupel (in uniform) in November 1928.

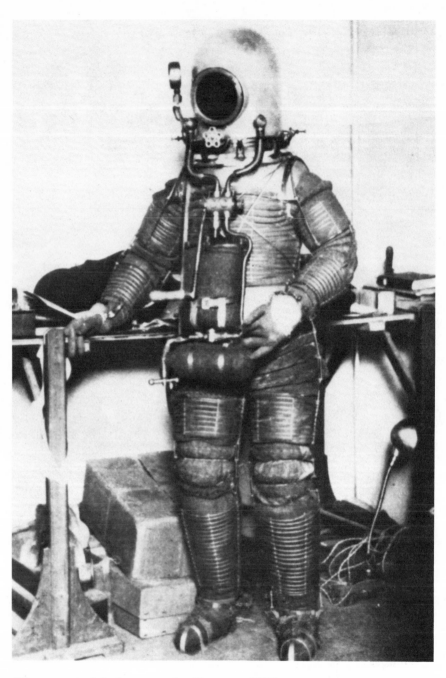

The space suit being worn by Herrera, 1936.

Left: Colonel Herrera, age fixty-six.

Below: At work in his study in Madrid.

Above: Herrera with the space suit helmet, Madrid, spring 1936.

Left: In his Paris apartment at age eighty-four.

Milestone 3: 1905
Age, 26 years

The military aerostatic service, under the command of Colonel Pedro Vives, was preparing for a group of free-flight scientific balloon ascents on the occasion of the total eclipse of the sun on August 20, 1905, which had to be observed from the highest altitude possible in order to compare the results with those obtained on the ground. The observations, both on the ground and in the air, would be made at Burgos, one of the points where the duration of the total eclipse would be the longest. Two military balloons had been prepared, and the Spanish aeronaut Jesús Fernández Duro offered to contribute his own balloon, *El Cierzo* [North Wind], on the condition that he be allowed to participate in the ascent.[14] A number of Spanish and foreign scientific personalities had been invited, and as they wanted me to participate to make a drawing of the solar corona, I had to get a license to pilot a free balloon before the date of the eclipse. I made four ascents, one of them an examination, which, together with the one I had made in 1903 completed the five required for the license.

Three balloons were chosen for the observation of the eclipse. The first was piloted by Colonel Vives, accompanied by the German aeronaut, professor and world altitude champion Arthur Berson as co-pilot and observer. The second had Captain Alfredo Kindelán as pilot and Professor Augusto Arcimis, director of the Spanish Meteorological Observatory, as observer.[15] I piloted the third, with Fernández Duro as co-pilot. I was also to draw the solar corona and study the phenomenon—then a mystery—of the "flying shadows," which some attributed to solar radiation, others to diffraction on the surface of the moon, and others to phenomena produced by the earth's atmosphere. These consisted of alternating bands of light and shadow observable at the beginning and end of total eclipse, eight or ten centimeters wide, wavering, and running in a direction parallel to the narrow solar slit visible at those moments. To facilitate observation of this phenomenon, my balloon was equipped with a board, a white square one meter and a half on a side, suspended horizontally below the basket.

At the hour of the eclipse, the first and second balloons rose without difficulty, but when I cast off, a few minutes before the beginning of totality, I noticed that the balloon was not gaining altitude in spite of my casting off ballast to accelerate the ascent. The cause of this delay was that, as we began to rise, the white board had caught the hilt of one of the soldiers' swords and unsheathed it, and it was on the point of breaking loose and falling on the heads of those below like a new sword of Damocles. The soldiers were making an effort to reach it and we were desperate because the total eclipse was about to begin above us and we couldn't see it because the sky in Burgos was covered with clouds. Finally the sword fell to the ground without wounding anyone and we began to ascend. We passed rapidly through the cloud cover, throwing off as much ballast as possible, but, to our dismay, we saw that above this was another, even thicker layer of clouds. After a quick consultation we decided to throw off all the remaining ballast; without it, we would just have to manage to land as best we could. The balloon, disencumbered of extra weight, entered the clouds at 5,000 meters, plunging us into profound darkness and despair that at that moment the total eclipse must be starting.

Suddenly, the most marvelous spectacle imaginable broke before our eyes. The cloud layer pierced, in the dark star-filled sky the solar corona glittered, ringing the black disc of the moon over a sea of violet colored clouds. We could see the earth in shadow at the bottom of an abyss five kilometers deep; all was surrounded by a luminous horizon where the moon's shadow, fleeing eastward, did not reach. This vision was so splendid that my companion began to jump up and down in the basket, shaking it and disturbing the drawing of the corona I was making by the light of an electric bulb fixed to my helmet.

As soon as totality was over, at the moment the "flash" or first margin of the sun appeared, I looked at the white board to see the "flying shadows," but I didn't see anything. Then Fernández Duro shouted, "Look at our hands!" And in fact, our hands and all the objects we had were covered with narrow stripes, about a centimeter wide, alternately light and dark, undulating from one side to the other, and generally parallel to the brilliant ray of sunlight visible at the edge of the moon, which had a moment ago obscured it totally. For the first time there was proof that the mysterious phenomenon of the "flying shadows" was produced by our atmosphere, since at an altitude of 5,000 meters—that is, when the mass of air the sun's light had to penetrate was half of that necessary to reach the earth—the width of the stripes was reduced to a tenth part. In an account I sent to the astronomy observatory at San Fernando I presented an explication of this phenomenon as produced by the interference of the sun's rays, which are very close to each other, as they travel through layers of air of different density—a phenomenon of the same order as the origin of the scintillation of the light of the stars.

After the eclipse was over our balloon, whose descent we could not control because we had no ballast, remained in equilibrium for a few hours and then descended slowly until it touched earth, assisted by some peasants near the town of Villasar de Herreros, in the Sierra de la Demanda, to the north of Burgos. The towns-people and their neighbors received us with enthusiasm, listening to the fantastic tale my companion told them about our journey— he told them we had flown so high that we had seen the eclipse from the other side, with the sun covering the moon. They helped us recover the balloon, found us a cart to transport it to the nearest railway station, invited us to supper, and put us up for the night in the town hall. They entertained us with a serenade, singing a verse that went: "We are all very happy, the town of Villasar, you came from the sky, and safely here you are."

The friendship that developed between Fernández Duro and myself during that ascent led to our participation, together, in the Grand Prix Competition of the French Air Club, which was to take place in Paris in the same year, 1905, one of the most im-portant years of my life. Twenty-two balloons from several countries participated in this competition, piloted by the most celebrated aeronauts in the world. Ours was the only Spanish balloon entered. The departure of the balloons took place in the Tuilleries gardens in Paris, around the edge of the lake. Strong prevailing winds made handling at the take-off difficult, and one balloon, half-inflated, was swept away by the wind and fell into the lake. When we were given the signal to take off, I was in charge of the altimeter and Fernández Duro handled the ballast, casting it off as I instructed. At once we found ourselves in the clouds, so low they touched the rooftops, and I saw that the altimeter indicated we were descending, so I asked that ballast be cast off. But the altimeter showed that we were still descending, and, by now alarmed, I asked for more ballast to be cast off, until blue sky appeared above us. The balloon ascended so rapidly that we passed through the cloud cover quickly. At this point I realized the cause of my error: the gradations on the altimeter, which we had bought in Paris, were reversed from the direction of those we were accustomed to using, so that when I thought I was reading descent, it was really ascent. This mistake of mine contributed in large measure to our success, because our balloon, very lightweight from the beginning, reached a high altitude where it remained stable all night, and we enjoyed the spectacle of a splendid starry sky with a full moon over a white sea of clouds drifting below that prevented us from seeing the ground or knowing in what direction we were moving. We only knew that we were being carried at high velocity. Through the clouds we could hear the sound of a real hurricane raging on the earth below us.

At midnight another balloon emerged from the clouds and rose to our altitude. From the basket they asked in French, "Who are you?" We answered, "Duro, Herrera," and they asked, "Spanish?" and we replied, "Who are you?" Then before they had time to respond their balloon descended and disappeared into the clouds.

So we passed the night without having the slightest idea if we were moving north or south, east or west, or if we were over land or sea. At dawn, when we expected to receive a boost from the sun—as it heated the balloon up it should have allowed us to gain altitude and prolong the trip—a black cloud appeared above us and flakes of snow started to fall. This soon developed into heavy snow that weighed the balloon down considerably, causing it to descend in spite of our efforts to keep it up by casting off all our remaining ballast. Passing through the clouds on our forced descent, we found ourselves flying eastward at lightning speed, first crossing over some snow-covered mountains and then over a snowy plain dotted with scattered trees and crossed by a few roads. We were flying at a speed of 100 kilometers per hour and we could not control the balloon's descent because we had no more ballast to cast off. The braking anchor, on a 100–meter rope, skidded through the snow, hardly slowing us down, so we decided to throw out the anchor on the 15–meter rope. This one, as it crossed a road, hooked onto a cart and overturned it, causing the balloon to pause momentarily and dashing the basket against the ground. As soon as the anchor came loose from the cart we resumed our dizzying flight until it caught once more, this time on the eaves of a roof built of wooden rafters covered with brush and stones on top of a little house, uprooting it and leaving the house uncovered and causing the basket to bang into the ground again. Loose once more, the balloon continued on its unbraked course and I saw with horror that an enormous tree with antler-like branches was advancing towards us like an express train. The crash was terrible. One branch pierced the basket, and the balloon, brought to an abrupt halt, burst like a hot chestnut, its cloth fluttering in the hurricane winds. We were stranded in the treetop, unable to move, tangled up in balloon cords and tree branches, until some men and women, all wearing high boots, came to help us get down from the tree which, with a few blows of the axe to the lower part of its trunk, fell to the ground along with the now empty balloon.

We could not understand the language they spoke, so to find out where we were we showed them a map, but these people had never seen a map and were unable to clarify the situation. Finally the schoolteacher from the next town pointed out our location with his finger. The town was called Weisskirchen, in Moravia, twelve kilometers from what was then the Russian border, and the snowcapped mountains we had crossed were in Bohemia.[16]

In order to retrieve the balloon, Fernández Duro drew them a picture of a cart, but it was so badly done that none of them could figure out what we wanted, so I, having better pictorial talents, drew another cart with mules and all, which was easily understood. They brought a cart from the town and then I drew them a picture of a train with smoke spewing from the locomotive, to let them know we wanted to go to the railroad station, and finally I drew a telegraph office complete with wires, and they understood that we wished to send a telegram. With some of our gold Louis (French coins that we carried as a form of international currency), we paid these good people for the use of the cart, the telegram and the train tickets, and compensated the owners of the overturned cart and unroofed house for damages.

When we arrived at the station in Vienna, we read in the papers that so far all of the balloons had landed in France. In one of them Santos Dumont had broken a leg, and only two were reported missing—that of the Frenchman Jacques Faure and ours.[17] As we were about to board the train for Paris we found ourselves face to face with Faure and his companion and immediately the four of us got down on hands and knees on the floor of the station platform with a map of Europe spread out, calculating the distances from Paris to our respective landing sites with a measuring tape. Faure's balloon had been behind us and had therefore been able to take advantage of the morning sun's extra boost, rising above the snow storm that had knocked us down and landing more to the south, in Hungary, beating us by a distance of 200 kilometers. They won first prize and we were awarded second. We had covered a distance of 1086 kilometers at an average speed of 87 kilometers per hour.

The French Air Club received us in triumph, gave us the second prize, which consisted of a medal and some aeronautical instruments, and the French Governor honored us with the cross of the Legion of Honor, Knight's rank. An account of this flight was published in the magazine *L'Aérophile* with one of my drawings (Figure 1), and we gave a lecture at the Air Club.[18] Queen Cristina was very interested in the details of this flight which had taken us to her country of origin, and when I told her where we had landed, she said, "I was born there," and I answered, "Madam, I was reborn there!"

Fernández Duro and I weren't satisfied with the success of that trip and began preparations for another one to try to beat the world distance record; we would leave Barcelona in a northeasterly direction when there was a low pressure area in France and high pressure over the Mediterranean. As we would have to cross the Gulf of Lyon at low altitude we furnished the balloon with two coco-fibre ropes, each 100 meters long, which would float on

Figure 1. A bruising landing for a second place finish in the 1905 Grand Prix Competition of the French Air Club.

the water and make it unnecessary to use up ballast in the first part of the trip. We set up our balloon in the gas factory in Barcelona, so we could inflate it when meteorological conditions were propitious for our project. But the Barcelona papers, informed of our intentions, announced every morning that the balloon would leave that same afternoon, so every afternoon an enormous crowd gathered around the gas factory, leaving, disappointed, at dusk, only to reappear the following day.

But the wind kept blowing inland for weeks on end, making our departure impossible and our situation became the object of sarcastic jokes on the part of the public who never got to see the *bomba* (Catalan for balloon) take to the air. At the time there was a zarzuela in vogue called *El arte de ser bonita* [The Art of Being Pretty], in which a chorus of fat sopranos sang, "Because the fatty, the fatty, the fatty, never goes anywhere and never will," and the crowd sang to us every afternoon as they left, bored with waiting,

"Because the balloon, the balloon, the balloon, never rises and never will."

One afternoon we were nearly lynched by an impatient and angry crowd. Although the low wind was from the sea, we suspected that at about 100 meters there was a favorable current, and we released a small balloon of the type bought for children at the Thursday bazaars, to see which way the wind was blowing higher up. But the crowd, seeing that silly toy balloon, thought we were making fun of them and burst out with hisses and insults until we had to call the police to protect us.

Finally, one afternoon a wind came up that, although not blowing out to sea, which was what we needed, was blowing parallel to the coast, and by this time sick and tired of waiting, we decided to leave. We drifted above the buildings located on the coast, with our long coco-fiber ropes trailing across the roofs. A photographer had set up his camera on a tripod, and was taking pictures of the balloon as it passed over one of the houses, when one of the ropes, passing over the roof, hit him and knocked him and his tripod to the ground. He quickly got up and set up the tripod again, when the second rope dealt him another violent blow, knocking him down again. This time we saw him on the ground with his camera, not even trying to get up for fear that more ropes were coming to knock him over again.

Once, the balloon dropped dangerously close to the crowd and we had to throw off an entire sack of ballast, which fell next to one of the editors of *El Diario de Barcelona*, who then wrote in an article we read on our return, "If the sack had fallen on my head, it would have served me right."

Finally the balloon passed out over the water, stabilized by its ropes, and travelled very slowly parallel to the coast towards France. At midnight it veered eastwards, entering the Gulf of Lyon, where it paused, then resumed progress to the south, a direction we categorized as "fishward," since if we continued on that course we would have ended our flight among the fishes. But after describing a great loop during the night the balloon began moving west towards the French coast, passing extremely noisily over the roofs of Salces, uprooting roof tiles with its ropes, and knocking against chimneys with a zinc box that hung from one of them (we had carried this to weight the basket with sea water against the boost of the morning sun's heat and were unable to release it because it had gotten stuck). To make matters worse, we were singing and playing the *Marseillaise* on an accordion we had on board. All the dogs of Salces barked furiously at us and all the inhabitants were rudely awakened. Past the town, we crossed a plowed field whose owner pointed a shotgun at us and shouted, "Stop that balloon or I'll shoot you down!" We landed between Perpignan and Narbonne, gave the accordion to a boy who helped us retrieve the balloon and returned to Barcelona having failed to beat the distance record but having made the first maritime flight using cocofiber stabilizers. The Air Club of Berlin awarded us their medal of the year with the motto, *Audentes coelus adiuvat* [Heaven helps the daring].

As had happened nine years before, this period of my life was marked by a great sorrow—the death of my mother in Granada—and I was not able to be with her in her last hours because a heavy Mediterranean storm prevented travel between Melilla and the peninsula.

My service in Africa over, I petitioned to be assigned to the air station in Guadalajara, commanded by General Vives, who had always honored me with his appreciation. Also at Guadalajara was Commander Rojas, master technician of the air station (who had been ill from the effects of a treatment against the bite of a rabid dog) who also supported me.[19] But Captain Calvo, my old drawing professor, was there too, and he opposed my nomination and considered me insubordinate, especially after receiving during my first months at the air station a police complaint against me for damages caused in a house of prostitution.

But I was finally appointed, as had been my wish since graduating from the Academy, to the aereostatic service in Guadalajara. My parents were dead, my sister was married and I was a confirmed bachelor. Alone and free, I dedicated myself totally to my favorite diversion—flying balloons, officially or privately. I resumed my old pranks whose victims were certain society people in Guadalajara, among whom I acquired a bad reputation. One evening at the theater I noticed a blond girl sitting a few rows away who reminded me of someone I had known ten years earlier. I realized that she was none other than *El Ternerillo*, the little girl who used to amuse us with her songs and mischief when I was a freshman at the Academy. I kept looking at her out of curiosity and she returned my gaze, which led me to repeat the experiment, with equal success. After a little mental calculation in which I determined that there wasn't a disproportionate difference in our ages, I made a firm decision to renounce all my anti-matrimonial convictions and make the "Little Calf" my life's companion. There were many obstacles to be overcome, not the least of which was the unfavorable impression conveyed to my intended's family by others. The mothers of other eligible girls went so far as to tell their daughters they would rather see them dead than married to the likes of me.

This struggle touched off several outrageous incidents that, while adding to the bad opinion proper people already had of me, at the same time enhanced my image as man of mischief and bravado that seemed to appeal to the girl I desired. I found out that her name was Irene and that after her childhood in Guadalajara she had attended the Ursuline School in Madrid, where she had been a rebellious student; her memories of the school were as bad as mine were of the Academy of Engineers. She demonstrated an absolute incompatibility with the multiplication tables, but had a talent for writing original stories. Once she got her name on the "black list" by bringing an enormous live grasshopper to school and playing with it at her desk, a long string about its neck to keep it captive. This aroused the curiosity of all those around her, and soon the nun noticed the commotion and ordered her to hand over the object she had in her hand immediately. At this Irene put the insect on the floor and walked very solemnly and with many pauses towards the teacher, leading the grasshopper like a dog behind her and provoking gales of laughter from the class. When she reached the front of the room she put the grasshopper on the table, and the nun let out a scream of fright, flew into a rage, and ordered Irene to get rid of the loathesome animal. Naturally that month, as every month—sometimes for more serious infractions—Irene got a zero in conduct on her report card.

During this period I made numerous balloon ascents (about seventy), some "comfortable" (without overturning the basket), some "good" (overturning the basket), and others "lucky" (getting dragged or other accidents). These terms are just a few of those in the official nomenclature describing descents, which is too lengthy to relate here in its entirety.[20]

I made one of these trips because I wanted to spend a pleasant Christmas Eve (*nochebuena*) alone in the air. I left the gas factory in Madrid at 10 P.M., seen off by some friends, including Kindelán, who brought me some candy bars to eat on my flight. In fact, this Christmas Eve had nothing good about it; it was totally dark, cold, and threatening rain. As soon as I cast off I was plunged into the most profound darkness, and soon it began to rain, which made the balloon descend until it practically touched the ground, but there was no wind. White objects loomed up out of the ground— they were the tombstones of the San Lorenzo Cemetery, I later confirmed. I threw off ballast to get out of this macabre place, and found myself in darkness once more until the balloon began to descend again, at first slowly, but then at full speed, in spite of my casting off ballast. The basket touched down, and I found myself surrounded by a group of men and women carrying *zambombas* [rustic drums] and wine skins, who were celebrating Christmas Eve in the Pradera de San Isidro. They had been pulling on the control rope of the balloon until they brought it to earth. They offered me a drink and insisted that I get out of the basket and go with them, which I resolutely refused to do. Then they tried to pull me out with such force that I had to threaten them with a revolver to make them let me go. Finally a woman shouted, "Let go of him and I hope he kills himself!" and I found myself free of these overenthusiastic Christmas revelers.

I passed the rest of the night in darkness at high altitude, wrapped in my greatcoat, and drenched with the water that streamed in any icy shower from the appendix of the balloon onto my head. At seven in the morning, still in darkness, I landed in the snow covered mountains of the Sierra de Guadarrama, and when dawn broke a shepherd who was less than ten years old came to help me collect the balloon and find a cart to transport it to the station at Cercedilla. Thirty years later, while I was visiting at the house of Juanito La Cierva, the butler, an aloof, bearded man wearing an elegant frock coat, greeted me by asking if I had once landed on Christmas Day in the Sierra de Guadarrama. When I said yes, he responded, "Well the shepherd who assisted you was I." On All Souls' Eve, the first of November, I made a nocturnal ascent from Guadalajara. The view of the countryside was extremely strange and moving, with all the village cemeteries lit up with thousands of little lights to the limits of the horizon, in otherwise total darkness.

Another flight made under peculiar circumstances had been

arranged to give a newly appointed captain his baptism by air. The balloon was all ready and the captain and I in the basket when a squall came up that made it impossible to stabilize the balloon on the ground. The wind threatened to carry it off in spite of the soldiers' efforts to control it. Because of the situation, Colonel Vives ordered the new captain to get out of the basket and told me to go up alone. Once I was in the air I remembered that the captain, as the older of the two of us, had been the one carrying the money for the landing, and I had only a *duro* in my pocket.

After the flight, I landed on a plateau in the province of Guadalajara in a field where a group of priests from the nearby villages had gathered to eat a paella. The priests and some peasants came to help me retrieve the balloon, but I only accepted help from the priests, saying it was a very ticklish job. The real reason was to avoid having to give tips, which was impossible since I didn't have any money. They invited me to have paella with them, and the owner of a nearby house came to offer me—gratis—a cart, into which he, the priests, and I loaded the balloon and took it to the station. There, by showing the flight plan I carried, I was able to ship the balloon to Guadalajara and obtain a second class ticket without having to pay anything. In the station in Madrid I remembered that I still had my one duro, and it occurred to me to continue first class by paying a supplement. When the train started I asked the conductor to change my ticket from second to first class and, with very bad manners, he asked me why I hadn't informed him before we left the station. I said because I hadn't seen him, and he rudely answered, "Well, you didn't look very hard because I was right here." At this point, fed up with his impertinence, I said, "Then it was because I didn't feel like it." He responded angrily, "In that case you have to pay double the difference." "All right," I said, "Charge me double," and I handed over my only duro in triumph, which he threw back saying, "This duro is counterfeit." Fortunately I was friends with the owner of the restaurant at the station in Guadalajara and when we arrived I asked him to lend me a duro to pay the strict conductor.

On another solo ascent I had a "good" landing, that is, one where the basket overturned, leaving me on the ground enveloped in cords, instruments, and sacks of ballast, unable to move. Finally I was able to untangle myself, and raising my head from the ground I found myself surrounded by twenty little girls with their schoolteacher. When I could sit up, I asked one of the girls, "Manolita, recite the lesson on aerostatic balloons for me," and the child, blushing, said promptly, "Aerostatic balloons. Aerostatic balloons are based on the principle of Archimedes. They are filled with a gas lighter than air—hot air, combustible gas, hydrogen, or helium . . ." and she continued to recite some not so commonly known facts of aerostatic science. I congratulated the teacher effusively.

On one of the maneuvers we conducted over the Pyrenees, I made a free ascent from Pamplona, accompanied by Lieutenant Balbás, also a pilot, towards the east, traversing the entire mountainous zone of the high Pyrenees.[21] After using nearly all our ballast, we cast off the braking rope in the bottom of a valley that narrowed into a true canyon, with vertical walls 500 meters high. A gusty wind came up that battered the balloon against these gigantic walls, putting a spin on it like a billiard ball. Throwing off all our remaining ballast, we managed to rise up from the bottom of this dead-end alley, appearing on a high plain where there were two villages, Espierva and Diesa, whose inhabitants witnessed a balloon emerging from the bottom of a gorge instead of coming down from the sky in the usual manner. These people, who had never seen any balloon at all, believed that ours was a ship that had escaped from the sea, an idea enhanced by the fact that when the balloon split open on landing, it discharged a violent blast, shooting streaks of flame all around us. Balbás and I were unable to move, with empty sacks and ropes on top of us on an angle. Balbás, who had been educated in France as a child and always spoke French in awkward situations, shouted "Ecoute! Je ne peux pas bouger," and I, following his example, replied, "Moi non plus."

Finally the village people arrived, people who had never seen a cart—the only way they could get to us was by goat path—and they helped untangle us, fold up the balloon and put it in the basket, cover it and padlock it as if we were going to send it by rail, and push it over the cliffs to the bottom of the valley, where there was a town called Bielsa from which it was possible to travel by mule. We descended by goatpath, and in Bielsa we took the balloon out of its basket again and organized an expedition with four mules: one for the balloon cloth, one for the empty basket, one for the instruments, and one for us. Before undertaking the trek to the nearest railroad station we tried to get a drink at the inn in Bielsa, where we asked the innkeeper if she had beer. She said yes, and when we asked what kind, she said all kinds. So we asked for two Aguila dark bocks, and she actually brought us two glasses of water with two white envelopes of bicarbonate and two blue ones of citric acid.

I made another interesting ascent from Guadalajara with Lieutenant Gordejuela. When night fell over La Mancha, we dropped the braking rope without realizing we were heading for a telegraph line. On reaching a telegraph line one of two things can happen, depending on wind velocity and the amount of rope thrown out: either the rope passes over the wires, or else it winds itself around them several times. In this case the latter happened. The rope wound around the telegraph wires and the balloon was caught, agitated by the wind. This situation was aggravated by the fact that the telegraph line ran alongside a railroad bed, which was on an embankment. The wind was blowing across it in such a way that our rope intercepted the path of the train. There we were, already in darkness, unable to to disentangle the rope, when we saw the lights of a train approaching. We were horrified because the rope, if it became entangled in the locomotive's wheels, could derail it and cause the whole train to fall off the embankment. Our only recourse was to cut the rope where it joined the balloon. We watched anxiously as the train passed over it where it lay on the tracks, but it did not get caught in the wheels. We finally breathed easily when the train had passed by without apparent interference.

The balloon, freed of the weight of the brake rope, reached an altitude of 6000 meters by dawn, offering us a magnificent view of all Andalusia, with the whole coast of North Africa visible and the Sierra Nevada at our feet, recognizable only by the white dots of its highest peaks, and the Mediterranean and Atlantic united in the Straits of Gibraltar, all under a pure blue sky. We landed near Granada, where my sister and her husband and children lived, and they put us up in the house of my childhood.

I could go on recalling many more free balloon ascents on the Peninsula, each one different from the others, leaving from the aerostatic park in Guadalajara, or the gas factories of Madrid or Barcelona, or from other points where ports had been established. Once I crossed Las Hurdes at night; another time I fell into the

Beira Baixa in Portugal; on another trip, leaving from Barcelona in a distance competition, I reached the Pyrenees. and, gaining altitude to pass over them, I ran into a high north wind that would have sent me back to Barcelona, so I brought the balloon down near the border. I won first prize because the other participants did not notice the change in the wind's direction and were carried further south than I. Another unexpected change of wind made me look ridiculous in front of colleagues in the service. Over large rivers there are air currents running parallel to the water's flow, which we called the aerial highway of the Tajo, the Ebro, and so forth. One day my balloon was travelling rapidly down the "Tajo Highway." When it reached the Portuguese frontier, I released the messenger pigeons—as there were difficulties with releasing them in a foreign country—with the message: "In a few minutes I will land in Portugal." Unfortunately for me, all the pigeons reached Guadalajara just as the wind changed, reversing its direction, and I made my descent in the province of Alicante. After that I had to endure jokes about my poor sense of direction during the discussions I had with other pilots after every ascent.

In all my descents in the most rugged and isolated regions of Spain I could not fail to appreciate the noble and generous character of the Spanish people, so different from what one encounters in foreign countries. I admired the enthusiasm and interest with which we aeronauts were received everywhere by these good people, the energy with which they handled the ropes to bring the balloon safely to earth, the emotion with which they embraced us, as if we had escaped from grave danger, exclaiming, "You are safe!" All offered us their labor, their means of transportation, their food and their homes. They regaled us with serenades in which the popular muse invented songs in our honor, like the one I remember in a village of Old Castile: "If ever we are challenged to war by some nation, Lieutenant Herrera will win it with balloon and cannon."

The mayor of a town on the banks of the Tajo asked me, "When you are up in space, do you have orders to look down?" I answered that we had no orders but we did look down, and he replied, "Well, El Guerra would not be able to do that," to which I responded, "And I, in turn, would not be able to face a bull."[22]

Once I made a solo flight in a tiny balloon from Madrid in a competition followed by automobiles, landing at nightfall in Navalagamella. I left the balloon inflated, tethered to a street light in the public square (the light was out, of course), around which a popular dance was going on that lasted all night. When the sun rose the balloon heated up and became light enough to continue the journey which I made with great difficulty because of the quantities of food I had been given to take along, and I had no ballast. After just missing landing in the waters of the Tajo, I came down in Talavera de la Reina, where I was picked up by a car, having achieved the maximum distance and first prize.

On the other hand, I do not have such good memories of the ascents I made abroad. In the first Gordon Bennett Cup [1906] I left Paris with Colonel Francisco Echague, military attaché to the Spanish Embassy, in a light wind towards the Normandy coast.[23] Towards dusk we saw a curious phenomenon. A very wispy thin cloud covered the whole Paris region, but it had a smooth surface that reflected the moon like a mirror. When it was already dark we heard voices shouting at us from below, "Come down, you are going towards the sea, you are going to your doom!" Then we saw the lighthouse and landed on the beach itself near Cabourg.

In the darkness, some black shapes with white fronts approached us. They looked like men in formal dress, and we thought there was some aristocratic party taking place on this fashionable beach, but the gentlemen turned out to be Normandy cows which charged us in such a threatening manner that we fired shots in the air in an effort to chase them away. Unsuccessful, we went to the village to ask for assistance, but at the town hall they told us that the beasts could not cause any harm. We returned to the beach to find that the balloon and basket had been destroyed because the cows had amused themselves by goring it while we were gone. We spent the night in what was left of it. When people came in the morning, we asked several of them to sign the flight plan to verify the place of descent, but they said they would not sign unless we gave them 100 francs each. We declined and only paid them the amount they charged to help us retrieve the balloon.

On another ascent from Paris with Colonel Echague, after a good lunch in the basket with ample rations of oysters (the shells we threw out as ballast), my companion mentioned what pleasure it would give him to smoke a good cigar, and to satisfy his whim we made a stop in the middle of the country, taking advantage of a lull in the wind, so he could get out to smoke. Then we continued the trip to the vicinity of Epinay, always paying in solid gold for the help we needed to aid us in landing.

In the Gordon Bennett Cup in Berlin [1908] I competed solo. The balloon was prepared and equipped by a military aerostatic crew under the direction of a captain. When the preparations were complete, I could not make up my mind whether to offer a tip to the captain, who had a mustache and bore a general resemblance to the Kaiser. Finally I decided to do so and I offered him a few gold Louis, saying, "For the soldiers." The captain kept them, clicked his heels, gave me a military salute and said, "Thank you." When my balloon took off with its Spanish flag I heard shouts of "Viva España!" and I answered back "Deutschland über Alles!" An American balloon that had just taken off ripped open over a Berlin railroad station, crashing into the roof without injury to the crew, who stayed cool-headed enough to take pictures as they fell.

Alone in the basket, I prepared to spend two nights as peacefully as possible. The balloon had stabilized at low altitude over a sea of fog that covered the whole German plain—the cover was so low that the chimneys of the factories rose up through it. As the fog was moving in the soft wind at the same velocity as my balloon, I seemed to be standing still, and the chimneys moving, leaving a wake in the surface of the mist.

In addition to the great quantity of ballast sacks I was carrying— with which I was counting on making a flight of at least forty-eight hours—the balloon was equipped with anchor, brake rope, altimeter, statoscope, postcards with German stamps affixed to them, a little parachute, and a recent photo of the girl from Guadalajara. Our tenacity had overcome the familial and social opposition and we were engaged.

In order not to waste energy I got ready to spend the night as comfortably as possible; I curled up on some ballast sacks, using one as a pillow to rest my head on, keeping the altimeter in view to indicate the altitude. I was not afraid of colliding with mountains, as in this country there were none. My fiancée, gazing coyly from her portrait, seemed to be amusing herself guessing what was going to happen to me. So I passed several hours, alternately dozing off and awakening to make sure my altitude had not changed. It was a clear, serene night under a bright moon.

Suddenly I was awakened by the sun shining directly in my eyes. It was seven in the morning and I found myself drifting at

2,000 meters over a large city I could not identify. I wrote a postcard to my fiancée, saying I had passed the first night in peaceful sleep, was over an unknown city, and expected to spend another night aloft. I threw this overboard with a note saying, "Bitte, in den nachsten Briefbehälter zu werfen." [Please throw into the nearest mail container.] My fiancée received the card, which we still have, a few days later, accompanied by a message saying it had been found on the roof of a house in Magdeburg.

I was thinking about how lucky I was to have made such a good start when I noticed that the balloon was beginning to descend. I tried to stem this by casting off ballast, but instead of stabilizing, the balloon accelerated downwards into a dizzying fall. Glancing up I was horrified to see that the rip panel had come open and all the gas was leaking out through it. The soon-emptied balloon was falling like a closed parachute, attached by the appendix to the basket. It was useless to throw out ballast. Nothing could save me from death, I thought; my fiancée smiled mockingly from her portrait at my desperate situation. The balloon was snapping violently from side to side as it fell, when one of these jerks freed the rope that bound the appendix to the basket's suspension ring, and all the cloth rose to the top, forming a kind of parachute. This saved me by braking the fall, and although the collision with the ground was violent, I escaped with nothing worse than a twisted ankle and some broken instruments. The neck broke off a bottle of Rhine wine but its contents did not spill. The field where I crashed had been tilled and the ground was very soft; next to it was a road leading to the station in Magdeburg. Some motorists who had witnessed my accident stopped their car beside my overturned basket and ripped balloon, made some remarks that produced gales of laughter, and left without paying any further attention to me. Later some peasants came, and I asked them to help me recover the balloon and put it in a truck. This accomplished, a man who said he was the owner of the truck demanded that I pay for its use. I gave him a few gold coins, which satisfied him, but then everyone who had helped pestered me for coins all the way to the station.

I had already unloaded the balloon to send it to Paris when another man came up and asked me to pay for the use of the truck. When I told him I had already paid he said that the first man who claimed to be the owner was a swindler and that he was the real owner. After arguing with him I decided to pay what he asked, but this touched off a general attack by all the others who had by now become greedily determined to strip me of all the money I had. Finally the stationmaster had to rescue me by locking me in his office while those wild men tried to beat down the door. At last the train came, and I was able to leave that inhospitable country.

What had caused the accident was this: The rip panel rope was caught by a kink in the appendix ring, which in turn was attached to the basket's suspension ring, so that when the balloon was full and spherical in shape the rope did not pull on the rip panel; but when the balloon became elongated, the rope pulled taut and opened the rip panel.[24]

My long-time associate Fernández Duro died in St. Jean de Luz of typhoid fever and a year later the Aero Club of Southwestern France organized a balloon competition in his memory, and I had the honor of accompanying the celebrated Captain Ferdinand Ferber on his "baptism by air."[25] We landed in Mios, a village in Les Landes that had decided to award a prize—a silver cigarette case—to the pilot of the first balloon to land there. This was presented to me by the town officials. Captain Ferber, one of the pioneers of aviation, died testing a rudimentary airplane of his own invention.

With the goal of finding a mathematical solution to the problem of whether the brake rope will wind itself around electric cables when passing over a telegraph line, I presented a paper to the Spanish Mathematical Society (of which I was Vice-President) on the continuous pendulum, with a series of photographs showing the oscillations of a continuous pendulum made of flexible gold chain. We were able to formulate the differential equations in this problem, but we could not integrate them. We consulted Italian mathematicians at the Mathematical Society of Rome, but they could not find the solution either, so we asked the Aerostatic Service to perform some experiments with brake ropes suspended from captive and free balloons. For one of these experiments I piloted a free ascent, taking as passengers the mathematics professors Esteban Terradas, José A. Sanchez Pérez and Fernando Lorente de Nó, leaving from Guadalajara and landing in Brihuega.[26]

The Aerostatic Service organized a captive balloon trip from

Guadalajara to Zaragoza, with me as pilot. Arriving in Zaragoza we parked the inflated balloon in a clearing near the city, anchoring it securely with stakes, and I went confidently off to a barbershop. While I was getting a shave a man came in and announced that the balloon had escaped and fallen in flames on a sawmill. I leapt up and ran out, my face covered with lather, to see that what he said was true—a strong wind had come up that wrenched the balloon from its moorings, and as it rose it was struck by lightning and burst into flames, falling on some enormous stacks of wooden beams and igniting them. In spite of this disaster the town officials held a reception in our honor.

One ascent in a captive balloon nearly ended in tragedy. We were trying to accomplish the maneuvre of passing an obstacle with the balloon towed by mule cart. The obstacle was a telegraph line on the Guadalajara highway, near the Aerostatic Park, and the wind was blowing so hard that it knocked down the Guadalajara wireless antenna, making the mules rear and back up. The balloon was jerked about so violently that I had to hold onto the basket ropes with both hands to avoid being thrown overboard. Suddenly the jolting stopped and the balloon was perfectly still— the steel cable that held the balloon captive had snapped, and, now free, I found myself receding at high speed from the cart and its crew. This was a dangerous accident because a captive balloon (comet-shaped or "sausage" balloon) is not equipped for free flight. It lacks an appendix, so it can burst if the altitude of equilibrium is greater than that of explosion.[27] Because of its shape it is more sensitive to disequilibrium, and lacking the traction of the retaining cable, it assumed a vertical position, so that its lower part, which functioned as a rudder, was now covering the basket. We had heard of a similar incident in Germany in which the pilot broke both legs. As soon as the balloon was free, the cloth of the rudder enveloped me and I was barely able to see the ground through its folds. Still, I could appreciate the altitude I was gaining, and I was able to manipulate the valve and bring the balloon close to earth over a plowed field. It was almost night. When the guide ropes touched the ground I opened the rip panel and fell to earth with a crash, enveloped in cloth.

Captain Navarro, who was directing the maneuver from horseback, raced cross-country to help me. His horse tripped and they both fell but he got up and continued to run on foot, arriving exhausted and panting to find me safe and sound. Unfortunately this courageous effort proved fatal for Captain Navarro, who had a chest ailment. The next day he vomited blood and died soon after.

Another ascent which nearly ended in catastrophe was a night flight I took with Balbás as co-pilot and a young infantry lieutenant who was to receive his baptism by air. It was a splendid night with a brilliant moon and not a breath of wind. We weighted the balloon with precision. Balbás and I each loaded a sack of ballast to be used against any unforseen descent, while the lieutenant held onto the ropes, and then I gave the order to cast off. At that very moment, when the balloon had not even reached one meter in altitude, a violent gust of wind that no one could have forseen battered the basket against the ground with such force that Balbás and I were thrown out and left lying on the ground face down along with our sacks of ballast. I felt the guide ropes pass over my back and sensed that the balloon was leaving without me. Balbás also felt them and then realized to his horror that one of the ropes had wrapped itself around his ankle and was lifting him into the air, head down. I got up and ran after the balloon, but it was rising rapidly, disencumbered of my weight and the two sacks of ballast, with Balbás hanging by a foot and shouting "Au sécours!" He always reverted to French in moments of distress. Meanwhile the incipient aeronaut found himself alone in the basket without knowing what to do. Finally we shouted at him to pull the cord with the national colors on it—which was the valve—and not the red one, which was the rip panel. He understood us and the balloon, already 100 meters above the trees on the riverbank, descended smoothly and we were able to rescue Balbás from his perilous position.

My relations with *El Ternerillo*'s family advanced full steam ahead, in spite of the obstacles, to the point where Colonel Vives, my superior, went to ask for her hand, which was granted. The wedding took place on January 7, 1909, to the great disappointment of my fiancée, whose main interest in the event was not marrrying me, but going on our honeymoon by balloon, a promise I had made but was unable to keep because my associates at the Aerostatic Service forbade it. For this hoped-for honeymoon above the clouds we substituted a more prosaic trip to Paris, limiting the altitude of our matrimonial flight to the 300 meters of the Eiffel Tower.

The tranquility of our new life together did not last long. A few months into our marriage, when we were already expecting our first child, some bloody events occured in Melilla, culminating in the disaster of Barranco del Lobo. Our company was ordered to that zone of military operations, under the command of my friend Captain Gordejuela, also recently married and expecting a baby. He stayed with the company, but I felt it was my duty as an aeronaut and member of the company to volunteer to share the risks and difficulties of the first deployment of aeronautical forces in war. And so, in the fourth month of my marriage, I joined the Aerostation Company in Africa.

We set up camp in Nador and I acted as observer in almost all the operations carried out, among them a reconnaissance in a towed balloon at 1,000 meters, from which I took photographs, made maps of the terrain and directed artillery fire by telephone from the basket, thus enabling our forces to drive the Moors into retreat.

Our mission accomplished, we began our return towards camp. The Moors interpreted this move as a retreat and congregated by the thousands along the horizon, watching me hurriedly giving orders to the artillery to contain them. As the Moors saw that the shells were falling on target when my balloon was in sight, they believed that I was firing at them, and they began to shoot at me from everywhere. Fortunately they were ignorant of the curvature of trajectories when firing into the air, and they aimed directly at the basket, so the bullets passed below me. One of them, however, cut the telephone line and left me without communication, alarming those below who thought I was wounded or dead. Returning to camp we stood heavy fire all night from the Moors, who had pursued us almost to our position. During that operation several soldiers and Commander Perinat of the Infantry were killed.

I took part in other operations on land which were completed with no casualties, including the taking of the Alcazaba de Zeluán with a cavalry charge, the taking of a town in Nador from which the "pacos" fired on us in spite of our artillery fire, and the recapture of Barranco del Lobo, where I was horrified at the terrible spectacle of the corpses of our poor soldiers, mutilated and run through, with prickly pears in their eye sockets.

During these operations my first son, José, was born on October 27, 1909, to whom we had already given the nickname Petere, the name he uses in his literary work. We celebrated this happy occasion by sending up a little weather balloon carrying as crew a celluloid baby. It lost itself in the air over the tribal lands of the interior of Morocco.

The military operations finished and the zone pacified, we were received in triumph in Madrid, where we marched through the streets decorated with wreaths of laurel. I was proud of these branches, but my horse found them so appetizing that it was all I could do to prevent him from eating them. After the parade I met my son, who was three months old.

Soon after this we acquired the little dirigible "Astra España," in which I made the ascents necessary to obtain the international airship pilot's license. There were exceedingly few conditions under which we could navigate this airship. All that was needed was a light wind to prevent it from returning to base at Cuatro Vientos, and we could not travel far even on calm days. One day we ventured as far as the station in Guadalajara but a little breeze sprang up and prevented us from returning; the aviation troops and passengers from a train that conveniently arrived tugged on the guidelines and got us down.

One day when Kindelán and I were at Cuatro Vientos with the dirigible inflated in its hangar, the King arrived unexpectedly, accompanied by the Chief of the Engineering Division, and ordered us to bring out the balloon because he wanted to make an ascent. Following orders, I took charge of the ground work. Kindelán, the King, and the general climbed aboard while the mechanic was trying to start the motor. As frequently happens on such solemn occasions, the motor refused to start in spite of the mechanic's continuous cranking. The general suddenly felt ill and had to get out of the basket. Then the motor started and the dirigible rose with only the King, Kindelán, and the mechanic on board. They made a short flight over Madrid and the Casa de Campo and landed without difficulty at Cuatro Vientos under my direction. I breathed a sigh of relief after the success of this royal, but clandestine, operation, for which I was fully accountable; the ascent had been made without the knowledge or authorization of the government.[28]

That year marked the beginning of the era of aviation in Spain.

I made my first airplane flight, from Cuatro Vientos to Alcorcón and back, with Benito Loygorri, who had obtained his license in France, as pilot.[29]

The Spanish government acquired three airplanes, two Henry Farmans and one Maurice Farman. There were three Farman brothers—Henry, Maurice and Dick.[30] The first two were old and celebrated balloonists and pioneers of aviation; Dick, who was occupied with the commercial part of the business, had never been in the air. They tell a curious story about Dick's first balloon ascent. At a reception of the French Air Club, a French *aficionado* of the theory of air navigation overheard someone say, "That gentleman is Farman," and the aficionado asked, "Could you introduce me to him, because I would very much like to meet him." After they were introduced the aficionado invited Dick Farman to make a free balloon ascent. He accepted with enthusiasm and a balloon was made ready at the Airclub Park.

Arriving at the park, Dick Farman and his new friend got into the basket, cast off and went up into the air. Both were enchanted with the marvelous view from such a height, and noticing that they were slowly approaching the sea, each looked at the other to see what would be done next. When they were already over the coastline, the friend said to Farman, "We are already over the water. What do we do now?" Dick answered, "Whatever you say. You're the pilot." The friend replied, "But aren't you Farman, the famous pilot?" and Farman answered, "I am Farman, but I am Dick Farman, and I have never gone up in a balloon before. I thought that you, as pilot, had invited me to make the ascent." So there were the two of them, with no notion of how to fly, alone in a balloon drifting out to sea. Dick Farman remembered hearing his brothers talk about two cords that could be manipulated—one for the valve, to make the balloon descend, and the other for the rip panel, that would cause it to drop like a stone—but he didn't know which was which. Finally, he pulled one of them, fortunately the valve cord, and they began to descend over the water. Luckily an onshore breeze had come up at lower altitude and they were blown back towards the coast where they landed with the help of some fishermen. Thus happily ended a double baptism by air, without any baptist.

Two flying teachers, Osmont and Dufour, accompanied the Farman airplanes. They had passed their tests simply by flying a circle, but they required other tests of us, among them to describe a figure eight, which required two complete loops, one to the left and one to the right. The first thing they taught us was how to taxi on the ground without taking off, but they neglected to tell us what position the control stick had to be in; they warned us not to take our eyes off the oil gage for a moment, and to stop if it ceased functioning. With no more information than this, I put the plane in motion, watching the oil gage but not realizing that I had the control stick back and the next thing I knew the plane lurched into the air, went into a spin and crashed. The plane was destroyed but I was unharmed.

The students at this first flying school in Spain were five captains from the Engineering Corps: Kindelán, Arrillaga, Ortiz, Barrón and myself.[31] Our planes were so precarious that they could only be flown at dawn before sunrise and at dusk after sunset. While the sun was up the tiny eddies in the lower air layers caused the planes to oscillate and become unmanageable and dangerous. Furthermore we could not fly if there was even a light breeze, and turning to the right was dangerous because the gyroscopic effect of the propeller and rotating engine caused the plane to go out of control into a spin.

To be able to fly at all under such restrictions we had to leave Madrid at three o'clock in the morning. All of us, students, teachers, and mechanics, met at the Puerta del Sol, where a truck was waiting to take us to Cuatro Vientos. We were seen off by the ladies of the night, who were making their last rounds at that hour. The guards at Cuatro Vientos were quartered in the crates the planes had been shipped in, with beds and a bit of furniture allotted by the administration. In the dirigible hangar a small repair shop had been set up.

One morning I was flying over the village of Villaviciosa near Cuatro Vientos when the sun came up and my plane began to pitch so badly it was impossible to return to Cuatro Vientos. I landed on a threshing field near the village. Several villagers came to help and said that the Archbishop of Madrid was spending the summer in town, had heard of my landing, and wished to see me. I went immediately and was cordially invited to have hot chocolate.

I telephoned Cuatro Vientos asking them to send an instructor to pick up the plane, but when they said they would come after sunset, I said that by then I would not need an instructor and would be able to take off by myself. The plane remained in Villaviciosa all day guarded by some soldiers, and when the sun went down I got in, started the engine and took off triumphantly to the cheers of the whole population of the village and the blessing of the Archbishop, who came to see me off. After finishing this ten kilometer flight, I was as proud as if I had crossed the Atlantic.

In order to pass the pilots' test the International Aeronautics Federation required that we overcome two obstacles. First, to reach an altitude of more than 100 meters, and second, to make a loop to the right. The first was simply a matter of patience. During every flight one could gain a little altitude while flying against the wind, but this was lost with a tailwind or if one passed over a little depression in the earth that our instructors grandiloquently called the "Valley of the Eddies." As for turning to the right, our teachers said it was the same as to the left, but they themselves refused to try it.

Finally the students solved both problems by themselves. One day Ortiz began to fly one circle after another, gaining altitude meter by meter, until he reached a maximum of 100 meters. When he landed after this feat we all applauded and asked him how it felt to fly at such high altitude. "Boys," he said, "it was delightful, not one wobble, not one eddy! I will never fly low again."

Another day we watched in amazement as Arrillaga took off and began a turn to the right which resulted in a perfectly round circle. We welcomed him with an ovation, but he couldn't understand why—it turned out he thought he had been turning to the left.

After these rehearsals we were all flying at 100 meters and turning to the right—first the students, later the instructors. All five of us were now able to pass the tests needed for the FAI pilots' license. After we were all licensed there were two serious accidents, one of them mine. I took off against the wind on a very gusty day and immediately reached a respectable altitude. But when I changed direction and the wind was behind me, I began to lose control, and when I pulled on the stick to keep from descending the plane pitched, and went into a spin, and I saw I was going to crash in the ravines that then still surrounded Cuatro Vientos. I recall that all I could think of during the fall was that in my pocket I had two tickets for Wagner's *Siegfried* at the Teatro Real, which my wife and I were to see that evening.

It was a spectacular crash. The plane came apart in pieces on top of me and the engine fell on my right foot giving me a swollen ankle that kept me confined to the house, unable to walk, for forty days. In spite of this, hobbling and supported on my wife's arm, I went to hear the sylvan murmurs of Wagner's opera.

Arrillaga suffered the second mishap, which gave him a serious cerebral concussion that put him in the Military Hospital at Carabanchel unconscious for several days. As Arrillaga was extremely religious he always carried a rosary in the pocket of his flight jacket. Doubtless he was praying at the moment of the crash, because during the entire time he was in a coma he never stopped praying, and every time he came to the "Gloria" he would grab the ice pack they had put on his head and throw it across the room with all his strength. After this accident he was so unnerved that he had to give up flying.

Now that we were pilots we were authorized to carry army officers and members of the Spanish Air Club as passengers, but prohibited from carrying women passengers. Since my wife, who had already gone up with me in a captive balloon, wanted to fly in an airplane too, she joined the Air Club, and as she was a member, I flew her around the vicinity of Cuatro Vientos. This earned me a reprimand from Colonel Vives, whose understanding was that the prohibition on female passengers extended to members of the Air Club.

A flying competition for military airplanes in France was won by the Nieuport monoplane, a machine with flight capabilities vastly superior to those of any of the competitors. This induced the Spanish government to buy three Nieuports, two of eighty horsepower and one of twenty-five. I was chosen to learn how to fly these new planes, at the school at Pau. The control system of these planes was different from that of the Farmans. In the latter, the stick controlled altitude (forward and back) and warp, or lateral inclination (side to side); steering was controlled with the feet. In the Nieuport, however, the stick controlled altitude with forward or back motion and steering with side to side motion; warp was controlled with the feet. This meant having to forget everything that was already done instinctively and substitute new reflex responses. In a few months, under the tutelage of Dr. Espanet, I learned to fly the new planes, and back in Madrid everyone was astonished at how easy they were to fly.[32]

At the school in Pau a number of events happened that are worthy of mention. Some were tragic, like the death of Lieutenant Ducorneau.[33] He was flying 500 meters above us, trying out a new type of propeller called a Neri, when one of the propeller blades broke off. The other one, spinning the plane at twenty times per second with a centrifugal force of several tons, produced an effect like that of a bomb exploding in the airplane. The propeller blade flew off in one direction, the fuselage in another, the wings in another, and the poor pilot in yet another. He fell like a rag doll, arms and legs outstretched, to the bottom of a pond near the airfield. In those times, in spite of the relatively small number of flights, such catastrophes were common, with a probability of one death for every 200 hours of flying time.

Perhaps the most outstanding student of all was a woman who had been Miss America; she certainly had the longest flight sessions with the instructor, who ended up marrying her.

One international event was responsible for sowing seeds of discord among the students. Italy declared war on Turkey, and among the students were a Turkish captain, Fena, and two Italian lieutenants, the Count of La Torre and another. The latter were very close to me, respected my captain's rank, and consulted me on questions of honor. When the Turco-Italian war was declared, they came to ask me if they ought to challenge Captain Fena to a duel. I advised them that it was not necessary, and that they ought to avoid him so as not to provoke a touchy incident. They did this, and at the large table in the dining room where all the students ate together, the two Italians seated themselves at one end and the Turkish captain at the other. This captain, who was very likeable and a bit of a joker, lowered his head to table level and, looking directly at the Italians, pointed his finger and fired a piece of bread at them, saying "Bang!" This provoked gales of laughter from everyone but the two Italians, who didn't know how to react.

We had to take tests for a military pilot's license at Cuatro Vientos that were considerably harder than the FAI tests. They included a round trip flight to Guadalajara and a glide, motor stalled, from a height of 200 meters to a landing at a designated point. For me, with my new Nieuports, these tests were extremely simple, but this was not so for the others who had to fly the Farman biplanes. Because of this, when I was ready to take the tests Colonel

Vives asked me to wait until Kindelán had taken his, so he would have the satisfaction of being the first Spanish military pilot. I agreed, as Kindelán was older than I and we were very close friends. I took all the tests for the pilot's license except one—the glide—which was the easiest for me, delaying it until Kindelán finished his. During this visit the Infante Don Alfonso of Orleans asked me to take him up as passenger in the Nieuport.[34] At 2,000 meters the motor stalled and, with the propeller motionless, I landed on the spot designated for the test, but I did not present this for validation so as not to break my promise. A few days later Kindelán took his tests and was named the first military pilot, and right after that I made my glide officially and was awarded the second license.

For the second round of pilot training officers came from all branches of the army and the school was divided into two classes. Kindelán was in charge of the Farman biplanes, and I of the Nieuports. One of my students was Luís Dávila, my old schoolmate in Granada, who had followed in my footsteps, attending the Engineering Academy, where we lived together like brothers, becoming a balloon pilot and finally an airplane pilot under my tutelage.[35] Later he established the Granada airfield in Armilla, where he was burned to death in a flying accident. The airfield was renamed in his honor—Dávila Airfield—but this name has unjustly fallen into disuse. My other students were Jenaro Olivié (an engineer who was my associate in all my scientific work), José Monasterio of the Cavalry, Carlos Alonso Hera of the Quartermaster Corps, José Valencia (Infantry) and Dr. Antonio Pérez Núñez (Medical Corps).[36]

We had not had one death during the first round of training, but the second saw the inauguration of the by now long list of Spanish aviation fatalities with the death of Infantry Lieutenant Celestino Bayo, a brother of two other students, Captain Alfonso Bayo and Infantry Lieutenant Alberto Bayo. When we brought his body to the cemetery at Carabanchel the gravedigger suggested we buy a parcel reserved for aviators, as it would be less expensive. Naturally we indignantly rejected this advice, but later we realized he was right. Only a few days later another colleague, Dr. Cortijo, was buried in the same cemetery and more followed.[37]

In Madrid my wife was thrown into a state of alarm every time the news vendors announced "Tragedy today at Cuatro Vientos!"

One day she was really frightened. A friend of mine—a French pilot—left a message at my house that I had gone up with Colonel Vives, that he had been hurt, and that I was missing. She ran frantically from airfield to hospital to try to find out what had happened. In fact, I had gone up with Colonel Vives but in Guadalajara he changed planes and went up with a French pilot who had an accident—Vives suffered only light injuries. I, meanwhile, had stayed in Guadalajara for the day and returned to Cuatro Vientos in the afternoon.

In another incident Captain Emilio Jiménez Millás was a passenger in a Cuatro Vientos plane when the plane suddenly pitched and he was thrown out and killed.[38] I gave the sad news to the Air Club, but they got the names confused and told the press I was the one who had been killed. This prompted a wave of condolence telegrams to my "widow" from all over Spain and North Africa and obituaries ending with "he is survived by a young son. May the unfortunate flyer rest in peace." A close friend of mine telegraphed my wife that he was leaving Seville for Madrid to attend my funeral. I reassured him by telegram that I was safe, but he was just as upset to hear of Millás's death.

Events taking place in Tetuan obliged the government to send an aviation squad there under the command of Captain Kindelán and accompanied by Colonel Vives. I also felt it was my duty to volunteer, as I had before, and I requested permission to outfit one of the Nieuports with an extra fuel tank—using the passenger weight allowance—so a non-stop flight from Madrid to Tetuan could be made, which would beat the existing world distance record.

While these preparations were in progress some journalists visited Cuatro Vientos, found out about my projected trip, and published the news. This flight would have to pass over Gibraltar, and the English government informed Spain that they would not authorize this and that if we made the flight they would open fire on the plane over Gibraltar.

The Minister of War passed this prohibition on to me, and although I assured him that I would not be in danger because I would be passing over Gibraltar at an altitude higher than the range of their cannon—an altitude I needed to reach anyway to cross the Straits, as the Moroccans would surely fire at me—he stood by his decision and I had to travel the ordinary way to Tetuan, by land and sea.

Colonel Vives and Captain Kindelán returned to Madrid leaving me in command of the air squadron, whose job was to correct the direction of artillery fire, observe the enemy camps, and bomb their positions, especially the installation in the Cañón de la Concha, from which the Moroccans were firing on our camp. General Marina, Chief of Army Operations, had given us orders not to drop bombs on any position where women were present. They could be distinguished from the men, who wore dark djelabas, by their white dress. Naturally as soon as the Moroccans found out about this they decided to dress in white like women, except for those heroes who preferred to be shot at rather than sacrifice their trappings of masculinity. In spite of this the General stood by his order, preferring to inflict less punishment on the enemy than to kill women or children with Spanish bombs.

Flying over this African war, at heights from which the outlines of the star-shaped forts, impossible to recognize from the ground, could be clearly seen, I arrived at the next milestone of my life.

Milestone 4: 1914
Age, 35 years

In the camp at Tetuan we heard that the King had arrived in Seville. The weather next morning was splendid and I jumped out of bed to wake my friend Ortiz Echague, General Marina's nephew, and ask him if he would ask his uncle to write a message to the King that we would deliver by hand, bringing it by air. He thought it was a good idea and at eight o'clock we were in the General's office. After we reassured him that we could do it without difficulty, he agreed and handed us a letter addressed to His Majesty. We decided that I would pilot the Nieuport monoplane and Ortiz would take aerial photographs.

As soon as we took off, following the coast northwards from the mouth of the Río Martín, we were fired upon by the Moroccans, but this was quickly silenced by our artillery. When we reached the Straits we set our course directly for the Rock of Gibraltar, feeling rather smug about defying the British prohibition that had inconvenienced me earlier. This was to be the first time in centuries that Spanish colors would fly over the British fortress.

It was thrilling to see—from a height of 2,000 meters—the terrible battleships and enormous pieces of artillery converted into little toy boats and tiny cannons; spread out below us, they looked as if they could be destroyed with a single shot. Only then did I realize what a rude blow the immense power of the British Empire had been dealt by the coming of aviation.

Below in the British fort the stir caused by the appearance of a Spanish plane in their hitherto unviolated air space was enormous. Lacking anti-aircraft artillery (which did not yet exist), they gave orders to raise the firing angle of the cannons, so they could shoot us down. But they did not have enough time, and we continued on to Seville, whose white walls were already visible on the horizon. As the engine made its final revolutions on the last remaining drops of gasoline, we landed in a pasture at Tablada amidst the bulls; more peaceable than the cows of Normandy, they fled from this strange flying animal without harming us at all.

The spot where we landed was near a shooting range where the King and his friends happened to be. They saw the odd arrival of a plane in Seville, something never before seen in this city, and a few minutes later we were received by the King, who embraced us and ordered us to meet him at the station that night, as he and the royal family were about to leave for Madrid, and he would give us a reply to General Marina's letter. That night Ortiz and I were royally entertained by the townspeople with a banquet and dance in our honor at the Casino. We left our plane parked where we had landed, so we could give them a flying demonstration the next day before we left.

When we met the King at the station, he handed me the letter for General Marina and told us that when we returned to Madrid he would make us both gentlemen-in-waiting. Ortiz was listening very hard, trying to absorb what the King was saying, and the King said to me, "Explain it to him, as he seems a little deaf." We slept off the day's excitement in a hotel and arrived early at the landing field, where a large crowd had already gathered, only to find, to our distress, that hurricane force winds had come up during the night, wrenching the plane from its moorings and turning it over. The wheels were in the air and one wing had been destroyed, so we had to return to Tetuan by train and boat.

The English government promptly sent an energetic protest to Spain, calling for punishment of the pilots who had violated British sovereignty. The Spanish government informed us of the complaint and we made the best excuse we could, claiming that one cannot judge the true position of an airplane from the ground; we went unpunished.

New disturbances in the Melilla zone obliged the government to send a squad of Nieuport monoplanes there under my command. We set up camp in the vicinity of Alcazaba de Zeluán, and carried out daily reconnaissance and light bombardment of enemy positions. One day I was ordered to bomb the residence of a rebel *caid* who was preparing to stage an attack, and as I was not familiar with the location of the house, a Moroccan friend of mine offered to come along as passenger and show me the site. I dropped a few small bombs on the house he pointed out, but it turned out that the Moroccan had been mistaken and it was not the rebel's house after all. Nevertheless, the operation was fruitful, because the *caid* who lived in the house I had bombed was on the point of going over to the enemy and the bombing apparently made him change his mind; on the following day he presented himself at command headquarters with gifts for the General and protestations of friendship.

We also explored the then mysterious region of Guerruan, on the other side of the Kert, which was the entrance to this "basin," and in the course of my daily observations from air and land I noticed a curious phenomenon. Every morning I would fly over the port of Melilla and I always saw four ships in the harbor. After the flight I would go by car to report to the General, but when we drove by the port we could only see three ships. Intrigued by this discrepancy and not thinking it probable that one of the boats left the harbor every morning and returned in the afternoon, I observed the situation more attentively and saw the explanation: of the four boats I saw in the morning, one had a light greenish tint; this boat was in fact sunk beneath the water and therefore could not be seen from land, but because the water was so clear, it could be seen perfectly from the air.

When World War I began, I returned to Madrid, where I was named gentleman-in-waiting by Alfonso XIII and promoted to Commander for my service in Morocco. I could not accept this rank because in my corps (military engineers) promotions earned in the course of war had to be declined—instead I accepted the honor of the Cross of María Cristina.

When I presented myself to the King to thank him for the distinction he had awarded me, he said, "I assume you will not refuse the post of Commander" and I had to answer, "Sir, I have no choice." He replied, half joking and half serious, "I promoted you to Commander because I think you will be of more value there than as captain, so why do you throw this in my face and insist on remaining a captain?" I answered, "Sir, I am very sorry, but I must do this because I gave my word of honor." "All right," he said, "but promise me that you will serve as Commander for the six months that the law allows before you resign." I promised to do this and did not offer my resignation until six months after my apppoinment.

The English government asked for an officer of the Spanish Air Force to come visit its base of operations in the Somme, and I was chosen to represent us. I spent a few weeks in Amiens, where we were twice bombed by the Germans, and observed the front at Arras, accompanied by Captain Fraser (who had lost an eye when a mine exploded in a trench he was in) and later by General Wilson, who took me to places where there was more action so I could see the "real thing."

In one heavily bombarded town there was a church with a statue of the Virgin on top of its tower, holding the baby Jesus above her head with his arms outstretched in the form of a cross. The second time I passed this town, the Virgin, hit by cannon, was lying face down, still holding the baby, his arms still outstretched. The third time the Virgin and her baby had been totally destroyed along with the rest of the tower.

The Spanish government had acquired some American Curtiss planes, some of them hydroplanes, which had to be test-flown in the United States and in Canada. Navy Lieutenant Juan Viniegra and I were assigned to this mission, and we left Cadiz on May 1 on the transatlantic liner *Manuel Calvo*. Our arrival in New York on May 14, 1915 coincided with the sinking of the *Lusitania* by the Germans, and we found the Americans, the majority of whom were pro-German, profoundly alarmed by the turn the war was taking. In a New York theater a spectacular review was being performed, in which a succession of actors appeared representing the heads of state of all the nations at war, each followed by a retinue of government officials in uniform. Each delegation had to descend a wide staircase in order to reach the level of the stage, and as they marched down each was received with applause. But when the Kaiser appeared at the top of the stairs, with his silver helmet and white uniform, descending with measured steps to the stage, where he drew himself up square and gave a stiff military salute, the audience rose to its feet and gave him a delirious ovation. The show ended with the peacemaking intervention of the United States, and all the heads of state represented came together in one big embrace, thus ending the war.

We were met in New York by the Curtiss Company's representative, Mr. Moos, who arranged all our affairs and visits to all the airplane factories in the United States: New York, Washington, Detroit, Dayton, Chicago, San Francisco, Los Angeles, San Diego, and Hammondsport on the Canadian border. We visited the inventor Thomas Edison at his home in Orange, where he showed us his latest models of the phonograph and made us a drawing of the Iberian Peninsula, whose outline he recalled perfectly. He also told us about his recent research on lightweight batteries, but denied that they were made of aluminum, as some reporters had said.

The flight tests of our Curtiss airplanes could not be made in the United States because they were equipped with a control system patented by the Wright Brothers' company, so we had to go to Toronto. There we learned how to fly them and accustomed ourselves to the control system, which was all done with the steering wheel. You turned it like an automobile steering wheel for direction, pushed it forward or backward for altitude, and side to side for warp (lateral equilibrium). The foot controls were used only for acceleration. As Toronto is very close to Niagara Falls, we spent our days off there, seeing the celebrated cataracts, the cave of winds, the Torres Quevedo aerial tramway, and the power plants which we found fascinating. On one of these trips an American policeman asked us for our passports while we were crossing Lake Ontario. In those days, even in the midst of a world war, one could travel all over the world without passport, visa, or any other documents, and Viniegra and I had done just that, from Europe to the United States and then to Canada. When we explained that we had no passports, the officer asked for some other form of identification, but we had nothing. Finally he requested a calling card, but as it happened neither of us had any left. At this point he said, "O.K., put this card in your hatband," and he gave us each a little white card with the letters *U.S.* printed on it. We did, and when the boat docked he said, "All those with cards in their hats over here," and we got in line with many other passengers, men and women alike, who also had cards in their hats. We were all ushered onto a bus and driven to a place where they locked us up. Some of us were already beginning to get impatient, when the door opened and a policeman called my name and brought me before a kind of tribunal of American police, who asked me for my name, age, profession, the object of my visit to America, whether Spain was going to enter the war (I answered this by saying I didn't know), and if I had come alone or with someone else; I told them Viniegra had come with me. After calling him to be questioned, the chairman of the tribunal apologized for the inconvenience they had caused us, said the government of the United States welcomed us, and we were at liberty, but he advised us to carry at least a calling card in the future. He explained that the reason we were detained was that the night before some German spies had blown up an English munitions factory in Canada near Toronto, and because of this they had tightened security at the border.

I was in New York when the six months of my term as Commander was finished, and I submitted my resignation to the Spanish Consul there. From there it was sent to the Embassy in Washington, then to the Ministry of State in Madrid, then to the War Ministry. All these procedures took another six months, and still the matter of my resignation was not resolved. The problem was that I was the oldest pilot in the Air Force and was therefore entitled by seniority to the position of Chief of this branch of the service, as Commander Bayo, also promoted for merit in warfare, had been promoted after I had. So for a few months I was Chief of the Air Force until my "demotion" was published in the *Gaceta Oficial,* and Bayo was named to the position.

This promotion and demotion caused a big stir among my colleagues in the Engineering Corps, some of whom felt that I should break my word and accept, as the King himself had requested. But I refused absolutely, saying that my word of honor had been given to *all* officers of the Army and as long as even one of them held me to it, I had to uphold it.

A few months after a trip my wife and I made to Covadonga, our second son was born in Madrid, on May 6, 1917, and we named him Emilio Pelayo.[39]

The war was over, and we had witnessed the great advances made by the Zeppelin dirigibles in the area of intercontinental travel, particularly the trip from Jamboli, Bulgaria, to central Africa and back non-stop, carrying a cargo of three tons of provisions, munitions, and medicine for the besieged German garrison.[40] It had covered 4,225 miles and had enough gas left to go another 3,750. In light of this accomplishment, I proposed the establishment of a dirigible airline which would fly between Seville and Buenos Aires non-stop, using a rigid dirigible of my design. This plan attracted the attention of the King, the Marqués de Comillas (President of Transatlántica Española, who visited me at my house) and some Basque financiers. Together they formed a society called "Colón" [Columbus] to carry out this project, with the Zeppelin Company acting as consultants.

In order to study the feasibility of the project, Colón arranged a trip to Buenos Aires in 1921 for Commander Hugo Eckener and the pilot Lempertz, both of Zeppelin, and myself, on one of Transatlántica Española's liners. During this trip we held the parties customarily associated with crossing the Equator which were enlivened by the performance of Pastora Imperio, who sang some marvelous flamenco songs in my honor. Pastora revealed her rather picturesque personality during this voyage. Although the sea was very calm for most of the crossing, Pastora became seasick at the slightest motion of the ship, and dreaded crossing the Gulf of Santa Catalina, where the sea was generally a little choppier. When the fateful day arrived the ship rocked just a little, but this was enough to cause poor Pastora to lie prostrate on her couch in the dining room, getting up only when she had to go to the rail to empty her stomach. After lunch all the passengers went to the dining room for coffee and there was Pastora, pale as a corpse, showing no signs of life. Suddenly the boat rolled a little more sharply than usual and Pastora arose, grasping at the walls as she made her way to the rail, vomited what little she had left into the sea, and came back. Then, hanging onto the doorjamb, she screamed at all the ladies and gentlemen who were drinking their coffee, "Shit on Saint Catalina and on her father too!"

The Colón Company, to which I was assigned by the government as technical adviser, began to build the huge hangar necessary to accommodate the Zeppelin at Tablada, Seville, but because of poor management, lack of official support, the rapid progress of airlines using planes, and political changes the project failed. So, as professor of aerodynamics at the Cuatro Vientos Aerodrome, I approached the next milestone in my life.

Milestone 5: 1923
Age, 44 years

As part of my job in the Technical and Educational Service at Cuatro Vientos, I was in charge of the construction and direction of the Air Force Aerodynamic Laboratory, where we installed, in addition to separate departments for mechanical and chemical research, a closed wind tunnel, three meters in diameter at its narrowest part (the largest then in existence in all of Europe), with an aerodynamic balance to trace the "polar" [drag and lift coordinates] of the profile of the wing or model plane being tested. At international conferences in London and Paris I publicized the Spanish installation with its enormous wind tunnel. In Paris I proposed the establishment of a liaison among all the aerodynamic laboratories in the world, so that all of them could study the characteristics of the same model in order to isolate the influence of each tunnel's design on the results obtained. The engineer and pilot Louis-Charles Breguet seconded my proposition, and it was unanimously approved by the congress under the title "Breguet's Proposal."[41]

In 1922, the Portuguese aviators Carlos Gago Coutinho and Artur Sacadura Cabral flew the hydroplane Lusitania from Lisbon to Rio de Janeiro, using the Brazilian islet of Penedo de San Pedro, near the Equator, as one of their stopping-off points.[42] This islet is located directly on the route of most ships crossing between Europe and South America. As it was uninhabited and had no lighthouse, it was a navigation hazard and ships had to sail past it in daylight, when visibility was good, as I had learned during my trip to Argentina. When I heard of the Portuguese landing, I published an article in a Spanish daily titled, "The Island of Penedo de San Pedro should be ceded to Portugal," in which I said that to commemorate the exploit of the Portuguese aviators, who had used this island for the first time in history, Brazil should cede it to Portugal so that the latter could install a lighthouse, thus making navigation safe in the area and at the same time providing a fitting memorial to the first fliers to cross the Atlantic Ocean.[43]

This article was translated and published in Portuguese and Brazilian newspapers; the topic was debated by the Brazilian Chamber of Deputies, and they voted to cede the island to Portugal, as I had suggested.[44] The Portuguese Embassy in Madrid showed their appreciation at a reception and banquet, and the Ambassador presented me with the insignia of the Portuguese Order of Christ, and the rank of knight commander.

Around this time Einstein visited Spain, and the Spanish mathematical Society, of which I was vice president, organized a series of sessions to study the theory of relativity in depth and draw up a list of points we wished to have clarified. We presented this list to Einstein at a meeting, and he explained clearly all the concepts we had been in doubt about and said that he had enjoyed this meeting more than any of the other lectures he had given in Europe. He was also very interested in my aerodynamic laboratory. Another person who expressed interest in it was the American engineer and patron of the arts Harry Guggenheim, who visited the War Ministry during his visit to Europe.[45] When asked by the Minister of War what had interested him most of all the things he had seen in Spain, he mentioned the aerodynamic laboratory, and was astonished that the Minister didn't know of its existence.

At the end of the war, the victorious nations had formed an association composed of all their aviators called CINA (International Convention of Air Navigation) which Spain, along with other countries who had not taken part in the war, was invited to join, but with second-class status, all the important rights being reserved to the victors. Spain refused to join under these conditions on the grounds that her geographical position as the focal point of air travel between Europe, Africa, and North and South America entitled her to first-class status in the organization. As CINA refused to accept Spain's demand, we remained isolated. However,

I initiated relations with pilots from all the Ibero-American countries, and with the cooperation of the diplomat Juan Cárdenas of the Ministry of State, CIANA (Ibero-American Convention of Air Navigation) was formed.[46] It was officially constituted in November 1926 at a meeting in Madrid attended by representatives of all the Ibero-American nations. CIANA adopted the text of CINA's bylaws as its own, except that all nations had equal rights and status. We agreed that if CINA would agree to modify its bylaws in agreement with this provision, all the Ibero-American nations would join it in a bloc.

I was appointed to inform CINA of this at their next meeting, where I read the bylaws of CIANA and stated that I was not authorized to introduce the slightest change in the text, so that if CINA accepted the proposed bylaws of CIANA, the merger of the two conventions would be accomplished with no further discussion. But if they required any modification, even a comma, the merger would have to be suspended. After I made this declaratiaon there was a long silence, and then the delegate from England rose and said that the United Kingdom was in favor of CINA adopting CIANA's bylaws. One by one, all the other delegates accepted the change in regulations, and with that CIANA ceased to exist and all the Ibero-American nations, including Spain and Portugal, became members of CINA, with the same status as all the other nations of the world.

Around this time the Military Defense Committees made their appearance.[47] I was hoping that the Corps of Engineers—the only division of the army that had never risen against the government—would not have anything to do with them, but this was not to be. My colleagues formed their own committees and sent me a manifesto to sign, declaring my allegiance to them. I replied that I would agree to sign, but only if they declared that in no case would their decisions be in illegal violation of military discipline. They in turn insisted that I had to sign without stipulating any conditions whatever. This I flatly refused to do, in accordance with my lifelong commitment to support my colleagues, to the point of making great sacrifices, whenever it was to the collective good; but by the same principle I refused to do anything that I regarded as improper, no matter how damaging the consequences might be for me. My colleagues, nearly all of whom had signed the manifesto, threatened to bring me before a court of honor if

I persisted in my opposition, but I refused to yield and they held a meeting to consider my "contempt." Their solution was to designate me as a member of the Engineering Corps defense committee in the Ministry of War.

At the first committee meeting I attended I was asked to sign a statement to the Minister which began "With the greatest respect but also with great firmness, this committee has decided to oppose the Royal Decree of this Ministry dated . . ." I read no further and said I was opposed to signing any such document. They begged me to sign, because the accords had to be taken unanimously in order to carry any weight. I still refused, and I was not invited to attend any more committee meetings.

During my relations with the Zeppelin Company in connection with the projected dirigible air line between Seville and Buenos Aires, and also through some calculations I made having to do with the construction of large dirigibles, I became very friendly with Dr. Eckener and other scientists at Friedrichshafen who were planning the first flight across the north Atlantic in the *Graf Zeppelin*, from Friedrichshafen, Germany, to New York and back. The date and time of departure, October 10, 1928, at eight in the morning, was announced months in advance, implying that the Zeppelin dirigibles had been so highly perfected that one could announce beforehand the exact day and hour of takeoff, no matter what the atmospheric conditions might be. I considered Dr. Eckener's certainty in making this announcement a bit bold, but I was confident that his expertise would see the project through as planned.

On October 9, the eve of the departure, I was in Friedrichshafen with the others invited to come along as passengers: two ministers of the German government, the director of the meteorological observatory, Grace Drummond Hay (an American representing the Hearst publications), and two military dirigible pilots—the American Commander Charles E. Rosendahl and myself. There were also two American passengers who paid their own fares.

The world awaited this voyage with enormous expectations. A delegation from the German government, reporters from all over the world, musical bands and a great crowd of spectators gathered at Friedrichshafen.

Dr. Eckener had become a virtual idol to the German people, in spite of his allegiance to the Kaiser in exile in Doorn, Holland,

and his sometimes peculiar behavior. On a test flight in the newly constructed *Graf Zeppelin,* which according to the announcement was to pass over Berlin, Dr. Eckener changed course and headed inland over the North Sea. The German and English radio and press announced that he had gone to pay his respects to the Kaiser, and that he had saluted him from a window, waving a handkerchief. When this news broke, the German government, alarmed, sent Eckener a radiogram, demanding an immediate explanation for his flying over Doorn. Eckener's answer was, "What do the people of Berlin think I'm doing, testing motors or spreading monarchistic propaganda?" Then he flew over Berlin and threw a bouquet of flowers to President Hindenburg.

In Friedrichshafen on October 10 the day dawned calm and blue-skied for the departure of the *Graf Zeppelin* on its first journey to America. I breathed a sigh of relief at Dr. Eckener's good luck in having chosen such a fine day. I went to the airport with my suitcase packed and ready to travel, but I found Dr. Eckener wearing a long face. He told me, "We have to delay our departure until tomorrow. The weather is very bad in the south of France and in the Straits of Gibraltar, and we will never be able to get to the Atlantic. Tomorrow, on the other hand, we will have rain and bad weather here but the rest of the route will be clear."

The passengers, the press, the authorities and the public were tremendously disappointed. Everyone went home crestfallen, believing the trip would not take place. The next morning it was raining and a strong wind was blowing in the wrong direction for our departure. When I left the hotel again with my suitcase, the doormen laughed at me, certain that the *Zeppelin* would not leave in such bad weather. But Eckener prepared for departure, although very few people had gathered to watch.

The American commander Rosendahl and I, seated in the pilot's cabin, were wondering how Dr. Eckener was going to manage to lift off with the wind at our backs, blowing across the field towards a nearby line of trees. In astonishment we watched as he ordered all five engines started and brought to full power while we were still in the hangar; the doors opened behind us and a tractor towed the huge dirigible out at full speed. Propelled by the tractor, the 2700 horsepower of the five engines, and the wind, we raced like lightning for the trees, and when we got there, Eckener pitched the dirigible upwards, as if it were a light plane. We grazed the tops of the trees and found ourselves aloft. The American and I looked at each other and I said, "Well, what did you think off the take-off?" Rosendahl, who spoke Spanish, gave me his opinion in so purely Castilian a choice of words that it is not possible for me to repeat them here.

The dirigible followed the Rhone route, crossed the Gulf of Lyon, and when we reached Barcelona Eckener handed me the controls and let me guide it to the best spot for the passengers to drop the letters they wanted to send. The great city, illuminated by its own lights and also by the dirigible's headlamps, presented a magnificent spectacle.[48] Soon we lost sight of it, as we proceeded down the eastern coast of Spain. When we crossed the Straits of Gibraltar we all went to bed in our respective cabins.

On Thursday, the twelfth, we passed over Funchal, dropping more mail. The next day, in the middle of the Atlantic Ocean near the Azores, we were gathered in the dining room and saw, to the west, a cloud in the shape of a horizontal column that covered the entire horizon in the direction of our route. The German meteorologist told me, "According to Bjerknes's theory, when we cross that cloud we are going to have rain and bad weather." Breakfast was served, and just as we began to eat the dirigible entered the cloud and immediately we were plunged into a true deluge, with water gushing over the windows. At the same time, without any sudden motion, the balloon began to pitch over slowly, but continuously, until we all lost our balance. Some were hanging onto the columns and others, including myself and the meteorologist, were rolling down the floor with the dishes, until we stopped at the back corner of the dining room, where I said to him, "Bjerknes was right."[49] When the floor was tilted at an angle of 30°, the roll reversed itself, and we tipped over, slowly, in the other direction. Finally we regained the horizontal and we thought the incident was over, although the rain continued and the sea looked very rough, with enormous waves breaking in sprays of white foam. The minister Brandenburg[50] and I had begun a game of chess when Dr. Eckener came in to tell us that the material on the tail of the dirigible had ripped and was wrapped around the rudders. We were left with no controls and four of the motors had stopped. They had radioed the United States to send a boat to rescue us. Needless to say this news ended our chess game, and we began making rather pessimistic remarks about the situation we were in, in light of the menacing appearance of the sea at our feet. The two paying passengers were talking in a corner. One said: "Swear that if you are saved and I am not, you will look after my wife and children," and the other promised to and asked the same favor from the first. This provoked Lady Grace's indignation, and she said, "It's shameful that men like yourselves are so afraid when I, a woman, am not." I responded that they were the only ones who had paid and that gave them the right to be as afraid as they wanted to.

We passed the day feeling very uneasy, although the crew walked around with smiling faces, making jokes, and from time to time the second in command Ernst Lehmann entertained us with a concert of accordion music in an effort to lift our spirits.

That night we slept very little, but the next day, the fourteenth, Dr. Eckener reported that his son Knut, one of the pilots, had gone out onto the dirigible, reached the tail, and cut away the material that was jamming the rudders. Now the balloon could be maneuvered, even without all its engines, and they had radioed the United States to cancel the rescue boat as we would be able to reach the coast, somewhat south of New York, probably at Charleston. On hearing this news, I asked Lady Grace to save me the first dance when we arrived at Charleston, and she said she would.

On the 15th we made better time but the wind made us drift to the south as we couldn't use all the engines due to the damage to the tail section. On the morning of the 15th Rosendahl and I sighted the first signs of land with as much enthusiasm as Rodrigo Sánchez de Triana had 436 years before, and together we chanted, "Three cheers for the red, white and blue!"[51]

This dangerous crossing provoked enormous excitement all over the world, especially in the United States, where the papers were ravenous for the latest news of the dirigible. Public prayers were said in Catholic and Protestant churches for our safety. When it was known that the *Zeppelin* was near its destination everyone went out and searched the sky, trying to spot the first appearance of the enormous silver cigar.

The *Zeppelin* entered the North American continent at Cape Charles, and proceeded from there to Washington. President Coolidge was presiding over a reception at the White House when he heard that the dirigible had appeared over Washington and

he abruptly interrupted the function and went out in the garden
to watch the giant airship pass over. A few moments earlier we
had received a congratulatory radiogram from him.[52] We went
immediately to New York, and the enthusiasm with which we were
received there was indescribable. There were people who had
been gazing at the sky for forty-eight hours, day and night, in
hopes of catching a glimpse of us. When the airship appeared at
last, after the terrible dangers it had been through, its tail broken,
triumphantly navigating after conquering the elements, the great
city was paralyzed. All traffic ground to a halt as pedestrians and
drivers stopped to watch us. The streets and rooftops were were
packed with people waving handkerchiefs, and every conceivable
method of making noise was put into action—automobile horns,
sirens, factory whistles, foghorns, bells—all burst into a deafening
cacophony as we made our two loops around the island of Man-
hattan. In the stampede to see the dirigible many were injured
and one killed.

From New York we went to Lakehurst Airport, where an immense crowd had been waiting for hours, held back by police
lines. The dirigible landed and was put into the hangar, which
was invaded by reporters and the public as well, who had broken
through the police barriers. I was the first to set foot on the
ground, and the crowd greeted me with a boisterous round of
whistles; this confused me, and I began to wonder if I ought to
ask their pardon for whatever I had done wrong and promise to
do better the next time. Finally someone explained to me that in
America whistling was a way of showing enthusiastic approval.[53]
The rest of the passengers got off and then suddenly the lights
went out and we were left in total darkness. During the subsequent
confusion someone slapped one of the German ministers in the
face, but it was never discovered who did it.

When the lights came back on a cloud of reporters fell upon
us, and Dr. Eckener said to them in English, "You are the most
dangerous kind of journalists in the world." The next day we made
our triumphal entrance in New York, riding down Broadway in
a cavalcade of cars, welcomed by the customary cheers, applause
and whistles from the street, and a rain of confetti and paper from
the windows of the buildings. Our destination was a reception at
City Hall and a huge banquet in the Ritz Tower, at which the
Americans demonstrated their absolute disdain for customary

protocol. The banquet was given in honor of the Zeppelin Company and the crew of its airship, and was attended by Dr. Eckener, who had built the ship, was its commanding officer, and had organized the trip. Also present were two German ministers, a lady passenger, and distinguished directors of scientific establishments. But passing all these over, the place of honor at the head table was reserved for the American Rosendahl, who had merely come along as a guest, like me. After the banquet we went to the Ziegfeld Theater where the operetta *Show Boat* was performed in our honor, and during which Dr. Eckener took it upon himself to say a few words to the public in English.[54]

Apart from the dangerous episode of the storm and the slap in the face to the German minister, there only was one other disagreeable incident, caused by one of the American passengers. Not understanding the meaning of the signs that said *Rauchen Verboten,* he started to smoke at the beginning of the trip, and had his tobacco, matches and lighter taken away from him. He protested by staying locked in his cabin, in bad humor, for the entire trip. When we landed he lodged a complaint against Zeppelin saying he had been swindled as he had been deprived of smoking for 111 hours although he had paid full fare.[55] On the other hand, there was an amusing incident too. A pretty American girl, having broken through the police barricade, threw herself on the young pilot Knut Eckener, whose daring had saved the *Zeppelin,* threw her arms about his neck and gave him a noisy kiss, saying "On behalf of all the women in America." Knut had a fiancée in Friedrichshafen, and wanted to get married when he returned, so he asked his father for a raise. Dr. Eckener answered, "You have earned it well, because you saved the *Zeppelin,* but I can't give it to you because I'm your father."

I did not return to Europe in the Zeppelin, but remained in New York a few days to wait for a ship to Buenos Aires, to continue my research on the projected dirigible airline between Seville and the Argentinian capital. While I was in New York, the telephone company held a banquet in my honor and invited me to call Madrid on the telephone and talk with whomever I wanted to for as long as I wanted. This would be my second phone call between Madrid and New York, the first having been the day before, when the King had called me. At the banquet I read over the diary I had kept during the voyage and at last chose to speak with my military boss, Kindelán, and my financial boss, my wife.[56]

I had received a telegram from the Mexican government inviting me to go there, and I asked Kindelán if I could accept, but he said no because it would delay my return to Spain too much. I also spoke with my wife and sons, who told me their studies were going well, and while I was talking a very beautiful woman who was standing near the phone booth asked if I would hand her the receiver for a few moments so she could say hello to my wife. I did, and the director of the phone company said to me, "It's fortunate that our telephone doesn't have television, because if your wife saw who you were with she would be very suspicious." The lady was the Countess of Yebes.

Every day in New York I received two American papers whose rivalry was intensified by the fact that one represented the United Press and the other the Associated Press. In addition, one was Democratic and the other Republican, a serious matter because there was a presidential campaign in full swing. Each availed itself of a thousand ruses in an effort to monopolize me and displace the other. One sent two bottles of whiskey to my hotel room, very expensive and very risky as well, as we were in the middle of Prohibition, but beyond that the drinks were poisonous because they caused insanity or paralysis. One night reporters from both papers were in my room until late, asking me questions until I asked them to leave and come back the next day. But five minutes later one of them came back and asked if I would let him sleep in one of the two beds in my room, so he would not lose touch for even a minute.

The next day I had some visits to make, and the reporter accompanied me in a taxi. When we arrived at a certain spot, he told the driver to stop, asked him to wait for us, and ushered me into an entry were there was a tiny door in the corner. He knocked a few times and the door opened partway, revealing only the nose of a mysterious gentleman. My companion uttered some cabalistic phrases and we were let into a place with a stairway down, at the bottom of which was a room containing some tables and about thirty drunks. My companion shouted from the top of the stairs, "This is Colonel Herrera who came over from Europe in the *Graf Zeppelin!*" The drinkers stood up with raised glasses and shouted, "Hello, Colonel Herrera!" I got out of this den of iniquity as fast as I could, afraid I would be arrested, because of Prohibition, even though I had not drunk anything.

I received an invitation to sail on a ship leaving New York directly for Buenos Aires that had every kind of accomodations and attractions, but fortunately I declined because I wanted to sail the Pacific route to acquaint myself with different Latin American countries. I say fortunately because this boat began to list as soon as it left New York, the captain refused to ask for help, and it ended up capsizing, keel in the air, and many passengers lost their lives.

I booked passage on the *Santa María*, which was going from New York to Valparaiso via the Panama Canal. Pan American airways offered to fly me from Key West to Havana, so I remained in New York a little longer before taking a train to Key West, flying to Havana, and there boarding the *Santa María*, which already had my luggage on board. During those last few days in New York the two reporters hounded me until the last minute, asking for statements and articles and even trying to contract for the publication of my memoirs. Both of them accompanied me on the train partway and said goodbye at the same station. But one of them only pretended to leave; as soon as the other left, he got back on the train and stayed with me the whole night.

In Havana I was greeted by a representative of *Diario de la Marina*, who invited me to dinner that night and to a party the next day to be given for me at a country house. I was not able to go to the party because the previous night's supper of octopus had made me ill, and I am afraid I offended them by my absence.

Aboard the *Santa María* I passed through the Panama Canal, observing the curious maneuvers involved in passing through the locks and Gatún Lake with its alligators, while we lunched on deck. Later I was entertained at every port of call by the Spanish community. In Talara (Peru) I was scolded for saying Talara and not Talará, since I was from Granada, and the founder of the city was from the town of Talará de las Alpujarras. In the town of Chan I could see the mysterious relation between certain features of the South American Pacific coastline and that of China. At every port I was obliged to speak to the people who entertained me, and I had prepared a little talk which I delivered, always the same, but with adaptations for each locality. But at one town I saw that the local press had published my speech from the previous stop

in its entirety, and after that I had to give a different speech at
each place. My stay in Lima was exceptional, because the Chief
of the Peruvian Army was the German General Faupel, who was
married to a beautiful Peruvian woman.[57] This general entertained me at a banquet given by the entire Lima garrison, and
afterwards, almost at the hour of the boat's departure, I was brought
on board by a hydroplane from the Peruvian Marine Corps. I
leapt off over the wing of the plane onto a rope ladder which
bounced me off into the water. The crew was quite amused at this
acrobatic number.

My attention was drawn on this trip to the foolishness with which
the Americans celebrated the crossing of the Equator. I had a
sextant with me and every day at noon I calculated our latitude
along with the other officers, and I could see that we were going
to cross the Equator at four in the morning of the following day.
That night, when all the passengers were having supper with the
captain and his officers, we suddenly heard a tremendous explosion, the music stopped, the lights went out, and the sirens began
to wail. We all started to run to find life jackets and take up our
lifeboat positions, when the lights came back on and the captain
said, smiling, "Don't be alarmed, it's just that we are at this very
moment crossing the Equator and this is how the boat celebrates
the event." I said to him that this was not so, that we would not
cross it until four in the morning, and he answered, "You're right,
but I wanted to take advantage of a moment when everyone was
all together in the dining room to announce this surprise." The
festivities were held the next day. It was announced that we should
all wear bathing suits, because we would all have to smear ourselves
with water and sand with a broom and after that Neptune, the
god of the sea, would shave us with a huge wooden razor and
throw us head first into the swimming pool. I was exempt from
this baptism because I had already crossed the Equator, but another passenger who refused to participate and locked himself in
his cabin had his door broken in by the sailors, and they threw
him into the pool with his clothes on. An old couple in their
eighties had to submit to the shave and the dunking along with
the rest.

Afterwards there were more agreeable activities, including a
three-legged race, in which the girls, dressed in bathing suits, had
to run in pairs, the left leg of one tied to the right leg of the other,

a sack race, and a race in which the girls had to start out fully clothed, including gloves, with a suitcase in hand. At the signal, they had to strip down to their bathing suits, put the clothes in the suitcase, and run to the other end of the track; there they had to put all the clothes back on and run with the empty suitcase back to the starting point.

My ocean voyage ended at the port of Mollendo (Peru), where I disembarked in a chair, surrounded by other passengers on foot, all hanging on to me, hoisted to land by a crane. In Mollendo I took a train that passed through Arequipa, crossed the Andes and stopped at Puno, at Lake Titicaca. I was afraid of getting altitude sickness, which afflicts those who take this train trip for first time, and I was advised to dress very warmly for the night. I did, and when we reached the station at El Alto (5,000 meters), I awoke with a feeling of pressure in my chest, which I thought was a symptom of altitude sickness. But I noticed that when I unbuttoned my jacket and took it off the pressure disappeared, and I arrived at Puno with no ill effects. There I boarded a boat to cross Lake Titicaca, at an altitude of 4,000 meters. The captain was a mestizo, very short, but dressed in an admiral's suit with gold braid. When I asked him what time we would arrive at the Bolivian port of Guaqui, he answered, "On this boat, as on every boat in the world, one knows what time one leaves but one does not know what time one will arrive." The view from this lake, the highest in the world, is splendid, ringed as it is by colossal mountains, including Sorota, 6,617 meters high, and Illimoni, 6,404 meters.

When I arrived at Guaqui, I found the director of Bolivia's principal newspaper waiting for me. He accompanied me by rail to La Paz, where the president held a reception for me and told me he was expecting a visit from Herbert Hoover. He was looking forward to this visit because, as Hoover was an engineer, he might be able to assist Bolivia in the development of her many natural resources. After my visit to the president I boarded the train for Buenos Aires, but this train did not run at night because of the steep grade of the railroad bed, which descended 3700 meters from La Paz to sea level, and we had to spend the night waiting at the highest point. During the night we heard the news that there had been a coup in La Paz and that the president, just a few minutes after my visit, had had to abdicate and flee the country.[58]

In Buenos Aires I was well received. I gave a few lectures and boarded the Italian liner Principesa Mafalda for Barcelona, where my Air Force friends Olivié and Carlos de Haya (both killed in the Franco uprising nine years later) were waiting with an airplane to fly me to Madrid.[59]

I was named director and professor of aerodynamics at the Advanced School of Aerotechnics at Cuatro Vientos, whose building I had designed.[60] At the same time I was apppointed director of the Aerodynamic Laboratory and Comptroller of the Aviation Service. This last job touched off a sequence of events that was to affect my life for seven years. In the middle of December of that year [1928], José Calvo Sotelo, Minister of Finance under Primo de Rivera, issued a royal decree ordering all government entities to pool all the funds at their disposal, whether they were committed or not, and they would be redistributed in years when there was a surplus, but not when there was a deficit. The reason for this was to show that the treasury of the dictatorship had a surplus. The Aviation Service had millions committed to the construction of airplanes and aviation materiel, contracted out to different factories and already under construction. Compliance with this decree meant cancelling all the orders, closing all the factories and putting workers out in the street. I consulted Kindelán about this dilemma, and he said the only solution was to treat all the equipment under construction as if it were finished and delivered, put the money in the safe until the finished products were delivered, and then pay the contractors. This put me in a position of tremendous responsibility, but seeing that it was the only way to avoid a conflict with the state, I agreed to do it, after talking to the Comptrollers of Artillery and the Navy and finding that they were doing the same thing in their respective departments.

So Aviation, like the other Corps, reported all the contracted work as if it were finished and received, and deposited the amount necessary to cover the cost. But the cashier, without authorization, loaned some of the funds to one of the contractors, and at the same time Commander Ramón Franco, hero of the flight from La Rábida to Buenos Aires in the *Plus Ultra* and Kindelán's secretary, found out about my failure to comply with the royal decree and denounced me to the Ministry of War.[61] I was then pressured into denouncing myself, declaring that I had not complied with the royal decree, and giving my reasons for this.

An infantry colonel was named as presiding judge. I was called to testify before him and he, who knew all the circumstances of the affair perfectly well, asked me, "Did any of your superiors advise you to violate the royal decree?" and I answered, "I did it on my own and no one gave me any advice." The Colonel then asked me again, "Listen, Herrera, you have only to say the word and you are cleared of all responsibility." He insisted that I say something, because if I didn't, he would be obliged to indict me for the crime of embezzlement. In the end he did just that because I refused to say anything more. The next day I called Kindelán to tell him about it, and he said he was sure that I had not violated the royal decree for my own benefit. General Fanjul asked to defend me because he said I had a good case, but the years passed and I continued under indictment but on probation at half pay.[62] One day I met Fanjul in the street and he asked me what had become of my case. I replied, "You should know, you're representing me." He made excuses for having done nothing because of his heavy political obligations, and I continued under indictment until 1935 (the Republic was now in power) when the lawyer Ricardo de la Cierva, brother of my friend Juanito de la Cierva, inventor of the autogyro, asked my permission to request the judge to give him the file on my case to study. After examining it, he sent a letter to the judge saying that in the entire dossier there was no charge against me except my own statement, that I had not caused any harm to the state nor to anyone else, that all the depositions were favorable, and that he should dismiss the case. He did; I was a free man, and all the pay that had been withheld for seven years was returned to me, although I received it during the Civil War, when the currency of the Republic was difficult to redeem.

In 1930 Zeppelin scheduled a flight for the *Graf Zeppelin* from Seville to Rio de Janeiro, New York, and back to Seville. Among those invited were Prince Alfonso de Orleans, myself, the writer Federico García Sánchiz, the journalist Corpus Barga, and the banker González Herrero, as well as other German and American passengers.[63]

The dirigible left Friedrichshafen on May 18, reached Seville by afternoon, spent the night taking on hydrogen and embarked for Pernambuco, Brazil, on the morning of the 19th. At midnight we passed over Tenerife, on the afternoon of the 20th over the

Cape Verde Islands, and on the 21st we prepared to cross the
Equator, the first time in the world for a dirigible. This presented
a serious problem because of the extra weight the Zeppelin would
have to contend with in the torrential rains of the equatorial zone.
Some pessimists were certain that a dirigible would never be able
to cross the Equator without being driven down by one of these
tremendous downpours, but Dr. Eckener was sure that these equatorial hazards could be overcome. He arranged for all the engines
to be run on gasoline before we reached the Equator, instead of
Blaugas (blue gas, a misnomer, as it was not blue, but its inventor's
name was Blau). Blaugas weighed the same as air and its consumption did not decrease the weight of the balloon; but it was
necessary to make the balloon lighter and for this reason we were
using gasoline.[64]

To prevent the balloon from rising because of this loss of weight,
we navigated with the nose low, tilted forwards, and in this position
we withstood two enormous squalls, pitching the balloon upwards
to give it ascensional force to counter the weight of the water
which drenched it.

We celebrated the event at a party given by the pilot Hans von
Schiller, and Lehmann played his accordion. Von Schiller, disguised as Aeolus, King of the Winds, baptized us, the women with
cologne, the men with seltzer, and gave us the new names we were
to use in the southern hemisphere. He changed the Prince's name
to L'Enfant Terrible, Corpus Barga's to Corpus Delicti, and mine
to Herr Lehrer. The Prince, first cousin to the King of Spain, had
his relative's sense of humor and open manner; he spoke Spanish,
French, English, German, Portuguese, Italian, and even a Swiss
dialect with equal facility. We occupied the same cabin, he in the
lower berth, I in the upper.

Among the passengers was an American woman who was spending her honeymoon "American style," as she called it, which is to
say, she was crossing the Atlantic on the *Graf Zeppelin* while her
husband toured the countries of eastern Europe. At our ports of
call she always received a telegram from him that said, "I am glad
to hear you still have not broken your neck."

This lady had a crush on the Prince, which was a great annoy-
ance to us as she would come to our cabin after supper and wouldn't
allow us to go to bed early so we could get up at dawn to see the
view in the early morning. Sometimes we had to ask her to leave

so we could get undressed, and she would say, "Well, get undressed, are you little girls?" (In those days "girls" did not get undressed in public.) When she drank champagne with the other passengers they played dirty tricks on her. Our bunks folded up against the wall during the day and were pulled down horizontal at night for sleeping. Some of her young friends pulled her bed up one night while she was in it until she was almost pinned to the wall, then let go of it suddenly. The ropes supporting it broke, and the lady, shrieking loudly, rolled out onto the floor.

After we crossed the equator I received a congratulatory radiogram from the King, which surprised me as I had not telegraphed him. Later I realized that the banker, named Herrero, had sent him a telegram and the King had thought it was from me.

We reached Pernambuco at eight on the night of the 22nd, sixty-two hours after leaving Seville, and we stayed two days visiting the people and attending banquets and receptions while the balloon replenished its supply of hydrogen. The Prince and I shared a room that had been reserved for us [at the Hotel Central], and when we went to pay the bill we noticed that they had charged us for five days, although we had only spent two. They explained that this was because they had held the best room for us three days before we arrived. We paid and left for Rio de Janeiro.

The wind was from the north and we reached Rio de Janeiro before dawn; the city was completely covered with clouds. The balloon circled slowly above the clouds, waiting for dawn, and the passengers were treated to one of the most impressive spectacles imaginable. Just as the sky began to lighten the clouds below started to disperse and El Corcovado, El Pan de Azucar, and other high features of the landscape emerged slowly from the mist, now visibly illuminated by the city lights. Soon it was full daylight, the clouds disappeared altogether, and the splendid city and its harbor appeared before our eyes.

The *Zeppelin* landed at Dos Alleuros, near the city, where a large crowd was waiting for our arrival, in spite of the early hour, as well as the authorities and, of course, the press. None of us disembarked in Rio, as we only stayed for fifty-five minutes. We were back in Pernambuco in twenty-four hours, where they held yet another banquet for us, to the great disgust of Dr. Eckener, who hated these affairs. "When one achieves a certain amount of notoriety, one must have an iron stomach," he commented.

The Prince and I stayed in the same hotel room we had had before, and when we went to pay the bill they again charged us for five days—for a room we had just vacated the day before. Again we protested and again they claimed that, since we were royalty, they had reserved five days for us in the best room. But this time the Prince, although he was royalty, refused to pay twice for the same reservation, and we paid only for the night of our stay.   In Pernambuco the *Graf Zeppelin* let off passengers and took on new ones, a boisterous group who wanted to stop in Havana. Dr. Eckener refused in view of the bad weather in the Caribbean Sea and set course for New York. This caused a spate of protests which were finally appeased by the intervention of the Prince. At Cape Hatteras we ran into a storm which we managed easily, except for a mild panic on the part of the new passengers.

After circling New York a few times, we landed at Lakehurst on May 30 and stayed for two days. The Prince and I went to Washington to see the Spanish ambassador, who put us up in the Embassy, where they had readied a magnificent room for the Prince and a slightly more modest one for me. The Prince, however, protested the separation, saying that he was already accustomed to staying in the same room with me and wouldn't be able to sleep if I weren't there, so we both stayed in the Prince's room and I left the following day for New York where I had things to do.

In New York I had a suite reserved in the Sherry Netherlands Hotel, at that time the most modern and luxurious in the city. The manager showed me my room, which consisted of a bedroom, office, sitting room, a bathroom with a pool you could swim in, a refrigerator, fresh fruit, and a magnificent view of Central Park. I was startled by such opulence and asked what the price was, but the manager just answered, "Never mind." The next day I asked for the bill, which amounted to $35 for one night, sweetened by the gift of a silver box full of chocolates.

During my twenty-four hours in New York, one of the reporters who had harrassed me two years before found me again and would not leave me alone until the departure of the *Zeppelin,* where he managed to get through the police barrier and talk to me through a window of the ship. During this last conversation he gave me his fountain pen and his camera and then said, "Would you like to meet my wife? I will give her to you too." I declined this last gift. When we were aloft he sent me a message over the radio, wishing me bon voyage.

One of the passengers on this New York-Seville flight was Commander Richard E. Byrd, the celebrated polar explorer. On June 3 the *Graf Zeppelin* arrived in Seville, after passing over Lisbon. Because of a stormy cloud over the Straits of Gibraltar, the *Zeppelin* was not exactly on course and landed instead at Tabalada, where many people were waiting for us, including my wife and sons and Berta Dávila Wilhelmi, the sister of my unfortunate friend Luís Dávila; since his death she considered us her family. Thus ended the triumphal journey on which, for the first time, a dirigible crossed the Equator.

The municipal elections of April 1931 resulted in a republican victory, recognized by the King, who abandoned his throne and left the power in the hands of the people. In my opinion this change of sentiment on the part of the Spanish people—who had until then shown sympathy for the King—was due to the monarch's having overstepped the power vested in him by the constitution, which he had sworn to respect. Some of his behavior was welcomed with sympathy on the part of the public, such as certain impetuous acts performed without government authorization (for example, the dirigible flight related earlier). Other decisions were received with criticism by some people and approval by others, including the installation of Primo de Rivera's dictatorship, in emulation of the examples of Italy and Germany which seemed crowned with success. Most damaging of all was the military disaster at Annual in which the King appeared to be deeply implicated.[65] This, on top of the opposition to the monarchy, in principle advocated by the republican sector, made it possible for the result of the elections to favor the Republic.

When I took my oath of office, I had promised my allegiance to the King; but when he ceased to be king by the will of the people, to which he yielded, I was no longer bound by my oath as an army officer. As a gentleman-in-waiting, however, I had sworn allegiance to the person of Alfonso de Borbon, and I did not feel I was free of this oath. The day after the King left, I went to Paris and asked him for an audience in the Hotel Maurice. My letter said I continued to consider myself a gentleman-in-waiting, at his service, in compliance with my oath. He answered by thanking me for my offer and recommended that I accept the republican regime established by the people, as he did want any blood shed between Spaniards on his account.[66] In view of this, after a short detour to Geneva, where I had been called in by the League of Nations to consult on technical matters concerning airplane engines, I returned to Madrid where I signed, as all the other officers had (except members of the royal family), a promise, on my honor, to serve the Republic faithfully and loyally, to obey its laws, and defend it with arms. One of these oaths of honor carried the signature of General Francisco Franco Bahamonde. In addition to obtaining the allegiance of the army, the Republic received a collective letter from the church, pledging its allegiance to the new regime.

But this allegiance of the army and the church had been offered with the idea and the intent that the new regime would not limit the advantages that the military, the aristocracy, and the clergy had enjoyed under the monarchy. As soon as the first laws were enacted under the Republic, which introduced reforms affecting the army, did away with noble titles, projected agrarian reform, and separated the church from the state, all this allegiance was converted into overt or covert opposition. Criticism, attacks, and provocation against republican sentiment multiplied, to the point where it was feared that the people, unrestrained, would launch violent attacks against church property.

The writer Ramiro de Maeztu lived in the same building I did, Calle Espalter 15; he told me he was concerned that our nearby parish church, San Jerónimo, might be the object of an attack by the masses, and he wanted to know if he could count on me to organize its defense.[67] I said, in a case like that, the thing to do was to notify the police, but he countered that such an attack might happen so suddenly that there would be no time for the police to get there. I said that in that case he could count on me, but I informed him that although I was a military man, I had no weapons. He answered that this was not a problem, as the church had stocked enough guns for its own defense. A few days later, in response to provocation by monarchist elements, who played the Royal March in a house with the balcony doors open so it would be clearly heard in the street, groups of hotheaded republicans stormed and set fire to several churches. The government failed to send peace-keeping forces to stop them, in spite of Interior Minister Miguel Maura's recommendation to do so, fearing that any repression of these acts would end in bloody confrontation.[68] Fortunately no blood was shed, either in Madrid or the rest of the peninsula, where demonstrations of popular protest continued the following day. Our church, San Jerónimo, was not attacked and Señor Maeztu did not have to call out its defenders.

From then on the conspiracy against the Republic grew clandestinely within the army, the clergy, and the aristocracy, some of whose members had been stripped of their noble titles. After having given their word of honor to support and defend the Republic, sealed with their own signatures, they now claimed that as they had sworn their allegiance as titled members of the nobility, and the Republic had now dispossessed them of those titles, they were no longer bound by their oaths.

General Marvá nominated me to the Academy of Sciences and strongly recommended that I pay a visit to each of its thirty-five members to ask them to vote for me rather than for the university professor Enrique Moles, who had also been nominated.[69] I found the prospect of these visits very distasteful, as I sincerely did not consider myself more highly qualified for membership than Professor Moles. I could not bring myself to visit members of the Academy and ask them to commit an injustice in my favor. I felt that to leave my calling card at each of their houses was the equivalent of a personal visit, while to visit them and recommend that they vote for my rival would have been absurd and an embarrassment to General Marvá. On the other hand, I could not show any disrespect or lack of appreciation for General Marvá, to whom I owed a great deal. I did not know what to say to his constant exhortations that I make these customary visits, telling me that my reluctance to do it was an insult to the Academy members. All of them had in their turn fulfilled this duty out of courtesy, and they were complaining that I had not visited them yet, while Professor Moles had already made his visits.

I had reached a point of desperation, still unable to make a decision, when my salvation came in the form of a telegram from Geneva. Salvador de Madariaga, the Spanish delegate to the League of Nations, requested urgently that I attend meetings beginning the next day as a representative of Spanish aviation.[70] I lost no time in writing a letter to General Marvá lamenting the fact that I would not be able to make the visits of protocol because I had to leave for Geneva immediately.

Milestone 6: 1932
Age, 53 years

At this session the League of Nations was studying the problem of aviation disarmament, and they were classifying airplanes as either "angels" or "devils," only permitting the construction and use of the former—those suitable for peaceful uses—and prohibiting those that could be put to military purposes. I presented a chart representing all the different kinds of aircraft then in use by all countries, showing the relation between the power of the engine and the total area of wing surface. This ratio revealed a clear line of separation between two groups of planes—in fact, between the type of airplane permitted and the type prohibited.

While I was busy with this, I stopped worrying about the matter of my election to the Academy of Sciences, which I had given up for lost once I had abandoned the customary visits; I assumed I had defaulted to my rival. But on the night of May 4, 1932, I received a telegram from Madrid informing me that the Academy had approved my membership by a large majority. This unexpected triumph made me very happy, and I decided to contribute my knowledge of aeronautical science to the Academy—I was the first pilot ever elected to it. The motto of my acceptance speech, delivered the following year, was *Per Scientia ad Excelsia, per Excelsia ad Scientia*. The medallion I received bore the number fifteen, which had previously belonged to José Echegaray, Nobel Prize winner in literature and eminent mathematician.

When knowledge of my election to the Academy became public,

a certain colleague from the Engineering Academy who had brought about my near-expulsion for "being unworthy of wearing the honorable uniform of the Corps of Engineers" wrote me a letter asking my forgiveness and offering his friendship. I answered that there was nothing to forgive: on that occasion he had treated me excessively badly and on this excessively well, so we were at peace.

In 1935, as director of the Advanced School of Aerotechnics, I had to accompany the students in their last year of study on a trip to Italy, France, Germany, Russia, and England. We were well received at the principle centers of aviation in Italy, France, and Germany. The day before we were to fly to Moscow, according to our pre-established schedule, which had been approved by all the countries and pre-paid through agencies in each, I went to say goodbye to the Spanish ambassador in Berlin. He informed me that he had received a telegram from the Soviet Government denying us entrance into the U.S.S.R. When he asked them why, the Soviets answered that it was because the Spanish Republic did not have diplomatic relations with the U.S.S.R. They returned our air fare, but not the money we had paid for hotels.

In accordance with the motto I had adopted, to reach heaven through science and science through heaven, I presented a project to the Academy, Military Aviation and the Spanish Geographic Society, involving the ascent of a free balloon with a capacity of 25,000 cubic meters, to be piloted by myself alone in an open basket, wearing a space suit that would allow me to go up to 25,000 meters.

The proposal was favorably received by both Spanish and foreign scientists. I published several articles and gave many lectures on the potential of this project. A German company offered to supply the material (rubberized silk) at a greatly reduced price; the Zeiss company offered me a high magnification telescope of their manufacture so the balloon could be observed from earth at high altitudes; and the Swiss company Vulcan offered to give me a precision watch, made to my specifications, and other precision instruments I needed.

The Spanish and foreign press, including the Russian, published articles describing my project, and French Aviation offered to send a flying escort to follow the balloon and assist with the landing. A similar offer was tendered by my friend Juanito de La Cierva with his Autogyro.

The balloon was built in accordance with my plan in the workshop of the Aerostatic Service at Guadalajara. But we still had to resolve the problem of the space suit. We needed a suit that, while maintaining the air at normal atmospheric pressure inside, would at the same time permit liberty of movement in the stratosphere. To achieve this we would have to prevent the air pressure inside the sleeves and pant legs from making them rigid. I thought the way to accomplish this was to give the suit at each joint an accordion-pleated form, flexible but not extensible. That is, it would have the form of a bellows, secured with steel cables that allowed it to flex without stretching. I studied the form for each joint— shoulders, elbows, wrists, hips, ankles, and even the fingers—and at the same time the problem of resistance to the interior atmospheric pressure and the thermal problem of preventing natural body heat from being dissipated in space through the suit's material.

As a result of these studies and the testing that accompanied them, the first space suit in the world was built. It consisted of three suits: one, of wool, went next to the skin and enveloped the body completely from the neck to the ends of the toes and fingers; another, of rubber asbolutely impermeable to air, also covered the whole body from the neck to the extremities; a third tough protective layer was made of cloth reinforced with steel wire and pleated at each joint accordion-style with steel cables that did not stretch but did permit flexibility. The head was covered from the neck up by an aluminum helmet with a round visor in front of the face composed of three layers of glass, each of which was transparent to visible light rays. One was unbreakable, the second opaque to ultra-violet rays, and the third opaque to infra-red rays. These glasses contained an anti-fog substance, and the helmet attached by screwing onto a metal ring hermetically sealed at the neck to the rubber and outer layers of the suit. Inside the helmet there was a breathing tube which conveyed pure oxygen to the mouth, and a device to absorb the carbon dioxide produced by respiration. There was also a microphone for speaking to the outside by radio—a microphone I had specially built without the use of carbon, which could ignite spontaneously when exposed to the pure oxygen from the breathing tube. Both outside and inside the visor, where I could always see them, a thermometer and a barometer were installed to show me the temperature and air pressure inside and outside the space suit.

I also had at my disposal a cape made of silver lamé to put on if I felt too warm from the effects of the sun's rays—this would reflect the heat. In case of intense cold, I had studied electric heaters, but I found in the two experiments I conducted at Cuatro Vientos—each lasting about three hours—that a heater was not necessary. Standing with my suit on in a metal tunnel where the atmosphere was as close to that of the stratosphere as possible and the temperature held at 79° [C] below zero through the use of dry ice, I found that the temperature inside my suit stayed at 33° [C] above zero.

The ascent was planned for the month of October 1936, when it was predicted that meteorological conditions would be the most favorable, and during the wait I went to the summer session at the University of Santander to give a course on aerodynamics. The session was also attended by Professor Auguste Piccard, who had recently completed a stratospheric ascent in a spherical closed basket made of aluminum. He was very interested in my projected ascent and was constantly giving me advice. (In Madrid I had also met the Russian aeronaut Prokofiev, who had also made an ascent in a closed sphere and who was very pessimistic about the results of my project.)[71]

Meanwhile the political tension between the Republicans and the Falangists was increasing to a dangerous level. The conspiracy against the Republic, born at the installation of the new regime, grew more widespread every day. To give an idea of what was happening, I prefer to quote the words of one of the most active conspirators, the Carlist Antonio Lizarza, from his book *Memorias de la conspiración, 1931–1936: Como se preparó en Navarra la Cruzada* (Pamplona, 1953). [Herrera here quotes a number of pages from Lizarza's book, to demonstrate that the conspiracy between the military, the church and right-wing politicians had been carefully planned in advance of Franco's uprising in July 1936.]

I think that these words by the principal organizer of the conspiracy in Navarre are sufficient to convey the ambience in which the Republic had to develop throughout Spain. What stands out, in addition to the seeds of military rebellion, is the secret, belligerant, absolutely anti-Christian actions of a large part of the Spanish Catholic Church. Even when these acts became publicly known, not one member of the ecclesiastical hierarchy raised his voice to condemn them. Apostolic Roman Catholic that I am, I cannot consider as representatives of Christ those who conceal, prepare, or manufacture arms to assassinate their own brothers, whose only sin was to defend and support a legally constituted political regime, established through peaceful and democratic means. Nor do I condone those prelates who approved these acts by their silence.

Bands of gunmen from both sides began shooting at each other, with better and better aim. The burial of the victims of one encounter served as the occasion for more killing. Luís Jiménez de Asúa, professor of the University of Madrid, was attacked in the street, and the policeman accompanying him was killed. Lieutenant Castillo of the Assault Guards was assassinated by Falangists and died in the arms of his wife, at the door to his house.[72] One of his friends, keeping vigil over his body that night, swore that before dawn he would be avenged. Others joined in the oath and that same night Calvo Sotelo, leader of the opposition to the Republic, was assassinated by members of the Assault Guards.

The upset caused by this crime was intense, at the University of Santander and throughout Spain. Although we did not have the details, we already knew that the Falange was in contact with the Italian and German governments, that civil war was about to break out and they were counting on the help of Mussolini and Hitler to overthrow the Republic. It was natural that they would take advantage of these recent events to accomplish their goal.

In fact, on Saturday, July 18, 1936, the Army in Africa rebelled, and the revolt swept through the Peninsula. On Sunday, the 19th, the students and professors at the University of Santander drove through Asturias; in the villages some saluted us with the hand open, fascist style, and others with the clenched fist, communist style. Professor Piccard decided to leave, bidding me an emotional farewell.

We were faced with the problem of how to return to Madrid, with communications cut in the north of Castile and Irún fallen to the rebels. The only solution was to ask France to send a warship to San Sebastián to carry us to St. Jean de Luz, from which we could reach Madrid via Cerbere and Barcelona. The French government agreed to this plan, and, after we gave our word of honor to use it to return to Madrid, they granted us all safe conduct.

We reached San Sebastián on the last train running and found the city in a desolate state. We were put up in an empty hotel, without light or water, that was in the hands of a town committee which treated me very warmly, saying, "For you, everything you need, even water, but for the others, nothing." The French boat arrived and we boarded with difficulty because the sea was so rough. On our way to St. Jean de Luz we saw the fires burning in Irún, set by the rebels who had taken it.

In St. Jean de Luz we were met by the Prefect of the Lower Pyrenees, who told us that we were completely at liberty either to stay in France, to go to the rebel zone via Pamplona, or to the Republican zone via Cerbere and Barcelona.

The university rector asked us each to express our wishes, so he could make a list of names according to destination. I spoke up to say that we had all promised on our word of honor to return to Madrid and there was no need for a list. The rector, Blas Cabrera'[73] and the other professors pointed out to me that neither Daniel (a canon from Madrid who was with us) nor I could return to Madrid under such circumstances—the lives of all clergymen and all officers of the army, which had betrayed the people, were endangered, particularly mine, as I had been a friend and colleague of the rebel generals and a gentleman-in-waiting to the King. In fact, the Republican government, deserted and attacked by its own order-keeping forces, had had to resort to giving arms to the public, and even releasing prisoners from jail. The people, feeling betrayed and mocked by the army and the clergy, had taken it upon themselves to dispense justice with their own hands, even going against the orders of the government. To this I replied that Daniel should do what he thought best, but that I was the only military man there and since the general opinion was that the Spanish military went back on its word of honor, I wanted to show that I, at least, did not, and I was absolutely determined to go to Madrid as I had promised. Finally, we all set out for the frontier at Cerbere except for Daniel, a professor from the University of Valladolid who was ill with dysentery, and a student from Pamplona who had just read in the papers that one of his brothers had been hanged the day before.

Throughout this trip the professors and many of the students thought that it would offend the democratic values of the people, which were now sovereign, if they presented themselves in starched collar and tie, and they decided to dress as workers. But the result was counterproductive. If the people were offended by a bourgeois appearance, they were even more annoyed by that of a *señorito* dressed as a worker. So it happened that I, who made no changes in the customary clothing of a professor of that civilian university, was received everywhere with a courtesy and respect that surprised me, in contrast with the suspicious attitude directed at the other professors.

At the station in Barcelona, when the rector Blas Cabrera, who had an illness that made his hands tremble, presented our papers to the stationmaster, the latter shouted, "Why are you trembling? There must be something suspect if your hands are shaking!" I had to intervene and explain that he was a distinguished professor with a condition that made it impossible for him to keep his hands still.

In Madrid I found what I expected: an out-of-control populace master of the city. The rightists had taken refuge in the embassies, or they had fled, or they were in hiding. I have always been against running and hiding; I don't believe life is worth doing ridiculous things to save it. Furthermore I like situations to be clear-cut, so I went directly to the bull—which is to say, to the Subsecretary of Aviation, Lieutenant Colonel Angel Pastor, a good friend of mine.[74] But when the political regime changes, friendship counts for nothing. I told him, "I am here for you to do as you wish with me. I want you to know or remember that I was a friend and colleague of Franco and all the rebel generals, and a gentleman, and personal friend of the King, so you can shoot me if you think it proper. What I want is that in two or three months you don't say that you just found out these things, that you didn't know. I want you to know about them now. But I also want you to know that I have given my word of honor to serve the Republic loyally, and I am not one to break my word." Pastor answered, "We all know you perfectly well and we are certain you will keep your word of honor."

In fact, I was sent to the aerodrome at Los Alcázares as chief of instruction and technical services. I was in charge of training pilots, observers, bombardiers, mechanics, apprentices, radio technicians, and so on. They were scattered all over the zone, from Alicante and Cartagena to the Pyrenees, and I had to cover the area weekly, on nocturnal flights over the water, taking advantage of bad weather when we were less likely to be attacked by enemy fighter planes. Over land, we had to fly in absolute darkness, without even interior lights at our seats. To distract myself I learned to read Braille, using books and magazines I purchased in Barcelona. Several times we were fired upon by anti-aircraft guns defending Barcelona—seeing a mysterious plane arriving at dawn, they thought we were the enemy.

Although the best time had passed for my projected stratospheric ascent, I told Indalecio Prieto, the Air Minister, that everything was ready and that if he would authorize it I could make the ascent immediately.[75] He asked me why I wanted to do it in the midst of such circumstances, and I said, to provide some semblance of normality. Prieto answered, "And who are we going to fool? Of course you want to go up into the stratosphere, and I want it more than you do, but I don't think Spain is in any condition for balloon ascents."

The ascent never took place. The balloon was cut into pieces to make raincoats for the soldiers (it was rubberized silk), and the space suit, with all its instruments, fell into the hands of the enemy at Cuatro Vientos.

Meanwhile the rebellion had developed into a struggle to the death, with most of the army, the clergy, and the aristocracy against the people of the Republic. The enemy could count on not only the arms and personnel existing in Spain, but also on the Moroccan forces, the armies of Hitler and Mussolini, and (according to them) the "Fifth Column" operating clandestinely in the cities. Until the government was able to organize some forces to keep order, the people, attacked and betrayed, assassinated multitudes of persons they suspected of belonging to the Fifth Column.

The European Non-Intervention Committee and the American embargo prevented our government from acquiring any arms to defend itself with. Only the U.S.S.R. sent us any war materiel, which was paid for with gold from the Bank of Spain, which moved to Moscow when the rebel forces were approaching Madrid. When the first Russian shipment arrived at Los Alcázares, one of our army officers came to see me there, asking to see the materiel they had delivered. He was an old friend of mine, and a distant relative as well, so I showed it to him. A few days later most of the equipment was destroyed by a tremendous enemy air attack—the bombs were aimed precisely at the hangars where the Russian delivery was stored. After the war was over, I read in a pamphlet published in Spain that this officer who had visited me had been of great service to Franco's army, which he had secretly furnished with information about the location of our supplies.

It is only natural that among the defenders of the Republic there would be some—released from jail so they could be recruited for defense—who would behave in a criminal fashion. As for me, I can only tell of an incident that befell my own family. While I was in Los Alcázares, it was common for armed patrols to present themselves at houses in Madrid to search for and take away any money and objects of value they found. Because of this, our family collected all its jewelry and money and brought it to my in-laws' house, where it was buried under some tiles in the floor, the work carefully camouflaged. Within two days a patrol came to the house and the man in charge—a convict—went directly to the spot where the treasure was hidden and, tapping the floor with the heel of his boot, gave the order to lift the tile. They did so and found all the hidden jewels and money. After reprimanding the members of the family who, "in spite of having attended private schools, were ignorant of the law prohibiting the hoarding of objects of value," the patrol left with everything, and the family thought they would never see it again. The person who had denounced us was a maid who became suspicious when she saw some marks on the floor.

The family was friends with Julio Alvarez del Vayo, the Republic's Foreign Minister, and they wrote him a letter complaining about what had happened, explaining that they were left absolutely without money, as my sons and I were away serving in the army.[76] In a few days, they received a letter from the Secretary saying they could reclaim their valuables and money at police headquarters. They went at once to the police where they found, along with an infinitude of like goods, their own possessions, which were returned to them. The point of the story is that this unofficial armed patrol, led by a convict, had deposited everything they took into the hands of the Republican government, down to the last cent and the last piece of jewelry, in a search made on their own initiative and without government authorization. By contrast, I have never been able to recover any of my property that fell into the hands of the fascist authorities.

My older son José was attached to the Fifth Regiment, participating in zones of heavy action such as Madrid, Extremadura, and the Ebro, acting principally as a military historian.[77] My younger son Emilio volunteered to serve with Aviation before he reached the obligatory age for military service. The pilots were sent for training to flying schools in Los Alcázares, France, or Russia. My son chose the latter two and received his fighter pilot license at the aerodrome in Kirovabad, in the Caucasus. When he returned to Los Alcazares, he told me, very pleased, that he had been assigned to Santander, where the last pilot had been killed, and that he was leaving immediately. I asked him if we could have lunch, and as he didn't know I went to ask his superior Núñez Maza.[78] He told me, "Your son is not going to Santander because I care too much about him. When I asked for two volunteers for this dangerous assignment to Santander, your son was the only one to take a step forward. I prefer that he not go, but stay here with me as part of the fighter group I am organizing, unless you prefer that he go to Santander." I answered that I did not want to interfere, and that he should go where he would be of best service to the Republic. My son was very angry with me because he thought I had influenced the decision not to send him to Santander (which was on the point of falling to the enemy).

On June 7, 1937, Cardinal Gomá, the primate of Spain, sent a letter to all the cardinals, archbishops, and ecclesiastical vicars of Spain which said, "My friends and Your Excellency: On the 15th of May I wrote to the Reverend Metropolitans to inform them of a directive I had received from the Head of State a few days before, and to ask their opinion on the appropriateness of seconding it. The response was affirmative. The directive has been carried out in the form of a collective letter from the Spanish Episcopate to all the bishops of the world, and I have the honor of sending you a copy of this letter whose object is to second the Head of State's initiative, and to present, in an authorized manner, our impressions of the National Movement."

All who received this letter answered affirmatively, signing the collective statement in obedience to the Caudillo's directive—except for two, Cardinal Vidal i Barraquer and Bishop Múgica of Vitoria. These two were expelled from Spain and the former died in exile. The latter returned to Spain, blind and infirm, when he was in his nineties.[79]

In the collective letter that all the prelates of Spain (except these two) mailed to the entire Catholic world on July 1, 1937, they denounced the crimes committed by the Spanish "Reds," without mentioning the cause of these crimes (participation by the clergy in the conspiracy against the Republic, acquiring and hiding arms for the rebellion in churches and convents, manufacturing bombs in the parishes under the direction of parish priests, and so forth), without a single voice ever raised on the part of the Spanish Church to condemn these anti-Christian acts, the responsibility for which therefore falls on the church as a whole. The letter cites dreadful tortures inflicted on priests by the "Reds" (of which I never heard a word, although I covered the entire "Red" zone during the war); it says they pursued fugitive priests with packs of dogs which tore them to pieces, that they put out their eyes, cut off their tongues and hands, buried or burned them alive, slit them open, crucified them. They also denounced atrocities that were patently false, like the pillaging of works of art from the Prado and Palacio de Liria, the dynamiting of the Arco de Baza in Tarragona, and the theft of treasures from the Toledo Cathedral. All this constituted a crime of calumny at a moment when passions were at a peak and intelligence was impossible or very difficult to obtain. Now, after more than a quarter of century, when the truth is known, these lies are still upheld, without the slightest effort to rectify them by those who perpetrated them. These people deserve the condemnation of the human and divine justice that they themselves claim to represent.

On August 25, 1937, Santander fell to the enemy and on the 26th Count Ciano wrote in his diary: "The victory at Santander has assumed major proportions. It is not the beginning of the end—the end is still a long way away—but it is a heavy blow to the Reds in Spain. I have given orders for the aircraft at Palma to bomb Valencia tonight. This is the moment to terrorize the enemy."[80]

My son Emilio, head of his patrol, was part of a squadron of seven fighter planes that were operating on the Ebro front. He and his comrades found themselves confronting an enormous squad of twenty Italian bombers, supported by several more fighters, on their way to bomb Valencia. The head of our squadron, in light of the size of the Italian force, felt that to attack them would be suicidal, and he turned back from the attack and ordered the others to return to the base. This decision angered the pilots,

and in their name my son expressed their displeasure at having
fled from combat with the enemy. The captain answered that he
had acted to avoid the loss of the group in a fight that would have
been futile; but, because of the pilots' opinion, he said that if a
similar occasion presented itself, they would fight.

This opportunity arose a few days later, on September 4, and
the captain, keeping his word, sent a fighter squadron to defend
Valencia. He told me that he saw my son attacking a bomber, and
that three fighters attacked him simultaneously; when the captain
went to my son's aid, two other enemy fighters attacked him and
while he was defending himself from them, he saw my son's plane
fall in a spin, pursued to the ground by the three fighters, firing
at him with all their machine guns while he fell. Three pilots were
lost in this combat, one burned to death, his plane shot down in
flames.

I learned in Valencia that my son had not come back from
combat on the 4th, and I went by car with my son José to search
the front for the site of the crash; but we were unable to find the
lost planes, except for the one belonging to the pilot who had
been so badly burned. The grief caused by the loss of my son
among his comrades—all of whom had great affection for him—
was profound. On the night of his disappearance, when they were
all asleep in the barracks, one of them began to shout, "Herrera's
here! Herrera's here!" The others, abruptly wakened, said, "But
what are you saying? Where is Herrera?" and the first one answered sadly, "It's nothing, I was dreaming."

My son José and I were griefstricken by his loss. José had lost
his only brother, with whom he was united with a love deeper
than fraternal affection; they both felt a kind of adoration for
each other. For me, the death of my parents had caused me the
deepest pain of my life, but it was, nevertheless, a consequence
of the law of Nature. But to lose a twenty-year old son, in whom
I saw the extension of myself—he even had my name—produced
a sorrow that will never be erased, not only grief for his death,
but feelings of anger and hatred against that stupid war between
brothers, and against the depraved souls who had brought it to
pass.

This dreadful tragedy for us was an occasion for General Quiepo
de Llano to make a joke on Radio Seville.[81] He said, "Just as the

father has not been able to rise as high as he would have liked, so the son has fallen sooner than he would have liked."

The Spanish Red Cross told me where Emilio's body had been found behind enemy lines, riddled with bullet holes, near his plane. He had been buried on the spot near another pilot from his squadron, named Sardina, who died in the same combat. My family has petitioned to move his body to a cemetery; but in order to do this we needed the death certificate, which was granted by Franco's government but written as if he had died fighting against the Republic, and we refused to accept it. And so I pursued and will continue to pursue the matter until it is possible to bury him with all the honors that his heroic death deserves, in the course of which he fulfilled all the requirements for the Cruz Laureada de San Fernando.

In spite of the note from the Red Cross and a letter from Kindelán saying he had placed a cross on my son's grave, I have always suspected that in reality he did not die there, but that, shot down in combat, he had been taken prisoner and shot. The reasons for these suspicions are, first, during one of General Quiepo de Llano's chats on Radio Seville, he said that my son was perfectly all right. Then, two of Emilio's friends, at different times, told me they believed he had been shot. And finally, in early September, just a few days after the combat, a notice was published in the press saying that four Red pilots, prisoners, had been court-marshalled: one was Russian, one American, one Spanish who had been trained as a pilot in France, and the other a Spaniard who had been trained in Russia. The article gave the names of all except this last one and said all had been condemned to death. Suspecting that this unnamed pilot might be my son, I petitioned the English and American Embassies, to see if they could prevent the sentence from being carried out. The English Embassy answered that they would do everything possible, but the American one refused summarily. When I reminded them that one of the condemned men was an American citizen, they responded that he deserved the death penalty for having fought against Franco. The outcome of the court-martial, according to the papers, was that the Russian and American pilots were pardoned because they were foreigners; the two Spaniards were shot, and the name of the one trained in Russia was never mentioned.

From my point of view the American pilot was suspect. He had been taken prisoner on his first flight against the enemy, and the Francoist forces offered to exchange him for one of their pilots that we had taken prisoner. We refused, asking them to return the American without any exchange. The press published a picture of this pilot and that of a pretty girl friend of his who had written a letter to General Franco, enclosing her picture, asking clemency for her friend. Like the press, Franco indulged in an outburst of Spanish generosity, granting the American's pardon and saying, "I cannot permit those beautiful eyes to shed tears because of my actions." After the war, this pilot was employed by Swissair and became implicated in the theft of some bars of gold that disappeared from a plane he was flying.

The German and Italian Air Forces, together with the Spanish Francoists, stepped up their bombardment against our factories, military centers, railroads and even civilian centers, in order to "terrorize" the enemy. The brutal bombing of Guernica horrified the world. A violent attack on Barcelona caused many deaths and casualties among the civilian population. Prieto, the Air Minister, expressed his reluctance to retaliate by bombing civilian populations in the enemy zone, but he had come to doubt whether this policy might not be working against us and whether he ought not to respond to each bombing with a strong attack against a city occupied by the enemy; in this way perhaps the Francoist attacks would stop, as they were being carried out with total impunity. With this motive, he ordered the bombing of Salamanca by our air force.

The enemy responded with a frightful attack on Barcelona, on the 16th, 17th, and 18th of March, 1937, killing more than 900 civilians—120 of them children—and demolishing whole blocks of buildings. The University suffered damage also; one of the strangest things was that closed boxes containing laboratory microscopes burst open because of the sudden drop in outside pressure produced when the bombs exploded.

Prieto himself confessed to me, "Herrera, we cannot go on like this; we must admit that we are outnumbered." This bombing, carried out by the Italian fascist air force, was so cruel that it provoked the German ambassador to protest. He sent a telegram to Hitler saying that after such acts of brutality the Spanish people would end up hating the Italians and Germans who were helping the "Glorious Movement" of General Franco.

There were some curious events during the bombing. A bomb fell on a truck loaded with ammunition, each piece of which exploded in sequence, one after the other. Another fell beside a pedestrian, severing his neck and leaving him headless; in spite of this, he continued to walk a few steps, decapitated. A resident of an upper floor was in the bathroom when the bombing started and when he opened the door he found that the whole front of the building had collapsed and he was about to step out into empty space; when the all clear sounded he had to get down on a fire ladder. The family of a friend of mine, Ramón Ferro, a pharmacist-pilot with Military Health, composed of the couple, two daughters and a baby, were having lunch in the dining room near a balcony that faced onto the street when the bombing started. Thinking that room was a dangerous place to be, they moved to an interior passage and sent the maid to get the baby from his crib. One bomb killed them all, except for the maid who went to get the baby. Another friend of mine was walking on the Ramblas with his daughter. They were both thrown to the ground by a bomb that exploded nearby. The father got up unhurt, but the daughter was killed instantly. The employees in auxiliary aviation services wore the emblem of wings on their uniforms, even though they did not fly. When they tried to take refuge in the subway during the bombing the other people there threw them out shouting, "Pilots, out of the shelters! To your planes!"

[There follows a description of civilian deaths in Barcelona from Claude Bowers, *My Mission in Spain* (New York, 1954), pp. 376–377.]

During a bombing of Valencia a few days later, a bomb fell on a car parked in front of the door to the Aviation Headquarters building, destroying it. A sharp sliver of glass from the windshield was found buried in the iron railing of the balcony, embedded to a depth of three centimeters.

In spite of our decision not to conduct air attacks except on the front lines, the Francoist air force continued to bomb our cities and centers of civilian population, even the most defenseless ones and those that lacked any military character whatever. Every afternoon a hydroplane from the Balearics, which people called *El Zapatones* ("The Clodhopper"), drove up and down the coastal highways, riding on its pontoons, machine-gunning all the cars, bicycles, and pedestrians it encountered. More than once I had to conceal my car in the trees while it passed.

The strict order given by Prieto not to attack anything but the front lines was followed exactly by the pilots, and this provoked Prince Alfonso de Orleans, who was on Franco's side, to publish an article in the *Revista de Aeronáutica* saying that "the Red Air Force was so bad that although it was based only twelve kilometers from Zaragoza, it never dared to bomb the city and life went on as usual there with no concern." In spite of this declaration by a high authority, a paper in Zaragoza published an article stating that a Red plane had dropped a bomb on the Church of Pilar, but that the Virgin had miraculously escaped injury from the attempted sacrilege because the bomb had failed to explode, producing instead the sign of the cross on its impact with the church wall.

In exact compliance with the proposal made by the Non-Intervention Committee to both sides in the Civil War, the Republican government decreed:

1) to prohibit all aerial warfare outside the front lines of combat;

2) to respect the lives of prisoners of war;

3) to expel all foreign combatants from Spain.

The Non-Intervention Committee believed that with these measures the war would be humanized and fought only by Spanish combatants, leaving the road to peace open for both sides. But this was not the case. The loyal government fulfilled these three conditions faithfully, but the rebel army continued to bomb civilian populations, shoot prisoners, and use German and Italian divisions.[82]

In order to comply with the third condition, our side brought all the foreign combatants together in Barcelona and made preparations for a general parade on November 15, 1938, to say goodbye to them and see them out of the country, under the supervision of the League of Nations and the Non-Intervention Committee. The day was very clear, with a strong mistral wind, and the crowds flocked into the streets to bid farewell to the foreign survivors of our war who had risked their lives to defend our liberty.

I watched the parade with my son José and his wife Carmen from their balcony on the Diagonal. They had been married in Madrid twenty-one months before, in the middle of the war, and had made their wedding trip from Madrid to Los Alcázares on a truck loaded with bombs which was attacked several times by enemy planes. The parade had been going on for several hours, amid enthusiastic and emotional public acclaim, when the news reached us that the pilot Ramón Franco, the Caudillo's brother, had taken off from the Balearics at the head of a bomber squadron, intending to bomb Barcelona while the streets were crowded with people watching the parade. The occasion could not have been more propitious for a massacre even greater than the one of March 18. The city's entire population was in the streets, and it would be impossible to sight the planes approaching from the south with the midday sun behind them. The success of the operation seemed assured, but our intelligence in the Balearics warned us in time to clear the streets and order everyone into the bomb shelters, and dispatch fighter planes to defend the city.

The hours passed but the Francoist bombers never appeared; everything returned to normal. Finally we found out why this potentially deadly operation failed. When the squadron was within just a few miles of Barcelona, Ramón Franco's plane went into a nosedive and crashed into the sea. The other pilots, demoralized by the loss of their leader, turned around and returned to their base. Although there was a strong north wind blowing, it was not dangerous enough to be a problem for a flier as experienced as Ramón Franco, and no one could explain the cause of the sudden accident. Sabotage by the Republicans? Sabotage by the Francoists because Ramón had had a falling out with his brother? Various hypotheses have been advanced, but none was ever proven.

The Spanish government received an invitation from the Chilean government to attend the inauguration in Santiago of its new president, Aguirre Cerda, who had been elected on October 26, 1938.[83] Our government appointed a special delegation headed by Indalecio Prieto and he, wanting to distract me from the sad state of mind I had been in since my son's death, appointed me military attaché to his delegation.

I left Barcelona for Paris by car on November 29, 1938, stopped over in Lyons, and reached the French capital the next day, where I joined Prieto, his son, and his daughter Conchita, who were accompanying him on the trip. We had reserved passage on the *Normandie*, a beautiful transatlantic liner that was later destroyed by fire, but because its crew was on strike we had to sail on the

English liner *Aquitania,* leaving Cherbourg on December 3. We were accompanied on this ship by two invisible passengers—Anthony Eden and Douglas Fairbanks—who spent the entire journey in their cabins and never saw or spoke to any of the other passengers. Prieto tried to arrange a conference with Mr. Eden, communicating through his son (who spoke English) and Eden's secretary, but the English politician diplomatically refused to speak with the "Red" Spanish politician, excusing himself on the grounds that he didn't have a single free moment during the six-day voyage.[84]

Beginning with our arrival in New York on December 9, we were received with ever-increasing warmth at each port of call. In New York we were greeted effusively by the Spanish community and, of course, by the inevitable American reporters. My colleague from the Engineering Corps, Francisco León Trejo (an observation pilot and aeronautical engineer) accompanied us and entertained us throughout our stay. I also saw a Catalan friend, Miret, whom I had met in Barcelona when I was flying balloons with Fernández Duro. I told him about the horrors of the bombing of Barcelona and he was astonished, saying "Barcelona was bombed? I can't believe it. I have been told not to believe anything the Reds say about these bombings." I answered, "You can believe it or not believe it, but I saw these terrible things with my own eyes." I also met another friend who was living in the same hotel as Sr. Cardenas, the diplomat who had helped to organize CIANA with me and with whom I had been good friends. Although he was in New York as Franco's representative, I sent him a message saying it would give me great pleasure to see him, if he wished. He flatly refused to see me.

On December 15 we left for Miami by train, where the Spanish community gave a banquet for us and Prieto made a speech. The 17th we left on a Sikorsky hydroplane, landing in Cienfuegos, Cuba, Kingston, Jamaica, and Cristóbal, Panama, lavishly entertained at each stop. On the 18th we boarded a Douglas for Chile, stopping at Turbo, Cali, Tumaco, Guayaquil, Talara, Chiclayo, Trujillo, Lima, Pisco, Arequipa, Arica, Antofagasta and Vallenar. Finally we arrived in Santiago de Chile, where a huge crowd welcomed us at the airport with cheers for Spain, the Republic, and Prieto and his party. One cheer that particularly moved me was "Hurray for Petere's father"—it seems that my own fame had faded before the popularity my own son enjoyed in these distant lands.[86]

The officials who met us at the airport were the Chilean Secretaries of State and War, our ambassador Rodrigo Soriano with the whole Embassy staff, and a Chilean Air Force Colonel who had been appointed my personal aide, with a car and chauffeur at my disposal. At the Embassy Prieto called me aside to tell me that my aide, Colonel Florencio Gómez Flores, was a rightist and had protested against this assignment but the Secretary had insisted. Prieto advised me not to accept him as my aide, but I responded that the Colonel had presented himself for orders coldly, but in correct military form, and thus I did not think it proper to reject him.

Day after day he served me with absolute correctness, and one day he asked me if I would accept his invitation to supper at the Casino. I did so gladly, and after supper he told me, "General, I have to make a confession. When I was appointed as your aide I protested because I did not want to follow a Red general's orders, but they made me do it against my will." I told him I was already aware of this, and he said, "But now, after having gotten to know you, I consider it the greatest honor to have served at your command." Naturally I expressed my satisfaction with his having modified his preconception of the "Reds."

The Spanish ambassador to Buenos Aires, Angel Ossorio y Gallardo, telegraphed us that he would arrive in Santiago by plane at six in the morning the next day.[87] Neither Prieto nor Soriano—nor anyone else—were particularly disposed to get up in the dead of night to greet him, so to spare them this inconvenience, I arose at four-thirty and at six was waiting at the airport to represent both ambassadors. When Ossorio and his wife arrived I introduced myself and he asked what I was doing there. I explained that I was the military attaché with Prieto's special delegation. Then he asked me if I had any credentials for the job. I said I didn't know and he said if I had no credentials I had no right to be in Santiago. I told him I would do whatever Don Indalecio said and he insisted again that if I had no credentials I could not attend the inauguration as a member of the delegation. This sour reception put me in a pretty bad mood, not because I feared that—after all those miles traveled—I would not be able to attend the ceremony to which I was invited, but because if I had stayed in bed with the rest of the Embassy staff I would have avoided this dressing down.

In Santiago I went to lay a wreath of flowers at the monument to the Chilean Army war dead, and in my speech I made it clear that I did this in the name of the entire Spanish army, of both sides. After the ceremony the Chilean troops passed in review before me.

In Chile, the person in charge of passing out toys to children on Christmas Eve is neither Père Noel, nor Santa Claus, nor the Three Wise Men; instead it is "El Viejito Pascuero" [Little Father Christmas], that is, the father or mother dressed up in a long white beard. We were invited by a Chilean family to lunch on Christmas Day and the lady of the house appeared with bandages all over her face. The night before she had gone into the children's bedroom disguised as El Viejito Pascuero with beard and candle, when suddenly her beard caught fire and the children watched in horror as El Viejito Pascuero, screaming as his beard burned, was transformed into their own mother.

The inauguration of the president took place in the Palacio de la Moneda in Santiago, attended by a large audience which included all the diplomats stationed in Chile and all the Chilean authorities. When our special delegation entered the hall, the whole audience burst out in applause and cheers for Spain and the Republic. When the Italian delegation appeared, the public received them with whistles, stamping of feet, and cries of "Out!" and "Die!" This commotion was repeated at the entrance of the German delegation and even more noisily when the representatives of the Holy See arrived. By this time the atmosphere had begun to resemble that of a bull ring after a bad sword thrust by the matador. We didn't know how to react; while the devoutly Catholic Ossorio y Gallardo showed his approval, the atheist Prieto was indignant, protesting that no matter what one's beliefs were, it was scandalous to treat the Pope's representatives so rudely, as they stood for a spiritual power that must be respected.

On Saturday the 31st we set out for Viña del Mar, accompanied by my aide Colonel Gómez; after lunch we went on to Valparaiso to attend a banquet and reception. We returned to Viña del Mar for New Year's Eve, attending religious ceremonies in a church on the beach, where the prayers, recited in a Chilean accent, sounded very peculiar to my ears.

On January 1, 1939, we returned to Santiago, and after attending banquets for General Amiezena and the new President, we left on the 7th in a Douglas for Buenos Aires, flying over the Andes and stopping in Mendoza and Córdoba. There we were entertained at yet another banquet and consequently missed the plane and had to continue to Buenos Aires by train.

I will never forget that train trip, which lasted from nine at night until 8:30 in the morning. At every station we were greeted by a large crowd shouting, "Prieto, Prieto!" and begging him to say a few words to them. But Prieto locked himself in his compartment and refused to come out all night. At one station, the crowd surged through the train, banging on all the doors to make Prieto get up. I tried to quiet them down by begging them to let him sleep because he was tired and ill, but to no avail. The train continued on its way with the corridors packed with people shouting and knocking and calling, "Prieto, Prieto!" in rhythm with the noise of the train. Once I heard someone shout, "Let's set the train on fire if Prieto doesn't come out!" Luckily this threat was not carried out, and at eight in the morning the train pulled into the station in Buenos Aires, spurting steam on all sides to clear a way through the crowds standing on the track.

The train stopped, but it was impossible for us to get out of the cars through the tide of humanity that surrounded us; Conchita and I managed to exit onto the tracks, and were horrified to see Don Indalecio floating on a sea of heads—his admirers had picked him up and were carrying him on their shoulders. Conchita cried, "Oh, they're going to kill papa!" The Spanish Embassy had sent a car for Prieto; escorted by some troops of Argentinian mounted police, he was able to reach the car and get in, but a swarm of people lifted the car off the ground. The springs couldn't support the weight and the car collapsed, so they had to send another car and, again escorted by mounted police, we finally reached the Embassy. There, the crowd invaded the gardens, trampling the shrubs and flowers, and Prieto and I had to come out on the balcony and deliver improvised speeches.

Prieto and his children stayed at the Embassy and I was given a room at the Hotel Alvear Palace, next to the room where the lady representing Franco was staying. She slipped insulting notes under my door, telling me we shouldn't be proud that half a million people met us at the station, because there were four million people in Buenos Aires and three and a half million of them couldn't be bothered to come and welcome us.

A Señora García Martín came to visit me, and rebuked me—as I was a decent person—for associating with "those Red criminals." I explained what was going on in Spain, we argued about it, and finally, furious, she said, "I'm leaving, because if we continue to discuss this you are going to convince me, and I don't want to be convinced."

The people and the press of Buenos Aires heaped eulogies on us. At this time there was an Italian warship in the port of Buenos Aires, and this gave rise to some newspaper articles asking, "What do those assassins want here?" When the ship's officers walked in the streets people followed them chanting, "Guadalajara, Guadalajara . . ."[88]; finally the boat weighed anchor and left Argentina.

Several times I took a taxi between the hotel and the Embassy and when I offered to pay the fare, the driver refused, saying, "You are General Herrera and you don't have to pay a thing in Buenos Aires."

Every day I had to attend meetings and dinners with Prieto, sometimes as speaker. But the news we were receiving from Spain had become so alarming that I asked Prieto's permission to leave the special delegation and return to Spain immediately, because it was my military duty to be there at the end of the war and suffer the consequences and not to avoid them by running and hiding. Permission granted, I left on January 16 in a Douglas from the Moron Airport (Buenos Aires), and, stopping in Porto Alegre, I landed in Rio de Janeiro where I saw the Spanish ambassador José Prieto del Río. The next day I boarded a Sikorsky hydroplane and went to Recife (Pernambuco), after stops in Vitoria, Caravelas, Bahia, Aracaju, and Maceio. The day after, in the same plane, I flew to Natal, Areia Branca, Camocim, Luis Correia, São Luis (where I continued as the only passenger) and Belém de Pará, where I spent the night.

On the 19th I continued in the same craft to Cayenne, Paramaribo, Georgetown, and Port of Spain, where I spent the night at the Queen's Park Hotel; the weather and the countryside were delightful, but I lost my fountain pen there. On the 20th I flew in a four-engine Sikorsky Clipper, stopping in San Juan (Puerto Rico), San Pedro de Macoris (Dominican Republic), Port-au-Prince (Haiti), and Antilla (Cuba), where I had to spend the night because of engine trouble. I arrived in Miami on the 21st of January and took the "Florida Special" to Washington, where the Ambassador Don Fernando de los Ríos invited me to lunch.[89] By afternoon I was in New York, where I stayed six days, hosted by Colonel León Trejo, who took me to see the first television experiments being conducted between rooms in the Empire State Building. During this stay I saw a huge demonstration in Times Square in support of Spain and in opposition to the the arms embargo against the Spanish Republic, attended by thousands—men, women, and children—carrying placards and shouting, "Stop, stop, stop the embargo against Spain."

On the 28th I boarded the transatlantic liner *Champlain,* which stopped in Plymouth and docked at Le Havre on February 4. I spent that night in Paris at the Hotel Edouard VII. The next day I had lunch at the Spanish Embassy with the Ambassador, Dr. Marcelino Pascua, who told me it was impossible for me to go to Spain as the frontier was closed, and that he had no news of my family. On the 6th I returned to the Embassy and the doorman told me that a woman who said she was my son's wife had asked for me and had been told I was in America and it was not known when I would return; she had left a message saying where she could be reached.

A good friend of mine, Don Luís Echeverría, took me at once in his car—through a thick fog which made it very difficult to find our way—to the Villette neighborhood, where Carmen was staying with a Spanish family in a very modest house, along with their niece who had also left Spain. She was seven months pregnant. She and I were immensely glad to see one another, and we moved to a boarding house on the Rue Pasquier.

She told me her story. She had had to leave Barcelona alone because my son Petere was at the front, and given her condition and the fact that she was the wife and daughter of "Reds," when the city fell to the Francoists she became a burden on her friends, who advised her to go to France. She went by truck and foot, under enemy fire, to Perpignan, where a French family took pity on her, kept her out of a concentration camp, gave her a comfortable bed, fed her, and gave her money to take the train to Paris. Of her husband Petere, we had no news until his friend the poet and writer Louis Aragon found out that he was in the camp of Saint Cyprien, near Perpignan.[90] I tried to go and get him but

I was told that the police had orders to intern all Spaniards who crossed the border in camps. But Colonel Pastor, head of the Supply Mission in Paris, took it upon himself to go to St. Cyprien, arrange for Petere's release, and bring him to Paris. He arrived on February 19.

As the boarding house where we were staying was too expensive for the three of us, we accepted a French couple's offer—the husband, Joseph Miranda, was a Spanish native—to occupy an apartment that had been furnished for them. It was at 15 Rue Béranger, fifth floor, with no elevator, in the third *arondissement* near the Place de la Republique. We are still living there.

On April 13, I went with Carmen, whose baby was almost due, to the zoo at Vincennes, and we climbed to the top of the artificial mountain they have there; the next day my first grandson Emilio was born, while the Spanish community celebrated the eighth anniversary of the birth of the Republic. My son José was invited to go to Mexico along with some other Spanish intellectuals who were refugees in France, leaving Carmen, the baby and me in Paris. Meanwhile my wife and her sister were in Los Alcázares, taking care of her nonagenarian father, her octagenarian mother, an uncle (Lieutenant Colonel José Alvarez Campaña of the Engineering Corps), and a very old, blind aunt. They were all ailing, beseiged by air raids, and without food, because I had given strict orders to the food distributors not to give me or any member of my family a single gram more than our quota.

At the end of the war on April 1, my family moved to Madrid and my wife was able to come to Paris, alone, to join Carmen and me and meet her grandson. When she arrived in Paris and saw that we were staying in a fifth-floor walk-up, she said, "But why are you living here?" I answered, "For the two weeks our exile will last, we can well put up with these inconveniences." These inconveniences have so far lasted twenty-nine years.

In any case, my wife was delighted to be reunited with us and her grandson, and free of the bombings and restrictions of war which she had suffered for three years in Spain. She was sleeping peacefully the first night when we were awakened by the clamor of the first sirens, the prelude to the Second World War just beginning.

My wife and Carmen wanted their parents to meet their great-grandson and grandson, respectively, and Carmen wanted to go to Mexico to be with her husband. So the two of them went to Madrid, leaving me alone in Paris, when the *drôle de Guerre* was beginning not to be so droll. When they reached the Spanish frontier, the Francoist customs agent took away Carmen's passport, which she needed to order to go to Mexico. When she went to reclaim it, they told her that one of the punishments the "Reds" had to suffer was matrimonial separation. After a lot of negotiation in Madrid she was able to obtain a new passport and left for Mexico with her baby to join my son.

The German army, having taken Belgium, was marching towards Paris, and the capital's population began its exodus to the south. All the tenants of our building, including the custodians, departed, leaving only myself and an aged neighbor. She asked me anxiously, "What do you think will happen?" I answered that I thought the Germans would be there within three days, and she said, "But won't there be a Battle of the Marne?"

Sitting in a café on the Boulevard St. Denis, I saw the desolate parade that came down from the north via the Boulevard de Strasbourg, fleeing the invading army: the dispersed officers in cars; disorderly columns of exhausted soldiers, some comforted and given food and drink by a few women, but others jeered at; an endless line of fugitive families in every kind of vehicle or on foot. I remember a poor woman on a bicycle, loaded down with a huge sack and followed by a five-year old boy, also on a bicycle, pedaling furiously so as not to be left behind and crying, "Mama, mama!" There were no trains or any organized form of transportation, and everyone was looking for a vehicle to go south. The Miranda family, from whom we leased our apartment, was able to find a truck driven by a captain, and enough gasoline to get to Toulouse.

The Mexican embassy invited me to leave Paris with them; the Spanish embassy had forgotten my existence. But the Miranda family insistently offered me a seat in their truck. I, like a good general, had tried to predict the strategic plan the French and the Germans would follow, but I was completely mistaken. I thought that the disorganized French army would abandon the northern part of France, including Paris, but that they would establish a front of resistance in the Loire Valley, and that the Germans, in possession of Paris and the coast of the English Channel, would not attempt to cross the Loire and would direct their forces against

England, taking advantage of the latter's loss of morale. I felt that if I stayed in Paris I ran the risk of being taken prisoner by the Germans, and I would not be able to communicate with my family. On the other hand, if I went to Toulouse with the Mirandas, it would be easy to keep in touch with them. In the midst of this I had an operation on one of my eyes in the Hotel de Dieu Hospital, in which my friends Drs. Teófilo Hernando and Gregorio Marañón, also refugees, participated.[91] When it was over I went to Notre Dame to meditate on what I should do about leaving Paris. One part of me was attracted by the idea of not losing touch with my family, but the other was repelled by the idea of running away. Still undecided, I went home and, looking fixedly at a portrait of my dead son, I asked him to advise me, stating both alternatives. When I presented the choice of remaining in Paris, I had the illusion that he started to smile from his portrait, and at that moment I made the decision to stay. I told the dear Mirandas that I could not accept their offer and that I would stay in the city and look after their house and furniture.

This was August 13, 1940. Paris was deserted and without public services, awaiting the imminent arrival of the Germans. In the afternoon I went to say goodbye to the Miranda family, which consisted of two brothers, one married to Louise and the other to her sister Marinette. The truck and the captain who was driving it were ready to go, but the Mirandas, in their excessive generosity, had invited a couple with a dog to come with them. This couple took their places in the truck with the dog, but the captain said the dog had to stay in Paris. Then the invited wife said she would go on foot with the dog, and Marinette decided to accompany her friend and give up the truck they had gone to so much trouble to acquire. Her husband did the same, and the truck drove off carrying only the invited husband, Louise, and her husband, leaving Marinette, her husband, the invited lady and dog to go on foot. The moment they started off, some riding and some on foot, a storm sprang up and a bolt of lightning struck within a few meters of us, hitting the lightning rod on the Church of St. Elizabeth.

In the sepulchral silence of the city, unbroken even by the sound of bombs or artillery, I returned to my house and went to bed. In the morning I was awakened by the noise of low-flying planes— it was the Germans. I got dressed and went out, on foot naturally—

there were no buses or subway trains—to the outer boulevards where I saw the columns of German troops, the soldiers riding in trucks with their guns aimed at the balconies. The army was impeccable, both in dress and personal appearance; the few French who remained watched them with more curiosity than hate, but when some women approached the infantrymen in an attempt to be friendly, others objected and cried out, "Oh, là là, là là, là là!"

All the cafés I passed were closed except the Marceville on the Boulevard Montmartre, and I went in. A few French locals were sitting at one table and I sat down at another, when two German officers entered very slowly and timidly, almost on tiptoe, removing their hats, and sat down at a table in a corner. I watched with interest to see what attitude the Frenchmen would adopt towards the Germans, whether they would leave as a sign of protest or whether they would stay. They stayed, as if they hadn't seen them.

Then I went to the left bank to visit the Sables de Lutéce, which I had not seen. As I came out, I crossed paths with a German officer who was asking the doorman what the place was. The doorman said it was a Roman circus called the Sables de Lutéce, and the officer asked, "May I come in?" The doorman replied, "You may go wherever you like." The worst impression produced by the entrance of the German army was the appearance of a flag with a swastika on top of the Eiffel Tower. This sad spectacle caused a number of suicides, one of which affected me deeply. A doctor who had assisted at the birth of my grandson, a world-famous specialist in brain surgery, had lost a son in the war of 1914 and when war was declared on Germany a second time he had said lightly before a group of friends, "If the Germans enter Paris, I am going to shoot myself." On the 14th of August one of his "friends" called him on the telephone and said, "Doctor, the Germans are in Paris. When are we going to your funeral?" "To-morrow," the doctor answered, and he hung up and shot himself in the head.

The meagre population that had stayed in Paris had been afraid that the Germans would enter the French capital with blood and fire, so they were agreeably surprised by the correct manner in which they behaved and dubbed them "The Correct Ones," which led to some humorous modifications in the texts of the letters we were authorized to send by mail. The post offices made available paper with printed lines that served as letters, such as "I am sick,"

"I am well," "My wife is sick," "My wife is well," and so forth. We were prohibited from writing anything—we could only cross out the phrases we didn't want to send. Some jokers added some printed lines to these sheets, which said, "The correct ones are annoying me," "The correct ones are not annoying me."

It was apparent that the girls of Paris, the "Pajaritas," were trying to conquer the Germans with their charm, but they found that the Germans paid no attention to them. Sitting on a bench in front of the Petit Palais, I watched two Germans seated on a bench in front of a bank as two girls came and sat down beside them. The girls smiled and tried to start a conversation, and then they began to sing a song called "The Three Waltzes," at which the Germans got up and left.

Little by little, the Parisian chic conquered the forced coldness of the Germans and their dangerous nocturnal raids stopped, giving way to the appearance in the Metro—now functioning—of yellow announcements which read, "Inasmuch as a member of the Occupation Army was the victim of a cowardly assassination, this morning were executed . . ." and there followed a list of five, ten, fifty or even a hundred hostages who had been shot, at random, from among those who had been arrested for whatever reason.

I had two close French friends whom I saw every day. One was the editor Blondel la Rougerie, head of the aeronautical magazine *L'Aérophile,* to which I contributed. The other was the secretary general of CINA, Lieutenant Colonel Roper. One night, returning from dinner at Roper's house, I took the Metro at ten o'clock in order to arrive home before eleven, but the train stopped at the Place d'Italie and I was left alone, in total darkness, far from my house in a neighborhood I didn't know. Some guards asked me where I was going, and when I said the Place de la Republique, they said, "Well, you'd better run." I quickened my pace and they said, "Faster than that."

On the way I passed a few cars with loudspeakers which announced, "It's eleven o'clock. Any person found in the street will be detained." Whenever I saw a form in the darkness, I tried to hide in case it was the police, but I noticed that the form, for the same reason, tried to hide from me.

I finally breathed easily when I reached the door to my house. I saw figures nearby, but thinking that they would try to hide from me, I paid no attention to them and was opening the door when one of them came forward, shined a flashlight on me and asked for my papers. It was a policeman who had arrested a woman and a sick man and had them in a car. I explained that I was in my own house, but it did no good; he took me along with the others and locked us up in the city hall of the third arrondissement along with other prisoners who were already there. Seated next to me was the grouchiest of the prisoners, who continuously grumbled, swore and cast hateful looks at the guards, who had begun a game of *bélote* [a card game]. When one of them looked at him, he said, "Go ahead, look at me. I am a respectable Frenchman who is ashamed to see you, also Frenchmen, treating us, who are decent people, as if we were criminals, just to please the *boches*, who have you under their boots!" The guards didn't answer him and continued their game. As it was very hot, the door to the street was open and my neighbor, taking advantage of the guards' lack of attention, escaped, but they noticed he was gone and gave chase, and he was recaptured and brought back to the prison. The guards then said to us, "Next time you say that the French police are bad, remember that we delayed catching this friend of yours, who didn't want to be in your company."

All in all, however, the French police treated us well. At dawn they gave us all coffee, and a glass of cognac for the ladies, and they put the sick man to bed. At five o'clock they let us all go, even the grouchy escapee. It wouldn't have been the same if we had been arrested by the Germans, because they made their prisoners polish their boots.

The "correctness" of the invaders soon began to diminish. Certain theaters were reserved for their use exclusively, as well as certain sidewalks and even whole streets. They were especially irritated by the epithet *boche*, although they were ignorant of its significance. One day a group of French locals were in a store waiting their turn to make a purchase, when two German officers came in and stood "correctly" at the end of the line. When the shopkeeper saw them he said to the Frenchmen, "Wait a moment while I serve the *boches*." They made a lot of purchases and when it was time to pay the bill, they said, "We Germans pay for everything we buy, but the *boches* don't pay for anything," and they took their purchases without leaving a single cent.

Meanwhile my wife, in Madrid, did not know what had become

of me when the Germans entered Paris—whether I was still there, or if I had been taken prisoner or shot. Wanting to find out about my situation she went to see the Minister of International Affairs, Juan Luís Beigbeder, a relative and an intimate friend of ours since childhood, and a former classmate of mine at the Academy of Engineers, to ask what news he had of me. The answer he gave her was, "I have orders not to concern myself with anyone." While she was in his office he made a phone call, in which he said, "At your orders, Caudillo, I think it would be a good idea to permit Cardinal Segura to return to Spain because his exile is making a bad impression abroad." In fact, Cardinal Segura had been exiled because he opposed having the name of José Antonio Primo de Rivera inscribed on the wall of the cathedral in Seville, while the name of San Fernando, who conquered the Moors, did not appear there.[92]

After long and laborious negotiations, my wife obtained a passport to travel to Paris and arrived in darkness. She was let off the train half a kilometer from the station, with no one available to help her carry her luggage. Naturally I was overjoyed that my solitude in occupied Paris was at an end; my wife was to stay with me from them on. At the same time I was shocked by the amount of luggage she had brought from Madrid to compensate for the scarcity of food in Paris—we were condemned to the loathesome rutabaga. She had brought several whole hams and three heavy suitcases stuffed with food, but the French and German police were searching and detaining anyone carrying packages suspected of containing foodstuffs, which were absolutely prohibited, confiscating them and imposing heavy fines upon the carriers or even holding them hostage, to be shot in retaliation for some collective offense against the occupying army.

Finally we found two porters to carry the baggage with us on the Metro (there were no taxis, because all the cars had been confiscated) and we had the incredible good luck not to run into a single policeman, either in the Metro or in the street; we breathed a sigh of relief when we reached the fifth floor of our house in the Rue Béranger with all our comestible treasure intact.

My wife and I had to start our lives over from square one as exiles—we had been left with no means of subsistence. Thanks to good friends we had in Paris who knew me because of the balloon ascents, the editor of *L'Aérophile,* Mr. Blondel la Rougerie, appointed me a contributor to the magazine and published a series of illustrated articles, with many figures, which constituted a complete treatise on aerodynamics. At the same time I published another series on the advantages that could be realized by using duraluminum in the construction of airplanes in place of the wood generally used at that time. These articles yielded me a double advantage—I was paid not only by *L'Aérophile* but by the Aluminum Français company as well.

Nearly all the publishers of geographical maps in Paris published special editions that followed the progress of the war, and Mr. Blondel asked me to study an original projection for the maps he was thinking of publishing. I visualized and calculated a system of double projections, cyclindrical and polar, which would quickly resolve the problem of determining the minimum distance between any two points on the globe. One had only to form a right triangle in which one of the legs was the difference in latitudes in the cylindrical polar projection, and the hypotenuse was the minimum distance between the two given points.[93] The system was very successful and the double-projection maps sold well and were used by the French, the Germans and the United States. With these and other scientific works I managed to earn about 2,000 francs a month which, in those days, was enough for a couple to live on in Paris. I also devised a "flexicalculator" for integrals and elliptical functions, which was constructed by my good friend the Spanish pilot, Sr. Montalván. He donated it to the Palais de la Découverte, where it is still on exhibition in the Mathematics Gallery, which entitles me to a free pass to the Palace. Some other scientific work I published in that period gave rise to public controversy with the authors of certain projects that I criticized, such as my calculation demonstrating that given the current state of aereonautical construction, airplanes exceeding a total of 200 tons would lose aerodynamic efficiency, and another calculation demonstrating the limited efficiency of helicopters with propellers powered by jet engines.[94]

Milestone 7: 1941
Age, 62 years

T he director of the National Office of Aeronautical Studies and Research (ONERA) called to ask me if I would accept a position in the organization, having heard of my earlier scientific and aeronautical work, and I accepted with enthusiasm. When he asked what salary I expected, I answered, a little nervously, about 20,000 francs. Surprised, he asked me, "Per month?" and I, thinking I had gone too high, said, "Well then, whatever you like," to which he responded, "You can earn much more." Finally it was agreed that I would be paid 100,000 francs for the first three months, and this rose rapidly to 70,000 francs per month.

I began my work with ONERA as assistant to the director, presenting a calculation on the "stratospheric plane," which I explained in a lecture and which interested two French engineers who went to the United States where they published it in the *Artillery Review*. I also did some work on the "Explorer's Curve"—applying it to the problem of aircraft interception—whose differential equations had been published in Germany and the United States without having been integrated. I was able to arrive at the integration of this curve and it was published by the French Academy of Science along with the description of my "flexicalculator."[95]

The director of ONERA with whom I had been working was replaced by the mining engineer Maurice Roy, who had just returned from Spain, having visited there at Franco's invitation.[96] When he took over, he refused to see me and fired me from

ONERA along with all the other employees who were Spanish Republicans.

Back to square one again, I wrote to M. Roy asking permission to publish some of the mathematical works I had contributed to ONERA; he not only refused, he prohibited me from working on any aeronautical projects without his authorization. Naturally I protested, and this gave rise to a controversy through letters and the publication in the Italian *Rivista di Aeronautica* of an article of mine on supersonic jets. I described one (invented by Roy that was awarded a prize by ONERA's engineering board, presided over by Roy), which produced an extraordinary specific propulsion, but whose drag was five times greater.

The seige against me by the Francoist government did not let up. The French general Denain, who had met me in Paris and spoken on my behalf to General Franco, got this response: "You may think what you like of Herrera, but he is on one side and I am on the other. If he caught me, he would shoot me, and if I could catch him, I would shoot him." The Caudillo was wrong in the first part of this statement, because I never had the attributes nor the wish to act as executioner.

During the German occupation of Paris, I received a letter from General Faupel, on whom I had made a favorable impression in Lima during my Pacific trip. Finding out that I was a refugee in France, he invited me to come to Berlin at the invitation of the Hispano-German society, and, if I wished, to accept a job as engineer with the vibration laboratory in Berlin. In spite of the serious inconveniences acceptance of this position would cause me, I wrote thanking him for his invitation and asking for instructions about how I should proceed.

I did not receive a reply, and when I expressed my puzzlement to a German friend of mine who was going to Germany, he offered to visit General Faupel, to find out if he had received my letter. When my friend returned he said he had seen Faupel, who had received my letter and still wanted me to come, but because I was a Spaniard, he had had to ask for authorization from General Franco, and the Caudillo had categorically refused. Thinking to do me harm, the Caudillo had saved me from great danger, to which I certainly would have been exposed had I moved to Berlin under the circumstances.[97]

The Germans did not bother me during the occupation, except

for one incident. One day a German soldier came to my house and ordered me to go meet a commander that afternoon at the hotel in the Gare St. Lazare. The soldier met me at the hotel, and we talked while we waited for the commander to arrive. When he asked me if I wanted to return to Spain soon, I said no, because to do this I would have to ask Franco's pardon and I was not disposed to do so. The soldier started to laugh and said, "All dictators are the same!" He told me that he was an engineer in Germany and that he, with his wife and son, owned a shop which sold engineering instruments in Berlin. He had never been in-volved in politics, and he added, "70 percent of those who are here have had the same experience as I have." I told him a little about my life too, and then the commander arrived and gave a curt salute, without offering his hand, and said, "I called you because tomorrow your wife's brother will pass through this sta-tion on the way to Germany and he wants to see her here, but not you because you are a Red general. Is that true?" I answered, "Yes sir, I am a Red general." Then the soldier spoke to him in German explaining what I had told him about my life, and the commander said, "Well, if you gave your word of honor to serve the Republic you have no choice but to keep it, and General Franco has no reason to reproach you." I answered, "It's true, but it is the case that General Franco also gave his word to serve the Re-public loyally." The commander could not believe his ears when he heard that Franco had a concept of loyalty so opposite to his own. His attitude towards me changed; he offered me a glass of cognac, which I politely refused, and he gave me a firm handshake as he said goodbye.

As reports of the war's development became more pessimistic for the German army, the cruelty of the occupation forces against the Parisian population increased. News of the execution of pris-oners appeared daily on the walls of the Metro stations. One after-noon when my wife and I were coming down from the Basilica of Montmartre, two German officers were walking in front of us, and two boys about ten or twelve years old ran by playfully; one of them brushed lightly against one of the officers, who imme-diately drew his pistol and aimed it at the boy—he would have fired if the other officer had not stopped him.

The appearance of the occupation army had changed radically. The robust soldiers of the first months of the occupation had been

transformed into sick and worried old men or boys who bran-
dished their newly acquired guns as if they were toys at passengers
in the Metro. One began to see German officers dead drunk,
supported by comrades so they wouldn't fall on the ground. Others
danced in the Metro, animated by the rhythmic clapping of the
passengers. Every day the uniformed women of the German army
used to march in formation through the Place de la Republique
to the Rue des Archives, surrounded by French policemen on
bicycles to prevent their being teased by the French women. One
day they appeared in the Place carrying their suitcases. "Going
on a trip?" some French women asked mockingly, and they answered testily, "Yes, but we'll be back!"

My brother-in-law, head of the Spanish railways, returned from
his trip to Germany and told us his impressions of his visit. He
said the Germans were preparing a terrible weapon which in a
single blow could totally destroy London and the greater part of
England. The insistence with which he talked about this dreadful
weapon made me think that perhaps it was not a bluff but the
truth. In that case, it could be nothing else than a uranium bomb.
To clarify my doubts, as I could not consult any German officer
about the matter, it occurred to me to write an article for *L'Aérophile* entitled, "Will the Uranium Bomb End the War?" I expected
that if this was not the device they were preparing, the official
censor of *L'Aérophile* would permit the publication of the article,
but that if the Germans really were building a uranium bomb,
they would not allow the article to be published.

When the article was finished, I brought it to the censor, a
captain who had become friendly with me because he was a first-
rate mathematician and had been very interested in my "flexicalculator" for elliptical functions. He said he could not authorize
publication of the article without consulting Berlin. The article
was sent back from Berlin with an *absolute* prohibition on its publication. This confirmed my suspicion that Germany was building
a uranium bomb.

The news about the Afrika Corps got worse and worse for the
Germans. One day I brought an article to the captain for censorship, and he said, staring vaguely into space, "It's bad, it's bad." I
said, "What, my article is bad?" and he said, "Not the article, Tun-
isia." The aggression of the F.F.I. (French Forces of the Interior)
against the occupation mounted. On every corner one saw groups

of boys with their hands in their pockets and nearly all the streets were barricaded. The Place de la Republique was divided in two by a barbed wire fence with a sign saying, "Anyone passing this point will be shot immediately." On one side of the wire were the Germans with cannon, mortars and machine guns; on the other the French women strolled with their baby-carriages and their children. Every once in a while shots rang out and everyone disappeared as if by magic. The doors, windows and balconies had to remain open, but no one allowed themselves to be seen. One day my wife, not hearing any gunfire, dared to peek out stealthily from the balcony to see what was going on in the Place de la Republique, where they had installed a trench mortar to make high shots into the courtyard of our building, and where the F.F.I. gathered to load their guns and drink courage from their bottles. When she lowered her eyes she saw, on the sidewalk opposite, two German soldiers standing with their guns aimed at her. After that she set up a periscope on the balcony, made out of mirrors, so she could see what was happening in the Place from inside the house. The revolt of the French police against the German occupation forces marked a period of recrudescence of street battles in Paris. Many of the boys of the F.F.I. were killed, and dead Germans were carried down our street by their comrades to be buried in the Place de la Republique under their helmets and swastikas.

My wife and I went out every afternoon to visit friends and buy the underground newspapers. The news that Hitler had begun his march against Russia on the same date that Napoleon had was received with great jubilation by all our neighbors, who shouted through the windows "Bravo, bravo, the war is won!"

Although Jews did not enjoy much sympathy in Paris, the cruel persecution the Germans had subjected them to, making them wear the yellow star of Israel on all their clothes, prohibiting them to enter public establishments, and deporting them to concentration—or extermination—camps, produced feelings of commiseration. A Jewish center had been set up in our building where weddings and holidays were celebrated, and where the elderly and indigent could eat for 1.5 old francs. Those who could not pay were fed free. A Jewish woman acted as administrator of this charitable center. One day a German truck came and forced the thirty or so old men and women who were in the restaurant to get in. The neighbors advised the administrator to hide so she would not be arrested too, but she refused and presented herself voluntarily to share the fate of her charges. They were all taken away and no one ever heard what became of them.

Some other Jews, an old couple who lived on the floor below us, were also arrested and taken away in a German truck, and the next day another truck, in the charge of an elegant-looking German officer, came and took away all the poor couple's furniture. They were never heard from again either.

The streets and Metro stations were constant witness to heart-rending scenes of children crying and calling for their parents, from whom they were separated by force, the fathers loaded into cattle cars, the mothers in other vehicles, and the children in still others. They would never see one another again. A colonel of the Hungarian army, named Juan de Pablo, who had served as a colonel in the Spanish Republican Army after he adopted Spanish citizenship, was loaded with other deportees into a totally enclosed cattle car, the floor covered with lime, and destined for certain death.[98] He managed to save himself by breaking through the floor of the car while the train was moving and throwing himself onto the tracks through the opening. Two others who tried to escape with him died in the attempt.

Some cars equipped with loudspeakers cruised about the streets of the city ordering a cease-fire and declaring that the occupation forces were abandoning Paris. This announcement was followed by several hours of silence, while the F.F.I. discussed what they ought to do. Their decision was to fire more heavily than before, in order to secure the surrender of the German garrison, with all its weapons and ammunition, and not to let them escape and continue combat against the French. So the fighting continued more intensely than ever.

The day came when the Allies landed in Normandy and there were continual air raid warnings in Paris; Metro service was interrupted, and during these interruptions the Germans ordered French passengers out of the stations, leaving them without shelter. But in one station, not very deep underground and not designated as a bomb shelter, the Germans left and the French stayed, and the musicians among them formed a jazz band and the people danced on the platform while the alarm lasted.

A few days after D-Day, an open car passed through the Rue

Béranger, stopped in front of our building, and a man stood up and began to shout, "Frenchmen, General De Gaulle is at the gates of Paris, Vive De Gaulle! Vive la France!" Naturally, in spite of the prohibition, everyone came out to the balconies, windows and doors to answer with cheers, but the man in the car took out a machine gun and began to fire at the buildings. For a moment I thought the shots were an expression of jubilation, in the manner of the Moors when they explode gunpowder, but when I saw that a bullet had knocked the plaster off the wall above a window opposite, right beside the heads of two children who were looking out, I realized that they were firing to hit. The shots were not a joyous outburst, but a warning to the public not to show themselves no matter what they heard in the streets. The car continued down the street firing at any window where someone was visible.

General Leclerc's division was approaching Paris, the noise of cannon came closer and closer, the air raid alarms were more and more frequent, and the mortars in the Place intensified their fire at the courtyard of our house. The explosions shattered the glass in the windows, and to pass the nights in peace we had to go down to the shelters, where we made shadow-figures on the walls to divert the children. They didn't let us spend one night in peace. Once when we went up to our apartment for a cup of coffee, we heard on the radio that there was fighting on the Rue Béranger. Broadcasts from Buenos Aires and Mexico celebrated the liberation of Paris while the combat was in its most violent phase.

Now very near Paris, General Philippe Leclerc ordered his senior colonel to send a scouting expedition to the city. This colonel, relating his actions on French television on the anniversary of the war in 1966, said he accomplished this task by forming a column of tanks manned by Spanish soldiers because they were the best prepared as they had all fought in Spain. The expedition consisted of the tanks "Guadalajara," "Teruel," and others under the command of the Spanish lieutenant Amado Granell.[99]

According to Lieutenant Granell's report on the radio, the expedition encountered no resistance. When the tanks entered Paris the people were frightened and hid, thinking they were German reinforcements, until one woman asked, "Who are you?" and, at the answer, "Leclerc's division," jubilation reigned. When the troops arrived at the Hotel de Ville and presented themselves to M. Bidault, head of the resistance, he could not believe his eyes.

The high command of the German occupation army in Paris declared that they would only surrender to uniformed French forces, but the F.F.I. had other ideas, and the commanders, officers, and soldiers of the German army, with all their arms, had to surrender to the F.F.I. boys in their shirt-sleeves, among whom were many Spaniards, some of whose names are inscribed on the memorial stones erected on the sites where they lost their lives defending the liberty of France.

The news of the German surrender spread like wildfire and within moments the Place de la Republique was crammed with people singing, dancing, embracing and kissing each other, climbing to the top of the statue of Marianne, and waving French, English, Russian, or American flags.

When the celebration was at its peak, some Germans or French collaborators opened machine-gun fire from a window of the Magasines Reunis building into the mass of humanity that filled the Place, which my wife and I were part of. The packed crowd tried to run over ground riddled with holes, falling and getting up again. Some crawled on the ground in search of shelter behind the German cannons placed around the statue, or behind the garden railings or the statue itself. Finally, dragged along with the current, we were able to reach our house.

During the entire occupation the air raid alarms were so frequent that neither my wife or I paid much heed to them. Generally they were caused by American or English bombings of factories or railroad stations around the periphery of the city. Only once the English bombed the Butte de Montmartre, thinking it was a station, and another time an American bomber pilot stalled over Paris, and to avoid crashing still loaded with bombs, he dropped them all on the Rue Cherche Midi, destroying many houses and causing a number of deaths; among the victims were some Spanish refugee friends of ours.

But the last night of the occupation when Paris was left with no air raid warning system or any means of defense, and in addition had to suffer the rage of the Germans as they were forced to evacuate the capital, the situation was very different. I told my wife that if we heard any airplane noise during the night we would have to go down to the shelter, because the Germans might bomb the city center.

In fact, just as we were getting undressed, we heard an airplane engine, and without waiting, we began to walk down the stairs from the fifth floor. While we were descending, the sky lit up as bright as day, but with a red light, and we were deafened by an earsplitting noise. We thought we would not reach the bottom, but we did. We saw the next morning that a bomb had destroyed five adjacent houses in the Rue des Archives, killing most of the occupants. Amidst the ruins French and English flags could be seen decorating the windows and balconies. Another bomb destroyed three other buildings in the Place de la Republique, also very near our house.

Paris liberated, General de Gaulle made his triumphal march at the head of Leclerc's division, marching down the Rue Rivoli to the Hotel de Ville and Notre Dame. My wife and I went to watch the parade in the Rue Rivoli, opposite La Samaritane, feeling all the excitement generated by this great international event. But at the moment General de Gaulle entered the Hotel de Ville, with the French forces lined up to the left of the door and Lieutenant Granell's Spanish forces on the right, some Germans and their French collaborators began firing from the rooftops at all the people in the street. The newspaper *L'Humanité*, in its first non-underground issue, made this comment on the event: "When the shooting began, everyone ran for cover in the doorways of the houses, except for the Spaniards, who remained motionless and at attention."

My wife and I, though Spanish, did not follow the example of our compatriots in Leclerc's division, but took refuge in a doorway. From one we moved quickly to another, and yet another. We saw people falling in the streets, victims of the snipers. In one of our hiding places we found ourselves at the marketplace (Les Halles), where the teamsters [*les forts des Halles*]—men capable of picking up a steer and carrying it 100 meters—were making a joke of the rain of bullets. One of them threw a stone out of the door and when several shots rang out without hitting him, he jeered at the bad aim of the snipers. Another one stood with his arms crossed in the middle of the street, shouting, "You're going to see how a *fort de Halle* who earns 40,000 francs a month dies!" imitating the historic phrase uttered by a deputy from the top of a barricade. A woman suddenly took refuge in our hiding place and, still feeling unsafe, wanted to go down to the basement. But the *forts* said to her, "Madam, stay with us; when they kill you, we will put you in the refrigerator."

The firing continued and we decided to go home, taking advantage of a nurse walking by with a baby in a baby-carriage, as we thought the snipers would not fire at the baby. In fact they did not, and we were able to get home, walking fast.

I had the opportunity to talk with a Spanish soldier from Leclerc's division. He was from Málaga, and he spoke with such a clipped Andalusian accent that even I, also an Andalusian, had trouble understanding him. I asked him where they were staying and he said, "In a strange place far away from here," and he showed me a piece of paper with "Bois de Boulogne" written on it. When Lieutenant Granell returned from Germany, he told me that this youth had been killed in battle, and he related this curious story about him. One night the Lieutenant was reviewing the sentinels at their posts, and this soldier was one of them. When Granell asked him what he did if he heard a noise or saw something suspicious, he replied, "I shoot with the machine gun." Granell said, "You're not supposed to fire the machine gun, but to throw a grenade," but the soldier insisted, "I fire the machine gun." Granell asked him, "But why do you fire the machine gun when the orders are to throw a grenade?" and the answer was, "Because if I throw a grenade it shatters their wristwatches, but if I use the machine gun I can retrieve the watches intact."

With Paris liberated and Leclerc's division advancing towards Germany, the Spanish refugees regarded the war as over and, not knowing—after the death of President Manuel Azaña and the flight of President Diego Martínez Barrio to Mexico[100]—if any Republican government had been constituted, Don Miguel Maura, in exile in France, decided to form a provisional government, asking me to join it as Air Minister. I accepted this position on an interim basis until a legal government could be formed, when I would step down, as would President Maura. The French and English governments were sympathetic to this project, and the former provided a magnificent house to serve as Miguel Maura's residence. Maura and the ministers he appointed were preparing some announcements for the Spanish people explaining our intentions, when an unexpected event thwarted our plans. The German army, retreating towards the border, made a recovery and forced Leclerc's division to retreat towards Paris. This ended the favorable attitude of the French government towards the Spanish provisional government in exile and emboldened Franco, who massed his troops on the French border and declared (so they say) that he planned to be in Paris before the Germans.

This setback to the French forces was only momentary, Franco's hopes of taking Paris disintegrated, and our plans for a provisional government also vanished. Once the Cortes met in Mexico and chose Martínez Barrio as president of the Republic for the second time, there was no longer any need for it.

Martínez Barrio's arrival in Paris was the occasion for a delirious reception by all the Spanish refugees and a large number of Frenchmen. At a meeting organized by the French president in honor of our president, attended by his representative Bernardo Giner de los Ríos, I was moved by the series of speeches the French made, praising the Spanish people for their struggle which set an example for the rest of the world.[101] The French government, to show its disagreement with Franco's regime, had closed the border between the two countries. At the end of the meeting, seeing that no one from Spain had gotten up to thank the speakers, I asked for the floor and said how glad I was to hear such praise for my country. I pointed out that we would never forget the fact that we had received sympathy from all the countries of the world, but always without any threat to their own interests. The French, however, had shown their sympathy at risk to their own interests. The chairman of the meeting answered my statement by saying, "Likewise, the French will never forget that it was the Spanish who first marched into Paris when it was liberated."

Once the censorship was lifted in Paris—but the world war still continued—I thought it opportune to publish my article on uranium bombs and the possibility that such a weapon might end the war. I submitted it to *L'Aérophile* but they thought the figures I presented on the effects of the explosion of such a bomb seemed so fantastic as to be more appropriate to a science fiction story than to a serious scienctific article. Other magazines also rejected it and only *Le Génie Civil* agreed to publish the article "as a popularization of the theory of electrons and protons as constituents of matter." The article appeared in its entirety in the issue of July 15, 1945, and twenty days later the world awoke stunned by the explosion of an American uranium bomb that destroyed the Japanese city of Hiroshima.

My article had been the only published reference to the potential of atomic uranium bombs, and beginning at eight in the morning of the day Hiroshima was destroyed by a bomb of this type, my house was invaded by journalists wanting to know the details of this new and terrible weapon. I was obliged to write articles and give lectures on the nature of atomic bombs, a subject which had never been discussed in the press. One magazine, *Noir et Blanc*, asked me for an article with drawings, and I wrote one which explained the mechanism of the new bombs by drawing an analogy in which each uranium atom was a circle of dancers (electrons), whirling about with hands joined; if one of these circles should break apart, each dancer would be thrust outwards by centrifugal force, each colliding with another circle of dancers, breaking it apart in turn and scattering its dancers who would collide with other circles, and so on until all the circles were exploded. This article was translated into English and published in an American magazine with the editorial statement that it was the clearest way of explaining the disintegration of uranium in an atomic bomb.

This period saw the beginning of a close association with *Le Génie Civil*, which printed the confirmation of my prediction that the uranium bomb was capable of ending the war—a few days after the destruction of Hiroshima and Nagasaki the Japanese surrendered and the war was over. Unfortunately, I was completely wrong in prophesying that the first nation to have an atomic bomb would demonstrate its effects in an uninhabited locale, so that the enemy would be able to appreciate what would happen if the war continued. The United States, however, the first to have the bomb, ended the war not in the humanitarian way that I had forseen, by using the bomb as a deterrent, but through the annihilation of two defenseless cities with hundreds of thousands of inhabitants, most of whom were civilians.

In other articles in *Le Génie Civil* I discussed the possibility of constructing a hydrogen bomb, and this was also confirmed by events a few months later. A member of the Academy of Sciences, Hippolyte Parodi, called the publisher to express the Academy's dismay at the magazine's printing articles by a "Red Communist" like me.[102] The publisher, telling me of this call, assured me that he knew I was neither "red nor communist," but "since his magazine was scientific in nature, he had to go along with the Academy's judgment and found himself under pressure to terminate our association." I realized immediately that this unexpected and unjustified attack by the French Academy must have been instigated on the other side of the Pyrenees, in the Pardo Palace precisely, and the first inquiries I made to clarify the situation confirmed this.

The mining engineer Maurice Roy, friend and guest of Franco and new director of ONERA, from which I had been dismissed due to the influence Franco had on him, had been named a member of the Academy of Sciences and had spread his opinion of me, which he brought from Madrid, among the other Academy members. Among those who were convinced was M. Parodi, who then protested, in the name of the Academy, that a French scientific publication should not publish articles by a person with such a bad background as mine.

I wrote to M. Parodi asking him where he had gotten the idea that I was a communist and he answered clearly and also told me about the vicissitudes of his life. I also related some of the details of my life, and he was so convinced that he had been deceived about me that he called the publisher of *Le Génie Civil* to tell him that he took back everything he had said against me. As a result I continued my association with the journal, to the great satisfaction of both the publisher and myself.

Milestone 8: 1950
Age, 71 years

Among the scientific works on the subject of air navigation I had produced, there was an original procedure for determining the point measuring the elevation of two stars.[103] In this same year the French Academy of Sciences instituted a prize, called the Plumey, for the most effective such procedure applicable to aeronautical navigation.[104] In spite of the campaign against me by M. Roy, I had the support of several members of the Academy, including Professors Joseph Pérès and Francis Perrin. On the latter's advice, I presented my work as a candidate for this prize, and I won it, along with the title of "Laureate" of the French Academy.

During their participation in the Republican cause, General Corniglion Molinier and André Malraux made a film called *L'Espoir* (*Sierra de Teruel*, in Spanish), which was first shown in Paris before a group of Spanish refugees, including myself.[105] On this occasion General Corniglion told me of his intention to donate half of the proceeds the film earned to the most needy Spanish exiles, and he put me in charge of distributing these funds. I was assisted in this difficult task by the widow of Lluis Companys ([president of autonomous Catalonia] who had been shot in Barcelona) and another Catalan, and in all we distributed two million francs to Spanish exiles all over France.

When Félix Gordón Ordas became president of the Republican government in exile, he named me Minister of Military Affairs.[106] I fulfilled the duties of this office by 1) defending the rights of

Spanish military personnel in exile in France and elsewhere in the world; 2) writing an annual letter to my old comrades, the officers of the Francoist army, reminding them of the duty they had pledged on their word of honor, given freely in 1931, to serve the Republic loyally and defend, not attack it, with the arms the Spanish people had entrusted to them; 3) demonstrating our scientific capacity by presenting the calculations and a complete proposal for using one of the V-2's that ONERA had to make a vertical ascent to 180 Km and descend by parachute, and offering as crew members Spanish aviators living in exile in France (the project was approved by the Minister, General Corniglion Molinier, but rejected by Maurice Roy, the director of ONERA); 4) presenting the Academy of Sciences with a proposal to launch a French artificial satellite, which would have been the first in the world.

I have always considered Astronautics to be a French science. In lectures in Madrid and Paris I pointed out that the novels of Jules Verne, *From the Earth to the Moon* and *Round the Moon* were the first works of science fiction that had used the true mathematical formulas necessary for space travel. He had also assumed the use of jet engines—rockets—for correcting the trajectory (although not for propulsion). The first complete work on astronautics had been written by the Frenchman Robert Esnault Pelterie, who originated the word "astronautics," and whose precursor Captain Ferber, who died in a plane crash, had prophetically titled one of his works, *From Peak to Peak, From City to City, From Continent to Continent,* on which I gave a lecture to the Spanish Aero Club in Madrid, adding *From Star to Star,* a feat presently near realization. Because of all these antecedents I believed that French science (pioneer in aeronautics both in lighter-than-air and heavier-than-air vessels, and producer of such illustrious names as Montgolfier, Ader, Marquis d'Arlandes, Pilatre de Rozier, Renard, Krebs, and others) had a historic duty to launch the first ships and men into interplanetary space, as they had into atmospheric space.[107] I have never ceased to dwell on the idea that, because of me, this was not to be.

This is what happened. On a certain date I presented my proposal for a flight of a manned rocket to a specified altitude to ONERA, which was rejected by its director, Maurice Roy. On a later date I presented to the Academy of Sciences my plan for a French artificial satellite, which was published in the next issue of

Le Génie Civil and sent to a committee appointed to study it and make recommendations about the possibility of carrying it out. One Sunday I was attending Mass in the parish of Saint Elizabeth when the priest approached me and offered me his hand, saying "Congratulations." Not knowing what he was referring to, I asked him to explain, and he said he had read an article in *La Croix* which said that I, a Spanish technician living in exile in Paris in a fifth-floor walk-up, had done the calculations for an artificial satellite for France, which would soon be built, and that they would be publishing all the plans and information about its characteristics.

When I read this article and others like it, I realized that the project was doomed to failure because the French scientific establishment could not present as its own the scientific work of a foreigner, nor could it contribute a substantial amount of labor and money to realize an idea that was not its own. In fact, a year passed before the Committee made its report and, during this time, the U.S.S.R. launched the first artificial satellite, "Sputnik," which had characteristics similar to the one I had proposed. So Russia took the honors for sending the first man-made object into space, followed by the equally important launching of a man into space, Yuri Gagarin, the first astronaut in the world.

Perhaps if I had not offered France my proposals for the manned V-2 and the satellite, some other scientists from ONERA or another French scientific organization would have come forth with a genuinely French astronautical project that would have been supported and carried out, and France would have earned the recognition that her scientific community so well deserved for making the first extraterrestrial demonstration of human genius. But I obstructed this possibility unwittingly through my *trop de zèle* in trying to show my appreciation to the French nation for the friendship they had extended to me when I could not live in my own country.

The students at Oxford University asked the university authorities for permission to organize a seminar on the Spanish Civil War, with participants from both sides. Among those invited to represent the Nationalists was General Kindelán, who could not attend and sent one of his sons instead, who read a speech. I was one of those representing the Republican side.

My wife and I were splendidly welcomed by the University, all expenses paid, including round trip plane fare and rooms in a first-class hotel in Oxford. In addition we were invited to dinner, I with the rector, the professors and the students, and my wife with the professors' wives. In my talk and my answers to the professors' and students' questions, I made reference to the origins and vicissitudes of the war, and above all to the horrors of the Francoist, German and Italian bombing of our civilian population, contradicting the assertions of the Francoists that they had never done this, and that on the contrary, they had sent provisions to alleviate the hunger of the "Reds." These claims did not fool the audience, because among them was the rector of the University, who had been England's consul in Murcia during the war and was perfectly aware of what had happened in Spain. Professor Hugh Thomas attended my lecture and took notes on it, and I supplied him with a great deal of further information.[108] He came to Paris to fill out the information he had gathered in London, using books and other documents the government in exile placed at his disposal, and the book he published on the Spanish Civil War is one of the most complete and impartial treatments written, along with that of the American Ambassador Claude G. Bowers, *My Mission in Spain.*

Emilio Herrera last wrote in his memoirs seven days before his death on September 13, 1967. He was eighty-eight years old.

Appendix

*Instructions to Officers in Charge
of Free Balloon Ascents*

I. Before the Trip

The commanding officer shall, giving sufficient notice, designate the officer who will direct the expedition, those who will accompany him, and the balloon to be used.

The captain of the expedition shall be responsible for it and will have the same authority as the commanding officer over all the officers under his command. If any officer taking part in the ascent has more seniority or higher rank than the captain of the expedition, he shall still be under the commmand of the captain, who shall have, with respect to all who make the ascent, whatever their rank, the same authority as a ship's captain over its passengers and crew. During the preparations for the ascent and on returning, the captain shall retain his authority, but he shall refrain from giving orders to higher-ranking officers who, for these purposes and during these periods only, are considered assigned to the expedition.

The captain himself, or another officer he appoints, will fasten the rip panel and inspect the interior of the balloon, repairing any minor damage. If the rip panel has been fastened for more than eight days, the night before the ascent it shall be opened from the top for a length of one meter and re-fastened so there is no excess resistance.

Enough time shall be allowed to check all the cloth, instruments and other objects, making sure everything is in good condition.

The sand used as ballast must be absolutely dry and well sifted. The sacks must be in good condition and each should contain 15 kg of sand.

Generally the following objects should be carried on the expedition:

Pocket barometer and log
Statoscope
Aspirator-psychrometer
Binoculars
Camera, with plates or film
8 homing pigeons
Map on a scale of 1/200,000
General map of Spain
Railway schedules
A small case containing
    Pencil, eraser, passport, flight plan, message containers, post cards, telegram blanks, stamps, and a copy of these instructions
Overcoat or rain coat, according to the weather
Sharp jacknife
Sword, spurs, and gloves
Unloaded revolver and separate ammunition
Provisions, including wine and water
Ball of twine
Two books of cigarette paper
Dispatch flags for letters
Horn or whistle
Large net for the valve cord
First aid kit
Instructions for accidents
Pocket watch
Money (150 pesetas, 25 in small change)

All these objects, except those carried in the pockets, should be put aboard at least one hour before the scheduled time of debarkation, carefully weighed. The officers who will take part in the ascent shall also be weighed. The captain or an officer he designates shall oversee the inflation of the balloon (before it is taken out of the hangar). He will verify himself that the valve, the netting, and the balloon are in good condition, and that the cords for the valve and the rip panel are positioned correctly, without interfering with one another. No balloon may debark unless both cords are perfectly installed and independent of one another.

When loading the basket the baggage must be placed on the long side, opposite the side that will first touch the ground on descent.

When the balloon has been checked and the basked loaded, the two shall be attached, taking care that the brake rope hangs exactly under the rip panel, and that the basket hangs in such a way that the center of the long side opposite the side that will touch the ground first is exactly under the point where the brake rope is attached.

The ballast sacks shall be placed around the perimeter of the basket, properly secured so that they remain upright. If they do not fit in this manner, they should be placed on top of one another in staggered, parallel rows, or on the outside of the basket after it is attached to the balloon.

The closed sack of ballast,[1] double wrapped, which is to be used to facilitate landing, should also be placed inside the basket, with the end of its 15 meter rope tied to the suspension ring twenty centimeters from where the brake rope is tied.

The guide ropes should generally be tied to the suspension ring diametrically opposite the brake rope, but if the ascent is made on a very windy day they should be tied on the same side as the brake rope, so that the latter can also be used as a guide rope if necessary.

When the basket is attached, the balloon is weighted, the aeronauts having climbed on board already, as rapidly as possible but in an orderly fashion. On windy days the weighting of the balloon is facilitated considerably if the weight the balloon is to carry is determined prior to taking it out of the hangar; then by subtracting the weight of the aeronauts, the basket and the ropes, one can determine, without having to resort to trial and error, how many sacks of ballast will be needed to keep the balloon in equilibrium, and avoid the operation of weighting it in the open air, which under such circumstances can prove difficult.

If the brake rope is coiled, it must be checked to see that the loops do not form any tangles or knots, so there will be no difficulties in uncoiling it from the basket.

1. Used as an anchor.

The cords for the rip panel and the valve must be firmly fastened to the suspension netting of the basket, leaving sufficient slack so that even when there are great hygrometric changes they can never become taught.

As a precautionary measure, on days when there is a strong wind, during these preliminary operations one officer should keep his hand on the rip panel cord, ready to pull it in case of emergency. For the rip to be effective it is indispensable on windy days to have the guide ropes on the same side as the brake rope, as we have said.

The release of the balloon shall be directed by an officer who is not taking part in the ascent, appointed by the commanding officer, in accordance with tactical regulations, but he shall not give the order to cast off until he has consulted the captain of the expedition, and the latter has obtained permission from the highest-ranking officer present.

Before the balloon is taken out of the hangar the appendix will have been tied up, and the officer in charge of ground operations will untie it, pulling the cord just before giving the order to cast off. The captain of the expedition, before declaring he is ready to leave, will give a last look around, principally to see that the appendix is open and that the suspension and ropes are in order.

The officer in charge of ground operations will guide the brake rope until it no longer touches the ground.

Before getting into the basket, smokers will leave behind any matches or lighters they may have with them, and the officers will synchronize their watches with the captain's. The latter will assign the various duties that each is to perform in the basket, reserving for himself the job of keeping track of the progress of the balloon.

In general, on an expedition composed of three officers, the captain will act as leader; one officer will read the instruments, throw the pieces of [cigarette] paper out [to determine direction of movement] and watch the end of the brake rope. The other will take charge of photography and the homing pigeons. The captain or one of the officers will take charge of the money and expenses for the expedition.

Before the ascent, all the instruments are read and the readings entered in the log, in which other preliminary notations have already been made. The captain of the expedition will position himself at an angle adjacent to the brake rope, so as to better observe the ascent, and in a position from which he can comfortably see the barometer and the statoscope.

II. In the Air

Before giving the signal to cast off, the captain of the expedition will see that one or two of the crew members are ready with a sack of ballast at the edge of the basket, in order to pour it out in such quantities and at such times as he may order. He will continue attending to the ascent of the balloon, and as soon as the brake rope no longer touches the ground and all obstacles have been cleared, he reads the barometer and looks quickly around the basket to see that everything is in order, especially the suspension.

It is preferable to ascend a little higher in the first few moments than to be too close to the ground, especially on windy days,

As soon as the balloon is completely inflated, note the time, pressure and temperature, and inspect the interior from time to time, looking through the appendix. Take barometric and temperature readings every five, or at the most ten, minutes, as well as intermediate readings when unexpected movements are noted, always obtaining maximum and minimum readings.

If the ascent was begun with the brake rope coiled up, it is uncoiled with the necessary precautions as soon as the balloon reaches its zone of equilibrium. Avoid ascending higher than 2,000 meters above the point of departure, unless it was explicitly anticipated to try to reach a higher altitude, and always take care to economize on ballast as much as possible. Take all the notes necessary to reconstitute the ascent, and mark the route followed on the map. Note the times and places when pigeons are released, when photographs are taken, ballast cast off, the valve adjusted, or any other significant phenomena.

If signs of electricity or storms are detected in the atmosphere, descend as soon as possible. If the ground can not be seen, also descend as soon as possible, until it can be seen again and position ascertained, in order to avoid being inadvertently blown out to sea.

The principal job of the captain, while in the air, is to pay careful attention to the balloon's vertical movements as well as to its route or horizontal trajectory. Frequent observation of the barometers

and statoscope and the cigarette papers, even though the indi-
cations of these last are not always exact, is the means by which
the vertical movements of the balloon can be constantly followed.
Always, when passing over well defined points on the ground,
estimate the balloon's velocity.

A strong odor of gas indicates a gain in altitude or a great
expansion of the gas to due to a rise in temperature. Ringing in
the ears indicates very rapid vertical movement, and is more no-
ticeable descending than ascending. Contraction of the appendix
indicates a loss of altitude or lowering of temperature. In general
the wind is not perceptible, as the balloon moves with it, but
changes in direction and intensity, and above all eddies, can be
perceived. When moving over the brake rope the wind can be
felt, and sometimes the sound produced by the flapping of a slack
balloon is heard.

Under no circumstances throw any solid object out of the basket,
to avoid causing damage below.

In good conditions, the voice will carry almost 500 meters, and
sometimes one can communicate in this way with people on the
ground.

Always when travelling at low altitude, or when the balloon is
descending, whether due to manipulation of the valve or to its
own tendency, attention should be redoubled, in order to observe
the exact moment when the brake rope touches the ground, and
to execute the maneuvers necessary to obtain the desired result.

When beginning a descent take care of all the instruments,
wrapping the most delicate in blankets or overcoats to give them
added protection. Put full sacks of ballast on the aft side so they
will not be in the way.

Even in very favorable conditions of wind and terrain, it is
advisable to travel systematically over the brake rope, and it is
worthwhile, whenever possible, to stabilize in a vertical position
when the brake rope begins to touch the ground, with the object
of having the security of not making too rapid a descent, being
able to make a thorough examination of the terrain, taking note
of the wind velocity, and being able to choose a good site for the
landing. This equilibrium is analagous to landfall at sea.

From this point of equilibrium, depending on the terrain and
the velocity of the wind, either manipulate the valve or cast off

ballast if it is advisable to ascend again in order to avoid some obstacle or to make the descent under more favorable conditions.

If the ground is unobstructed, throw out the closed sack when the brake rope touches the earth. But if it is wooded it is preferable to proceed using the brake rope only and not to cast off the sack until the last minute. The Germans say that when moving over a forest at low velocity it is easy for the brake rope to become caught in the trees or underbrush, but that it is not difficult, on the other hand, to make a descent in woods with high winds.

In spite of this I believe one must avoid descents in forests whenever possible, and to pass over them towing the brake rope, as it is preferable to look for open ground so as to be able to use the brake rope and the sack simultaneously, trying, as far as possible, to re-establish a vertical position as soon as the sack touches the ground.

At this moment, provided that conditions are such as to assure that the brake rope will not lift from the ground again, unhook the ring of the rip panel cord and you are ready to open the balloon at the right moment.

As soon as the brake rope touches the ground, and the chief of the expedition makes sure that it is positioned in the center of the long side at the back of the basket, guiding it if necessary by hand, the aeronauts should position themselves on the long forward side of the basket, which will touch the ground first, ready to suspend themselves from the ropes and flex their legs just before the basket touches the ground. The captain should position himself in the right-hand corner of the forward side so as to have more freedom of movement, and watch the brake rope and the sack so as to use the rip panel, the valve, or ballast, whichever is appropriate.

To facilitate this maneuver, one of the aeronauts should have a sack of ballast ready at the edge of the basket, ready to cast off the amount ordered, and the other will hold the net with the rolled-up valve cord, ready to manipulate it according to the captain's instructions. The rip panel should be opened in general when the balloon has already touched the ground, or a few moments before if there is a very strong wind, but always after the sack is dragging on the ground; or if the sack is not being used, when the balloon is just a few meters above the ground.

If one makes sure that the balloon falls with moderate vertical speed, properly oriented, and that it can be ripped open the moment it touches the ground, the danger of being dragged almost disappears. The aeronauts must be ready to assist the captain in pulling the rip panel cord to make deflation as rapid as possible, and to rip it themselves if they see that the captain is not in the right position to do it himself the moment the basket touches down.

On windy days one must not ask people who may be in the vicinity to catch the brake rope; furthermore anyone who offers to must be prevented from so doing, to avoid any harm that could result, both to the balloon and those who are helping. Only when the balloon is moving very slowly is outside help appropriate and it can be very useful in avoiding specific obstacles or descending on calm days in hazardous terrain. In this case the balloon can be moved by having the people pull it by the brake rope or the basket rope to a convenient spot, and there the rip panel can be opened. If it is absolutely calm the balloon may fall on top of the basket, and to avoid this the captain must get out, substituting his weight in the basket with an equivalent weight, and pull on the net opposite the side of the rip panel to make the balloon tilt.

No one must leave the balloon until it is deflated and the captain gives the order, even if he is already on the ground. Any failure to comply in this respect will have serious consequences and will be judged as if an officer had abandoned a post of honor.

Once on the ground the time, barometer, and thermometer readings are noted and recorded in the log.

Smoking is strictly prohibited in the vicinity of the balloon when it is near the ground and during the deflation of the balloon and recovery of the equipment.

III. After the Descent

If people come to help, the captain should pick the first eight or ten to arrive, or those he considers most suitable, to assist in recovering and packing the material, avoiding at all costs, through the intervention of the officers, notable persons, authorities, or police, if there are any, anything that would produce confusion, making everyone understand the necessity of keeping order to protect the equipment and the absolute prohibition of smoking to avoid possible explosion.

The equipment should be placed in the means of transport available in the regulation manner.

As quickly as possible the commanding officer shall be notified that the trip has been completed, by telegraph, homing pigeon (if the weather and circumstances are suitable), and mail, repeating the message in case any of these means of communication is delayed. If sending a messenger to another point will save time in sending a telegram or speed the dispatch of mail, it should be done.

This message must be clear, concise, and legible, specify the town, country, and province where the descent was made and the circumstances of the descent, classifying it as *comfortable,* if there was no crash; *good,* if there was a gentle crash without being dragged and no danger of any kind; and *lucky,* if there were difficulties that were overcome without any injury. If any accident occurs it should be reported in the briefest, but most accurate, form possible; the captain should inform the military authorities in the region of the descent if it was a major accident and take whatever measures are pertinent.

Whenever the descent is more than 30 km from Guadalajara, arrange to return by public transportation; if it is less, and you think it convenient for a truck to be sent from Guadalajara to pick up the equipment, request it when sending news of the descent. When possible, also give the estimated time of arrival in Guadalajara. If the return trip is going to be slow, one officer can remain behind in charge of the equipment and the others can return by the fastest route. In any case, one officer appointed by the captain must see that the equipment is in a safe place and that there is no smoking near the basket.

If the balloon's descent has caused any damages and the owner of the property presents a claim, always pay a claim you consider reasonable, but if you consider the claim unreasonable simply give the address of the commander-in-chief to the owner and he can apply to him in the manner that seems best. In making restitution one must keep in mind that while it is right for the Aerostatic Service to pay for the damages a balloon may cause, it is not right for it to pay for harm done by people who gather at the scene only out of curiosity, when the balloon is already on the ground and they cannot be of any service to the aeronauts.

Give a small tip to the men who helped you, pay the cost of

transportation and any other bills, and submit an accounting on your return to Guadalajara. If one of the crew members is in charge of the accounts, the captain will endorse the expense account he presents.

On arrival in Guadalajara, the captain will give a detailed account of all the incidents of the journey to the commander-in-chief, and look over the balloon equipment again, delivering it to the warehouse after removing the rubber seal from the rip panel and repairing any minor damage that might have occurred. If there is any damage he cannot repair himself, he will notify the commander-in-chief.

Using the data recorded before, during, and after the trip, the captain will draw up a table, in accordance with the approved model, and give it to the commander-in-chief within three days of his return. If the nature of the trip seems to call for a written report to complement the data contained in the table, it should be written separately and cover all matters the captain considers relevant.

Guadalajara, July 31, 1902
Pedro Vives y Vich

Notes to Memoirs

1. *Hernani, or the Castilian Noble,* opera by Giuseppe Verdi (1844), based on a novel by Victor Hugo.
2. On the earthquake of 1884, see Gobierno Civil de la Provincia de Granada, *Estado demostrativo de los muertos y heridos y de las casas destruídas en los pueblos de esta provincia por consecuencias de los terremotos de 1884* [Report on the dead and wounded and of houses destroyed in the towns of this province in consequence of the earthquakes of 1884] (Granada, n.d.).
3. On the cholera epidemic of 1885, see M. A. Vida Roviralta and J. Sjmolka Clares, "La epidemia de colera de 1885 en Granada," *Actas, IV Congreso de Historia de la Medicina,* 2 vols. (Granada, 1973), I, 387–396.
4. *El rey que rabió,* 7th ed. (Madrid, 1894), a popular zarzuela by Vital Aza (1851–1911) and Miguel Ramos Carrión (1848–1915).
5. The widow Cliquot actually died in 1866.
6. On the *tajamadas* or fortresses designed by Herrera's grandfather, see José Herrera García, *Examen comparada del estado actual del arte de fortificar* (Madrid, 1853) and *Teoría analítica de la fortificación permanente* (Madrid, 1846).
7. A pale dry sherry.
8. Pío Fernández Mulero (1888–1936), military engineer, entered the Escuela de Aerostatación in 1916, licensed as a pilot in 1917. Headed an expeditionary force at Zeluán Aerodrome, Melilla, and saw war service in Morocco throughout the 1920s. Assassinated by the left in 1936.
9. Manuel Fernández Silvestre (1871–1921), impetuous cavalry colonel, later general, who destroyed the tenuous truce with El Raisuli in 1913, and was recalled as a result. In 1921 he committed his troops to

an indefensible position at Annual, where the Spanish suffered severe losses, and killed himself in humiliation.

10. al-Roghi: Jilali ibn Driz, religious leader who rallied Moroccan tribesmen to revolt by claiming to be a pretender to the throne. Fought the sultan from 1902 until defeated by Rif tribesmen who then turned against the Spaniards. *Askaris* were native soldiers in the service of a European power. This episode took place in December 1905.

11. The black minister was most likely al-Roghi's commander-in-chief, Jilali Mul'l Udhu.

12. The Restinga is a long peninsular strip to the south of Melilla.

13. *Chambergo*, a broad-brimmed soft hat worn by the Flemish Shomberg Regiment serving in Spain under Charles II.

14. Jesús Fernández Duro (1880–1908), aeronaut, founder of the Aero-Club of Madrid (1905) and pioneer of Spanish civil aviation. He earned his airplane pilot's license in France shortly before his death from typhoid fever.

15. Augusto Arcimis y Werle (b. 1844), French-born director of the Central Meteorological Institute in Madrid.

16. Fernández Duro and Herrera landed on October 16 at 6:30 a.m. near Neu-Titschein, Moravia.

17. Alberto Santos Dumont (1873–1932), Brazilian aeronaut and aviator who performed the first officially recognized heavier-than-air flight in Europe, in his 14-bis airplane (October 1906).

Jacques Faure (1869–1924), French artillery officer who transferred to military aeronautics in 1912. Subsecretary for Aeronautics in World War I, later a general. Faure landed at Kirschdraud, Hungary, a distance of 1314 km. He also landed in a tree; see photograph in *L'Aérophile*, 13 (1905), 257.

18. For account of the 1905 Gran Prix and Herrera's sketch, see *L'Aérophile*, 13 (1905), 259–260.

19. Commander Francisco de Rojas Guisado (d. 1920), in charge of production and compression of hydrogen, construction of balloons and other technical services at the Escuela de Aerostatación.

20. On the categories of descent, see Appendix, p. 157.

21. Balbás, author of "Enseñanzas artilleras deducidas de la Gran Guerra," in *Aeronáutica militar. Conferencias y ejercicios desarrollados en el curso de 1922* (Guadalajara, 1922), pp. 175–243. In 1923 he was an artillery commander.

22. El Guerra, bullfighter; probably Rafael Guerra Bejarano "Guerrita" (b. 1862).

23. Francisco Echague y Santoyo (1850–1924), military engineer who succeeded Vives as director of aeronautics in 1915. The first Gordon Bennett Cup (named after James Gordon Bennett, publisher of the Paris

Herald) began in Paris on September 30, 1906. Herrera and Echague travelled 184 km, landing at Dives Cabourg on the English Channel, in eighth place. In the same competition, Kindelán travelled 315 km to Rumboldswyke, England, and finished sixth. See *L'Aérophile*, 14 (1906), 215.

24. On the Gordon Bennett Cup of 1908, the third, see *L'Aérophile*, 16 (1908), 463. Herrera travelled 121.5 km and finished seventeenth, four places behind Kindelán. According to this report, Herrera's accident was the object of a serious investigation.

25. Ferdinand Ferber (1862–1909), French aeronaut, imitator of the Wright Brothers and builder of monoplane gliders.

26. Herrera was initially interested in the practical problem of under what conditions a brake-rope hanging from a balloon would or would not engage a telegraph wire or power line and wrap around it. This problem, in turn, required the determination of the laws governing the oscillation of a continuous pendulum. The Mathematical Society heard a number of discussions on the subject and in early 1928 Herrera and the mathematicians Terradas (1893–1950), Sánchez Pérez (1882–1958) and Lorente de Nó (1896–1958) conducted a number of experiments at Guadalajara from a captive balloon and, then, a free balloon at 600 meters from which a motion picture of the rope was taken. See Junta para Ampliación de Estudios, *Memoria correspondiente a los cursos 1926–27 y 1927–28*, pp. 255–56, and *Revista Matemática Hispano-Americana*, 2nd series, 3 (1928), 17, 95.

27. If the pressure inside the balloon reaches explosion level before the balloon stabilizes, it will explode.

28. The King's dirigible trip obviously impressed Herrera. Some years later he told the following anecdote apropos of airship safety: "When the King of Spain took his first dirigible trip, he lit a cigarette in the cabin. Someone told him it was dangerous to smoke on board, and naturally the Sovereign stopped smoking, but not before pointing to some sparks emitted by the motors. "Don't you think," he said, "that these sparks are more dangerous than my cigarettes?" (*La Nación*, October 17, 1928).

29. Benito Loygorri Pimentel (b. 1885), civil aviator, learned to fly at Mourmelon, France. In 1910 he became the first Spaniard to receive an international flying license, flying a Henry Farman byplane. Subsequently he became Farman's representative in Spain and sold airplanes to the Spanish army. On March 13, 1911, he performed tests on two Henrys and one Maurice, taking Herrera along as passenger.

30. Henry Farman (1874–1958), born in France of English parents. Flew balloons, then gliders and planes. He designed the first effective ailerons, applying them to his modified Voisin biplane in October 1908.

In World War I and the 1920s he built planes with his brother Maurice (1877–1961), the latter having also been an aeronaut since 1894.

31. Enrique Arrillaga López (b. 1884), entered the Escuela de Aerostatación in July 1908, making his first balloon ascent the same month. A member of the first promotion of military aviators, he received license no. 5. In December 1911 he crashed in a Farman #1.

José Ortiz Echague (b. 1886), received Spanish aviator's license no. 3. A graduate of the Academy of Military Engineers, he also piloted balloons.

Eduardo Barrón y Ramos de Sotomayor (1888–1949), military engineer, made his first balloon ascent in July 1908. Saw action in Melilla sector where he observed artillery fire from the basket of a balloon. Received pilot's license no. 2 in 1911. On November 5, 1913, he participated in the first military bombardment in history, flying a Farman to which he had attached a tube which served as a primitive bomb-sight. During the Civil War he was chief of technical services of the Nationalist air force.

32. Gabriel Espanet (b. 1883), trained as a surgeon, started flying Leyat biplanes and was then named head of Nieuport's flying school.

33. Robert Ducorneau (1877–1912) was killed in a plane crash at Pau on February 22, 1912.

34. Alfonso de Orleans (b. 1886), graduated from the Infantry Academy, then studied aviation at Mourmelon, France, receiving Spain's second international (FAI) license. A member of the first promotion of military aviators, he served in Melilla and built the first bombs used in Morocco in 1913. He led a Fokker squadron in Tetuan in the 1920s.

35. Luís Dávila y Ponce de Léon, third promotion of military aviators, also piloted balloons. In 1913 he served under Herrera in the second squadron at Cuatro Vientos. Assigned to Africa, he died in an aviation accident on April 18, 1925.

36. José Monasterio Ituarte (1882–1952), graduate of the Cavalry Academy, served as a cavalry officer in Morocco and later, as general, under Franco. Received pilot's license in the third promotion.

Carlos Alonso Hera, received pilot's license in 1911. In 1912 he flew a Farman to 2000 m. altitude. The following year he flew the first military aviation mission in history, in Tetuan, and in May 1914 served under Herrera on an expedition to Melilla.

José Valencia Fernández, fourth promotion of military aviators, served under Herrera, along with Alonso and Pérez Núñez, in 1913. Taught and flew Curtiss hydroplanes in 1918.

Antonio Pérez Núñez, medical officer, second promotion of military aviators, flew Nieuport with Herrera in Cuatro Vientos course of 1911.

Served with Melilla squadron in 1914; later specialized in aeronautical medicine.

37. Celestino Bayo Lucía (1879–1912), graduated from Infantry Academy and saw service in Cuba. He witnessed Armand Zipfel's attempt to fly at Tempelhof in 1908, then studied American and French equipment in France, embodying his observations in a book, *Los aeroplanos bajo el punto de vista militar* (1910). In July 1910 he flew a plane of his own making. He graduated in the second promotion of military aviators at Cuatro Vientos where, on June 27, 1912, he died in an accident.

Alberto Bayo Girón (1894–1967), graduate of the Infantry Academy, transferring to aeronautics in 1916. Director of the Civil Aviation School at Cuatro Vientos in 1920. He flew in North Africa in the 1920s until he was sent to the Legion because of disciplinary problems. Returning to aviation with the Republic, he led an abortive expedition to recover Mallorca from the Nationalists in 1936.

Carlos Cortijo, medical officer in second promotion of military aviators who became the third fatality of Spanish military aviation.

38. Emilio Jiménez Millás y Cano (1879–1917), assigned to aerostatics in 1902, served as balloon pilot in Morocco, 1913–16. Second promotion of military pilots, he died practicing for his aviation license.

39. Pelayo was the ancestor of the kings of Castile who turned back a Muslim attack at Covadonga in 722 A.D.

40. A Zeppelin made the first international airship flight from Jamboli to Khartoum and back in November 1917.

41. Louis-Charles Breguet (1880–1955), early designer of motors, then airplanes, obtained pilot's licence in 1910. During World War I, he designed and tested biplanes. His Type 14, which first flew in 1916, gave France air superiority in the War. In the 1920s he built planes with his own company.

42. Carlos Viegas Gago Coutinho (b. 1869), Portuguese geographer, admiral, and aviator. As a geographer he performed geodesic, topographical, and boundary delimitation projects in the Portuguese colonies. The year after the Lusitania flight, Sacadura (1881–1924) was forbidden to fly because of poor eyesight; he continued and lost his life in an accident over the North Sea.

43. "La isla Penedo de San Pedro debe ser cedida a Portugal," *El Sol*, May 2, 1922.

44. Herrera reported the cession in "La isla Penedo de San Pedro ha sido cedida a Portugal," *El Sol*, June 20, 1922.

45. Harry Guggenheim (1890–1971), American aviation pioneer. On a European tour in 1926, he conferred with Herrera and Juan de la

Cierva in Spain; see Richard P. Hallion, *Legacy of Flight: The Guggenheim Contribution to American Aviation* (Seattle, 1977), p. 37.

46. Juan F. Cárdenas y Rodríguez de Rivas (1881–1966), diplomat, later Francoist agent in Washington, 1936–1939.

47. The Military Defense Committees were *juntas* of army officers formed in 1917–1922 to protest bureaucratic irregularities in the army, as well as parliamentary control over it. They were dissolved by the Minister of War in 1922.

48. Cf. Rosendahl's description of Barcelona, "its geometrical streets glowing with brilliant illumination in a pattern of criss-cross streaks." As the airship flew over, Herrera passed around a bon voyage message from the King, which had been received on the Zeppelin's wireless (*New York Times*, October 18, 1928).

49. Vilhelm Bjerknes (1862–1951), Norwegian meteorologist who originated the theory of polar fronts.

50. Count Ernst von Brandenburg (1883–1952), early Germany military aviator. At this time, he was Minister of Communications in charge of civil aeronautics.

51. Rodrigo Sánchez de Triana, sailor with Columbus who first sighted the New World.

52. Eckener and the Zeppelin party, including Herrera, "the Spanish observer," were received by President Coolidge in Washington on October 19 (*New York Times*, October 20, 1928).

53. In Spain whistling at someone in public has a pejorative meaning. Nevertheless, *La Nación*'s reporter at Lakehurst observed that Herrera's face was "impassive, as always" (*La Nación*, October 16, 1928).

54. The Zeppelin party attended a performance of *Show Boat* at ten in the evening on October 16. During the intermission Eckener, accompanied by Lady Drummond Hays and Rosendahl, delivered a short talk from the stage (*New York Times*, October 17).

55. The smoker was Frederick Gilfillan, "the most miserable passenger aboard the Graf Zeppelin," who shared a berth with Dr. Robert Reiner. "Denied tobacco, he became ill the first day out." Gilfillan vowed never to make the westward crossing by air again, stating: "Coming this way, there are too many difficulties to be overcome" (*New York Times*, October 17 and 19, 1928).

56. See the accounts of Herrera's radio telephone conversations with Spain, made from the New York office of the International Telephone Company, in Raffe Emerson, "Atlantic Liner Airships," *American Review of Reviews*, 78 (1928), 623, and *La Nación*, October 25, 1928. Herrera publishd his diary in *La Nación*, October 27.

57. Wilhelm von Faupel (1873–1945), German general and Iberian

specialist. He later served as Hitler's ambassador to Nationalist Spain, 1936–1937.

58. The president of Bolivia in 1928 was Hernando Siles. He was not overthrown until 1930, however.

59. On November 19, 1928, Herrera lectured on "La Línea Aérea Sevilla-Buenos Aires" in the library of the Sociedad Científica Argentina, under the auspices of the Argentine Aero-Club (*La Nación*, November 20, 1928). According to *La Nación*, Herrera departed Buenos Aires on the Giulio Cesare, November 20. Carlos de Haya González (1902–1938), joined military aviation in 1925 and flew Bristol fighters in Melilla. In 1927 he performed blind-flying tests. On the Nationalist side in the Civil War, he crashed into a Republican plane over Teruel and was killed.

60. The Escuela Superior Aerotécnica was officially approved on September 29, 1928, and the decree establishing it published in the *Gaceta Oficial*, October 2; reprinted in *Madrid Científico*, 35 (1928), 315–317.

61. Ramón Franco (1896–1938), infantry officer, brother of Francisco, served in Morocco, then switched to aviation in 1920, commanding a hydroplane base in Morocco. His flight to Buenos Aires in the Plus Ultra in 1926 broke numerous world records for hydroplanes.

62. Joaquín Fanjul y Goñi (1880–1936), active conspirator against the Republic. As leader of the unsuccessful uprising in Madrid, he was court-martialed and executed by the Republic in July 1936.

63. Federico García Sánchiz (1886–1964), essayist, later an apologist for the Franco regime.   Corpus Barga, pen name of Andrés García de la Barga (b. 1887), columnist for *El Sol*.

64. Blaugas was a mixture of ethane and ethene, with the approximate density of air. Zeppelin's engineer Lempertz had the idea of using it in dirigibles in place of gasoline, making it possible to dispense with the volume of sustaining gas (hydrogen or helium) necessary to bear the weight of the gasoline. Its use, therefore, did not alter the vertical equilibrium of the ship and it considerably reduced the amount of sustaining gas needed, especially on long trips; see Herrera's account, "Aviación," *Enciclopedia Universal Ilustrada, Suplemento,* I (1930), 1101–1102.

65. Because of Silvestre's close friendship with the King, the high commissioner in Morocco, General Damaso Berenguer, was reluctant to restrain him when he committed his troops to the defense of a weak position at Annual.

66. Herrera's conversation with the King was well-known among Spanish conservatives. See account (with mistaken date of 1932) in José María Gil Robles, *No fué posible la paz* (Barcelona, 1978), p. 87, n. 13.

67. Ramiro de Maeztu (1875–1936), member of the literary generation of 1898, ambassador to Argentina in 1928. In the 1930s he became

a spokesman for authoritarian political views and was assassinated in the early days of the Civil War.

68. Miguel Maura Gamazo (1887–1971), liberal monarchist who joined the provisional government of the Republic as Interior Minister.

69. José Marvá y Mayer (1846–1936), military engineer and member of the Academy of Sciences. He gave the official reply to Herrera's discourse of acceptance.

Enrique Moles Ormella (1883–1953), physical chemist, reknowned for his research on atomic weight. He was elected to the Academy in 1934.

70. Salvador de Madariaga (1886–1979), Spanish ambassador to the League of Nations.

71. Commander G. Prokofiev, aeronaut, participated in Red Army stratospheric ascents in the 1930s. Under the code name Félix he flew for the Republic from August 1936 to May 1937.

72. Luis Jiménez de Asúa (1889–1970), socialist politician and law professor, major author of the Republican constitution of 1931. Lieutenant José Castillo, assault guard, assassinated by Falangists on July 12, 1936. The Assault Guards were a police corps with members chosen for proven loyalty to the Republic.

73. Blas Cabrera Felipe (1878–1945), experimental physicist, member of the Solvay Institute, friend of Einstein and a leading Spanish popularizer of relativity.

74. Angel Pastor Velasco (b. 1887), member of the fourth promotion of military pilots (1913), flew in Morocco (1913–14), was chief of aviation during the Second Republic and in the early days of the Civil War was undersecretary for defense in charge of armaments. Later he served as arms procurement officer in Paris.

75. Indalecio Prieto y Tuero (1883–1962), socialist politician, during the Civil War he successively held the portfolios of Navy and Air and National Defense in the Republican cabinet.

76. Julio Alvarez del Vayo (1891–1974), socialist politician, Republican foreign minister during the Civil War.

77. The Fifth Regiment was a crack Republican fighting unit, organized by communist militiamen in the first days of the war.

78. Carlos Núñez Maza (b. 1899), communist officer, Republican undersecretary for air.

79. The letter to the bishops of the world was drafted by the primate, Isidro Cardinal Gomá (1869–1940) on Franco's request. Mateo Múgica (1879–1968), then exiled in Rome, who sympathized with Basque nationalism, and Francesc Cardinal Vidal i Barraquer (1868–1943), exiled in Switzerland and friendly to Catalan nationalism, refused to sign the letter.

80. *Ciano's Hidden Diary, 1937–1938*, Andreas Mayor, trans. (New York, 1953), pp. 4–5.

81. Gonzalo Quiepo de Llano (1875–1951), nationalist general in command of the Seville region; used Radio Seville to taunt Republican forces in nightly broadcasts.

82. The Non-Intervention Committee was formed in England in September 1936, with representatives from England, France, Italy, Germany, Russia and, later, Portugal. It had the effect of embargoing arms shipments from western democracies to the Republic but not from the Fascist countries to Franco.

83. Pedro Aguirre Cerda (1879–1941), Chilean politician, leader of the opposition to the dictatorship of General Ibáñez, elected president by the Popular Front in 1938, serving until his death. On the Prieto delegation in the context of Chilean relations with the wartime Republic, see Paul W. Drake, "Chile," in *The Spanish Civil War, 1936–39, American Hemispheric Perspectives*, Mark Falcoff and Frederick P. Pike, eds. (Lincoln, Nebraska, 1982), pp. 273–74.

84. Anthony Eden (1897–1977), British Foreign Secretary, active in the establishment of the Non-Intervention Committee.

85. José Herrera Petere (1909–1977; he used his nickname as a surname) became known during the war throughout the Spanish-speaking world on account of his pro-Republican poetry, as well as his novels *Acero de Madrid* and *Cumbres de Extremadura*.

86. Rodrigo Soriano (1868–1944), Republican politician, ambassador to Chile, 1931–1939.

87. Angel Ossorio y Gallardo (1873–1946), conservative politician who supported the Republic; during the Civil War he was successively ambassador to Belgium, France and Argentina.

88. The retreat of Italian fascist troops from Guadalajara in March 1937 proved of great propaganda value to the Republic.

89. Fernando de los Ríos Urruti (1879–1949), socialist politician and law professor, Republican ambassador to the United States.

90. Louis Aragon (1897–1982), surrealist novelist and Marxist militant. St. Cyprien was a detention camp for refugee Republican soldiers.

91. Teófilo Hernando Ortega (b. 1881), pharmacologist and collaborator with endocrinologist Gregorio Marañón (1887–1960) on the *Manual de Medicina Interna* (Madrid, 1916–1920).

92. Juan Beigbeder Atienza (1890–1957), a fluent Arabist, he served in Morocco in the 1920s and was military attaché in Berlin on the outbreak of the Civil War, later Franco's staff colonel; Foreign Minister in 1942.

José Antonio Primo de Rivera (1903–1936), son of the dictator and leader of fascist Falange party. His execution by the Republic made him a Francoist martyr, as a result of which his name was written on the facades of cathedrals. Pedro Cardinal Segura (1880–1957) objected to this, denounced the Falange as irreligious and was exiled.

93. Herrera, "Sur les Cartes orthométriques à double projection," *Comptes rendus de l'Academie des Sciences,* 217 (1943), 275–297.

94. Herrera refers to his 1943 polemic with G. Hamel on mega-aviation and to two articles on helicopters written in 1947 (see Bibliography).

95. "Flexicalculator pour intégrales et fonctions elliptiques, son application au calcul de la 'courbe de l'éclaireur,'" *Comptes Rendus de l'Académie des Sciences,* 230 (1950), 1134–1136.

96. Maurice Roy (b. 1899), engineer, professor at Ecole Nationale des Ponts et Chaussées, 1926–1946, and Ecole Nationale Supérieure de l'Aéronautique, 1930–1940; director of ONERA (Office Nationale d'Etudes et de Recherches Aéronautiques), 1949–1962).

97. In his memoirs, the monarchist aviator Juan Antonio Ansaldo (1901–1958) claimed that he had obtained a position for Herrera "in the aeronautical laboratories of a great German firm." *¿Para qué . . .?* (Buenos Aires, 1951), p. 260. Ansaldo, a monarchist militant who held several air attaché posts under Franco in the 1940s, retained a personal relationship with Herrera.

98. Juan de Pablo was the code name of Dezsö Jász, Hungarian communist colonel and operations chief of the Republican Army of the North.

99. On Granell and the Spanish Republicans in Leclerc's army, see Louis Stein, *Beyond Death and Exile: The Spanish Republicans in France, 1939–1955* (Cambridge, Mass., 1979), pp. 173–174.

100. Manuel Azaña (1880–1940), Republican politician and president of the Republic from 1936–1939.

Diego Martínez Barrio (1883–1962), Republican politician and cabinet minister, elected president of the Republic-in-Exile in 1945. For another of Herrera's anecdotes concerning Leclerc's Spanish personnel, see Eduardo Pons Prades, *Republicanos españoles en la 2ª guerra mundial* (Barcelona, 1975).

101. Bernardo Giner de los Ríos, architect, Minister of Works in Second Republic, exiled to Mexico.

102. Hippolyte Parodi (b. 1874), engineer, professor of industrial electricity at the Conservatoire National des Arts et Métiers.

103. There is a line missing from the text at this point.

104. *Comptes Rendus de l'Académie des Sciences,* 231 (1950), 1366: "Prix Plumey. Un prix de 14.000 Fr est décerné a M. Emilio Herrera, aviateur, pour ses travaux sur la navigation aérienne."

105. Edouard Corniglion-Molinier (1898–1963), French aviator and

air force officer who flew Malraux (1901-1976) to Spain on July 20, 1936, to ascertain the armaments needs of the Republic.

106. Félix Gordón Ordas (d. 1973), Republican politician and minister of industry; wartime ambassador to Mexico.

107. Robert Esnault-Pelterie (1881–1957), French aviator who built gliders and planes before World War I. His interests were very similar to Herrera's. See his article, "Astronautique et relativité," *L'Aérophile*, 37 (1929), 135–137. In his book, *L'Astronautique* (1930), he included aerodynamic specifications for an artificial satellite.

Joseph Montgolfier (1740–1810) and his brother Etienne (1745–1799), inventors of the hot air balloon.

Clément Ader (1841–1925), the father of French aviation, inventor of a bat-like machine called *Eole*, after the god of winds, which was powered by a steam engine. Its flight in 1890 was the first of a heavier-than-air vehicle.

Jean-François Pilâtre de Rozier (1754–1785), made the first free balloon flight with the Marquis d'Arlandes in 1783. He died in a hydrogen balloon explosion.

Charles Renard (1847–1905) and Arthur Krebs, designed the electric-powered dirigible *La France*.

108. Hugh Thomas, author of *The Spanish Civil War*, revised ed. (New York, 1977).

Part II

Emilio Herrera
and Spanish Technology

Thomas F. Glick

In the aftermath of the War of 1898, Spaniards began a torturous process of reassessment of national goals and resources which fueled the engines of social, political, and intellectual change over the next four decades. The intellectual "Generation of 1898" included thinkers such as Miguel de Unamuno and Ramiro de Maeztu who explored the past and present potentialities of Spanish culture, and their scientific contemporaries were similarly concerned with the nature of the scientific enterprise in Spain and why it had been beset with constant failure. Santiago Ramón y Cajal, who won the Nobel Prize for medicine in 1906, believed that isolation from Europe had been at the root of Spain's scientific decadence. This latter theme was also developed by Joaquín Costa, who sought the regeneration of Spanish institutions through their Europeanization. The "Generation of 1914"—persons born around 1880 who came to public prominence just before World War I—attempted to institutionalize regenerationist goals. This was the generation of the political leaders of the Second Republic, such as Manuel Azaña and Indalecio Prieto, of reformist political thinkers and publicists such as José Ortega y Gasset and of the first truly modern group of Spanish physical scientists—Blas Cabrera, Miguel Catalán, Enrique Moles, and others—who were fully integrated into the European scientific community.

The analysis of Spain's technological backwardness, which acknowledged that the country's defeat in the War of 1898 ("The Disaster," as it was called in Spain) had been at the hands not of

American society but of its technology, proceeded from the same wellsprings. Europeanization here was a synonym for industrial and technological modernization, which were a prerequisite, in turn, to economic and social progress. In this context, it is wholly understandable that the leading technologists of the early twentieth century—Leonardo Torres Quevedo (1852–1936), Emilio Herrera (1879–1967) and Juan de la Cierva (1895–1936)—were drawn to aeronautics, a field viewed as a kind of royal road to modernization, one whose success depended on full integration with European technology, and which promised immediate military, commercial, and institutional rewards. Spain was the first country in the world to use aviation in battle (in Morocco in 1913). La Cierva's autogyro, a kind of hybrid between a helicopter and conventional plane, became a symbol of technological regeneration for the entire nation. It was tested in Herrera's research establishment, which included the largest wind tunnel in Europe and, after 1928, the best technical school of Spain—both Herrera's brainchildren.

Throughout the nineteenth century new scientific ideas had been made to withstand constant tests of congruity with the values of the conservative elite that held power in Spain throughout most of the century. Darwinism was undoubtedly an extreme case, as the Catholic hierarchy brooked not even the slightest accommodation to the new biology. If other areas of inquiry were not as sensitive, they were subjected to the same kind of ideological scrutiny which, at the very least, had the effect of discouraging innovation and even the pursuit of pure research. Even the discussion, current in all western societies, on the nature and value of science became in Spain a sterile feud between warring ideological factions: conservatives defended the nation's thin scientific tradition, boosting the claims of the mediocre, while liberals denied much of value that had actually taken place, charging their opponents with the failure of science.

In the years directly following the "Disaster" it became clear that, in the interests of modernization, scientific inquiry had to be removed from the arena of political ideology and its practitioners allowed, even encouraged, to discuss and evaluate new ideas freely and openly. This new condition of civil discourse in science provided the immediate background for the rapid maturation of fields like physics and chemistry, in which Spanish achievements in the nineteenth century had been slim. Herrera was both a product and a catalyst of these new conditions, which were suddenly very favorable to advanced research.

Herrera's intellectual and personal odyssey was typical of the other leaders of the generation of the Republic: performance at a European level, accomplishments unprecedented in Spain at the time. But the normal course of his professional growth was interrupted by the Civil War, and the thirty years of exile that followed could only be a pale imitation of what his career, if uninterrupted, might have been. Like a microcosm of the Republic itself, Herrera's greatest success—the invention of the space suit—became his greatest failure; his invention fell to the Fascists like Spanish democracy did, a victim of the Civil War. This double loss haunted Herrera for the rest of his days.

If in retrospect, Herrera's career now seems typical of an entire generation of frustrated Spanish scientists, the best of whom ended their professional lives in exile, he was nevertheless quite untypical of that group in his social and professional origins. Scion of an Andalusian military family, he embarked upon a military engineering career that was normal in every way except for the climate of technological innovation in which Spanish engineering was then immersed. He was a loyal monarchist, a socially conservative Catholic, and although some of his miltary colleagues remained loyal to the Republic most did not not. For Herrera, the open spirit which informed his attitude toward science and technology came increasingly to define his political outlook. Democracy did not arouse the same fears in him that assailed most of his fellow officers. His close association with British, French, and American technology brought him into frequent contact with officers of those countries whose views of the relationship of military to civilian authority were sharply different from those prevailing in the Spanish army. Herrera's modernity invaded all aspects of his professional life.

From Aerostatics to Aviation

Balloons had been used for military observation since the 1790s but only became effective militarily when the invention of the telegraph made instantaneous communication with artillery possible. Military balloonists saw action in the Franco-Prussian War and by the 1880s the armies of most European powers had organized balloon corps. In Spain a Military Aerostation Service was authorized in 1884, the same year as the German Balloon Corps was organized, but it did not become fully operative until equipment arrived in 1889. In that year Queen María Cristina made a much-publicized ascent in a captive balloon. In 1896 the Aerostatic Service was reorganized at Guadalajara as a fully autonomous unit under the command of Pedro Vives y Vich (1868–1938) who made the first free balloon ascent in Spain (he had obtained his license earlier in Germany) in 1900, along with Emilio Jiménez Millás. Between 1901 and 1908 Vives was the focal figure in Spanish aerostatics, making eighty-two ascents and training the first military balloonists: Alfredo Kindelán (1879–1962), Antonio Gordejuela (d. 1913), and Jiménez Millás, among others. When Herrera entered the service in 1905 he became, after Kindelán, the most active balloonist. By 1908 Kindelán held the Spanish record for distance (500 km) and Herrera, for altitude (6000 m).[1]

At the St. Petersburg meeting of the International Commission for Scientific Aerostatics in 1904, Vives presented a plan for observing the total eclipse of the sun due to take place on August 30, 1905. There he consulted a number of foreign experts who had been associated with meteorological ballooning, including Arthur Berson (1859–1942) of the Prussian Aeronautical Observatory and A. Laurence Rotch of the Blue Hills Observatory in Boston. Berson was subsequently sent to Spain as the Commission's representative. His chief interest was in temperature change during the totality (there was none) and Rotch's was the possible change in wind directon (the results were inconclusive because the earth was hidden by clouds.) Herrera, assigned to draw the solar corona from one of the balloons, was more successful. His description of the expedition's results, given in his memoirs, is complemented by another he wrote in 1934:

> We carried out spectroscopic and spectographic observations of
> the solar corona and of the flash, and meteorological
> observations of the air under the influence of the lunar shadow,
> whose position could be determined at specific moments on the
> broad horizon our elevated observatory commanded; the solar
> corona was drawn from this high vantage point, and
> photographs taken which exactly matched the drawings and

photographs taken from the ground, proving that the earth's atmosphere has no influence whatever on the appearance of the corona. We also observed the phenomenon of flying shadows on a white screen hung from the basket of the balloon I used in the ascent. At our altitude, where the density of the atmosphere between the observer and the sun was reduced to half of what it was on earth, the bands of light appeared about seven times narrower than they did on earth, but kept their same orientation and movement, which demonstrated decisively the atmosopheric origin (owing to interferences in the layers of air of different indices of refraction) of this curious phenomenon, until then of an unknown nature.

Aside from the scientific observations, we observed that the sky was dark blue, spangled with stars around the dazzling solar corona ringing the black silhouette of the moon in the center of the soft glow of the milky way. The immense stretch of horizon visible, partly covered by a sea of clouds, was illuminated by a pale violet light except at its farthest extremities, beyond the moon's shadow, where it was bright as day. This magnificent spectacle will live forever in the memories of those who participated in that first contribution of aeronautics to astronomical science.[2]

Herrera describes his war service in Melilla in 1909 as a balloon artillery observer. Soon thereafter, now primarily interested in the technical side of aeronautics and aviation, he wrote an aeronautical navigation textbook for balloonists. He was particularly interested in meteorological questions and wrote a standard account of the protection of balloons from atmospheric electricity, which, via a German translation, made its way to the United States, where it was published as a Technical Memorandum of the National Advisory Committee for Aeronautics.[3]

In the summer and fall of 1908 Wilbur Wright conducted a series of flying demonstrations in Le Mans, France, initiating an important process of technological interchange, which had a significant quickening effect on the early history of aviation. (From Wilbur the French learned three-axis flight control, which made it possible to fly in windy weather and to execute aerial maneuvers rather than simply flying passively; the use of slow-rotating, geared-down propellers which had more thrust than the air-screws then in use and which, in turn, permitted the use of less powerful engines; and the ability to carry two persons in all normal flying conditions.[4]) During Wilbur's stay, Le Mans became a Mecca for European flying enthusiasts, including a number of Spaniards. As Alfredo Kindelán later recounted, "I attended the unforgettable spectacle with my close friend Emilio Herrera. I will never forget that afternoon; it was October 4. The great marvel took place before our eyes. Herrera and I were mute with amazement. Later our mood turned to open enthusiasm until, finally, we nearly cried with emotion."[5]

In 1911, Vives established an aerodrome at Cuatro Vientos, near Madrid, purchasing two French biplanes, a Henry Farman and a Maurice Farman, for instruction. The first "promotion" or class of military aviators began classes there on March 15, with a French instructor. Kindelán was the first to be licensed (he held the third Spanish FAI license, Benito Loygorri and Prince Alfonso de Orleans having already been licensed in France) and Herrera, flying a Farman, won the sixth. The military licensing, described by Herrera in his memoirs, came later, with Kindelán earning the first and Herrera (in a Nieuport) the second.

Aviation was introduced into the North African war in 1913, when Vives set up an airfield on the left bank of the Rio Martin, near Melilla, to house a squadron which included four Farmans, four Lohners, and four Nieuports, the model that Herrera flew in this period. A series of historic firsts followed: the first military aviation mission, first aerial bombardment, and so forth.

During World War I Herrera began the transition from active pilot to technical expert: his mission to observe English aviation in France and his trip to Canada in 1915 to purchase hydroplanes are two early benchmarks. With the establishment of the Aerodynamic Laboratory at Cuatro Vientos in 1921 the transition was virtually complete and in 1928 he told a journalist that he recalled the original Curtiss monoplanes (probably the speedy Navy R-1 of 1921) "which we had to pilot well-lashed to the seat. Those experiments have already gone by for me. Today I rarely fly a plane myself, being fully satisfied to act as an observer."[6]

The Aerodynamic Laboratory

From 1921 until the Civil War, Herrera's activities were centered in the Aerodynamic Laboratory at Cuatro Vientos, of which he was director. For it, he designed a closed vertical wind tunnel which, when completed that year, was the second largest in the world. The tunnel's diameter was three meters in the experimental chamber, expanding to four at the point where the wind fan was located. It then widened again as it ascended to the second story, which it occupied completely and then made a symmetrical descent at the other end of the building, narrowing again to three meters as it neared the chamber. Closed tunnels are more efficient than open ones because they recirculate air already in motion, but the constantly circulating air acquires centrifugal force and does not reach the experiment chamber in a homogeneous current. This difficulty Herrera overcame by introducing a countercurve just before the wind entered the chamber. The fan was powered by an electric motor of 700 hp and produced an air current with a velocity of 200 km per hour, at 700 revolutions per minute. (The only wind tunnel then larger was the horizontal one at Langley Field, Virginia, which, however, produced wind of a lower velocity.)

Models tested in wind tunnels were affixed by wires to a balance which measured the aerodynamic efficiency (lift/drag ratio) of the model, but it proved difficult to eliminate the distorting influence of the wires used to attach the model to the balance. In Herrera's tunnel, this difficulty was overcome by the installation of a special balance (Figure 2), invented by Jenaro Olivié, which made it possible to measure the resistance of the wires before the model was emplaced and to make compensatory adjustments. In this tunnel, Herrera performed tests which led to the perfection of the autogyro, as well as many others recorded in his textbook *Aerotecnia*.[7]

Herrera lectured extensively on his tunnel at international meetings throughout the decade. At the First International Congress of Air Navigation, held in Paris in 1921, the director of the newly built aerodynamic tunnel at Isay-les-Moulineaux, an open tunnel as large as the Spanish one, suggested that the open form be designated the standard type so that results of aerodynamic tests would be directly comparable. Herrera opposed this motion and proposed instead that a technical commission conduct systematic experiments with identical models in different tunnels in order to establish the advantages of one or the other type. At the Third Congress (Brussels, 1925), Herrera and other participants visited the Belgian aerodynamic tunnel, a smaller version of the

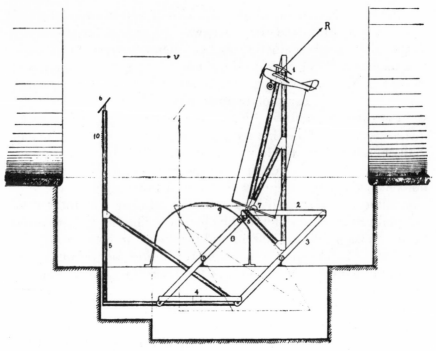

Figure 2. Diagram of the special balance used in Herrera's wind tunnel.

French type, and heard its director explain that the tunnel was useless because a whirlwind formed on the floor in front of the air intake and then crossed the experiment chamber, distorting results. Subsequent research showed that all open tunnels formed such whirlwinds, and Herrera conducted experiments at Cuatro Vientos to ascertain their origin. The whirlwinds were caused by the discontinuity in the walls surrounding the intake. Herrera presented this conclusion, which he believed demonstrated the superiority of closed tunnels, at the Fourth Congress in Rome, in November 1927.[8]

In 1929 Herrera was named director of the Escuela Superior de Aerotécnica, which he founded as an advanced center of aerotechnology. The School lacks a written history, but under Herrera's aegis it had great fame in Spanish scientific circles because he believed that mathematicians and physicists should teach their own disciplines there, rather than engineers. Accordingly he hired Pedro Puig Adam and Tomás Rodríguez Bachiller, two products of Julio Rey Pastor's Mathematical Laboratory, to teach mathematics , and Julio Palacios, a younger colleague of Blas Cabrera's, to teach thermodynamics. Bachiller, according to whom the school was "stupendous," also taught the theory of wings, using the Spanish translation of Yakofsky's Russian text, one of Herrera's favorites.[9] It is noteworthy that Herrera chose colleagues whose scientific interests were similar to his own. Puig Adam and Bachiller were two early Spanish exponents of relativity, the former having written his doctoral thesis on a number of mathematical problems related to the Special Theory, and Palacios, who in later life became a pronounced antirelativist, was at that time favorable to the theory and well-versed in its literature. With them, Herrera doubtless discussed Einstein's theories, as well as his own idiosyncratic cosmology.

Dirigibles

Herrera's first experiences with dirigibles were in 1909, when he made twenty or thirty flights in the Spanish army airship "España," which, he later recounted, was a dirigible in name only "because it was guided more by the wind than by its own mechanism." The vehicle in question was one of a series of dirigibles built by Torres Quevedo (now best remembered as a pioneer cybernetician), with the technical assistance of Kindelán. This was a semirigid airship whose shape was maintained by interior rigging and a large ballonet that was kept inflated with air blown into it by a fan, in contrast to the rigid duraluminum girders of the Zeppelins. On the basis of this experience Herrera earned a dirigible pilot's license, but soon afterwards the first airplanes arrived ("as rudimentary and imperfect as the dirigible just mentioned") and he dedicated himself completely to flying them.[10]

Nevertheless, in 1918 Herrera became interested in the possibility of instituting commercial transatlantic dirigible flights, which he believed should interest the Spanish government and business community because of the country's favorable geographic position: the shortest distance between Europe and North America is between Cape Vilano in Galicia and Cape Charles, Labrador. He pointed this out in a memorandum presented to the government in 1918 which further specified that, based on detailed specifications describing the German super-Zeppelins captured by the

French army during the war and which had been studied by Spanish engineers, it was clear that Spain possessed both the industrial capacity and the technical skills necessary to build and staff a transatlantic airship, since Spanish industry already was producing rubberized fabric, motors and other necessary elements, and Spanish aeronauts enjoyed prestige in this field, as proven by the military use of Torres Quevedo dirigibles, built in France by the Astra company during the war. King Alfonso XIII listened politely to Herrera's proposal but decided that the government's policy should be to support air relations with its former colonies rather than with North America. Still, interest in Herrera's original proposal seems to have remained alive until the British Navy airship R-34 made the first round-trip crossing of the Atlantic in July 1919.[11]

Soon after Herrera conceived the idea of establishing a regular airship service from Spain (first Sanlúcar, then Cádiz, and finally Seville were proposed as points of embarkation) to Buenos Aires, a project which he tirelessly—and fruitlessly—pursued for a full decade. This project brought Herrera into contact with Hugo Eckener (1868–1954), the Zeppelin company's indefatigable director of operations. Eckener must have found Herrera's plan attractive because the Spanish company that Herrera established (Compañía Transaérea Colón) would have provided the Germans with a base of operations at a time when, according to the Treaty of Versailles, Germany was forbidden to build or use transatlantic airships. Press reports from the summer and fall of 1921 indicate that both the Spanish company's ships and technical personnel would be provided by Germany. The company proposed to make 100 trips yearly, with each trip costing 420,000 pesetas. Sixty passengers would be carried at 5,000 pesetas each (around $800), in addition to 300,000 postal parcels or letters at two pesetas each, producing an income of 900,000 pesetas, approximately half of which would be profit.[12] These figures are interesting, because on the two voyages of the *Graf Zeppelin* that Herrera made in 1928 and 1930, although sixty persons were carried, approximately forty of these were crew. Indeed the high ratio of crew to passengers was one of the greatest hindrances to the commercialization of dirigible flights. Herrera was later to note, in connection with the possibility of a Spain-Cuba line (which he opposed), that the controlling feature of such enterprises, besides the availability of suitable docking facilities, was the flow of mail between the two ports, "since the postal portion is considered the preponderant element of the enterprise."[13]

The project came closest to realization in 1928 when Herrera joined Eckener, Charles Rosendahl, commander of the U.S. Navy dirigible *Los Angeles,* Lady Grace Drummond Hay and other passengers on the first transatlantic voyage of the *Graf Zeppelin* in October 1928. Prior to this trip there were three commercial dirigible plans afloat in Spain. The first was to build semirigid ships of the Torres Quevedo type with a capacity of only 50,000 cubic meters, for domestic mail service only. The second was to build Zeppelins of a capacity of 135,000 cubic meters (twice the size of the *Los Angeles*) at Seville, for transatlantic service. The third was to conclude a lease-purchase agreement for the *Graf Zeppelin* itself, whereby Transaérea Colón would pay a percentage of its income to the German company for the lease and amortization of the sale price. Herrera was reported to have concluded such an agreement on the trip, with the sale price reported to have been $1,200,000, but from published statements by Herrera it seems that he actually negotiated a lease agreement, whereby Colón would use the *Graf Zeppelin* until it was able to purchase its own airship.[14] The Seville facility was to feature concrete airdocks of an unprecedented size: a 190-foot arch with a span of 400 feet, or two city blocks, more than half again as large as the Lakehurst, N.J., airdock which was then the largest such facility.[15]

In his attempt to "sell" his plan to both the Spanish and the Argentinian public, Herrera took great pains to stress the safety of the 1928 trip, an interesting sidelight to the account in his memoirs because in the annals of dirigible history this flight is considered a failure. It proved that the *Graf* was too small for regular transatlantic service (it had an unfavorable passenger to crew ratio); it was too slow; and it could not cope with the meteorological conditions prevailing in the North Atlantic in mid-autumn.[16] In this light it is interesting to compare the low-keyed entry in Herrera's shipboard diary (written for public consumption in Argentina) describing the squall and accident of October 13 with Rosendahl's and the entry in Herrera's own memoirs, both of which give a more accurate glimpse of the real drama (and terror) of the situation. Herrera's diary notes: "It is 10:40 a.m. and we are having breakfast. There are sudden jolts. Winds are blowing in contrary directions making a target of the dirigible which, giving way, lurches upward. A squall. Some tables and chairs fall over, and some passengers fall. The photographic machines roll down the passageway. The covering on the port side of the tail rips. Lady Drummond Hay, a genuine sporting type of lady, smiles without becoming alarmed. The passengers show themselves to be in control of the situation in the face of so much serenity on the part of a member of the so-called weaker sex. We row through this zone of depression, which is very extensive, for ten hours. At 6:45 p.m. we see the first rays of sunlight and, shortly thereafter, the clouds begin to dissolve. Now calm, I send a telegram to King Alfonso, giving an account of the accident and indicating to him that the damage has been partially repaired."[17]

Rosendahl's published report is much more dramatic. It appears that Herrera's observation of the sportingness of Lady Grace was due to the fact that when the squall began and the nose of the ship thrust suddenly up, her breakfast eggs had landed in her lap! Rosendahl described white-faced officers and told of wiring the Navy to have rescue ships standing by.[18] Herrera's shipboard diary also notes that he and Rosendahl had spent a great part of their time in the command room, playing chess in moments of leisure, while Lady Grace, who was representing the Hearst chain (as well as *La Nación* of Buenos Aires) as a reporter, "did not cease depressing the keys of her typewriter and writing for a single moment."

In spite of the vision of serenity depicted in his dairy, Herrera was clearly troubled by the problem of squalls, which produced contrary pressures on different parts of the airship. In this case the prow and poop received violent upward currents while the center of the ship received a downdraft of equal force (in this very way the U.S. Navy dirigible *Shenandoah,* on which Rosendahl had been navigator, crashed in 1925). On his return to Spain, Herrera wrote a careful study of the meteorological problems encountered on the flight and their aerodynamic repercussions, calculating the trajectory of an ideal lurching pattern in hopes of providing a practical method of correction.[19]

While in the United States, in addition to accompanying Eckener to Washington, Herrera—"tireless," in the characterization of *La Nación*'s reporter—was taken on an inspection tour of the Lakehurst facility to view the mooring masts and other devices, was the guest in New York of the Fox International Corporation, the company which had contracted to build the Seville airdocks, and visited a hydroplane factory in Philadelphia.[20]

Herrera arrived in Buenos Aires on November 15, his primary mission there to discuss possible airdock facilities with a German engineer named Block.[21] The 16th he spent mainly in his hotel room studying topographical maps of the environs of the city, taking time out for social engagements with the Spanish ambassador Ramiro de Maeztu and with his colleague from the Madrid Mathematical Society, Julio Rey Pastor, who taught in Buenos Aires half of each year. On the 20th he gave a public lecture on the Seville-Buenos Aires project, attended by a great crowd that overflowed the library of the Argentinian Scientific Society and which included pilots, civil and military aeronautical technologists, and members of the Spanish community. Many who were unable to hear him speak waited in the street to greet him after the lecture, which dealt with meteorological problems encountered on the recent flight of the *Graf* and their relative lack of danger, the more favorable atmospheric conditions prevailing in the South Atlantic, and the airship's technical innovations—reversible engines, which greatly eased the docking process, and Blaugas, a fuel which had great advantages over gasoline.[22]

In spite of the favorable publicity and Herrera's bouyant public pronouncements, it was clear that the project was beset with difficulties. Herrera noted, apropos of Transaérea Colón's recent public stock offering of ten million pesetas, that Spanish capitalists were reluctant to invest in this kind of air project. The project had also attracted opposition within the Spanish aeronautical community. His enemies attacked him as a visionary, said Herrera, "and certain rival interests even reached the point of founding an aeronautical magazine in Madrid designed to attack the proposal." On the other hand, public opinion was on his side, as was proven by the fact that "all the political factions, who habitually fight each other over all matters, have in this case joined forces to secure the realization of my plans."[23] He was too optimistic. *El Sol*, Ortega y Gasset's newspaper which consistently favored scientific and technological innovation, went so far as to editorialize against the plan, which it thought imprudent in view of meteorological problems attendant upon a long trip. "For now," the newspaper concluded, "while air navigation has not arrived at even the minimal point of necessary solvency, it is the better part of discretion not to launch ourselves on dangerous adventures."[24]

Herrera made a second crossing on the *Graf Zeppelin* in the spring of 1930 from Spain to Brazil. By this time it was clear that the project had failed because of insufficient capital, in spite of Herrera's statements to the press to the effect that the primary problem revealed in 1928—lack of adequate meteorological data—had been overcome. It then became necessary "to prove that the dirigible could easily cross the zone of equatorial disturbances . . . which some regarded as a barrier which lighter-than-air ships could never breech." This problem had proven nonexistent and, therefore, "The project is still alive."[25]

Nevertheless this trip was more of a lark than a research mission. By now the *Graf* had a small coterie of habitual passengers. Corpus Barga, the Madrid columnist, noted that two women made the first leg of the trip, from Freidrichshafen to Seville: "Frau Vorley, who is accompanying her husband, and Lady Grace Drummond Hay, accompanied by her beauty. And also Dr. Jerónimo Megías, who comes on all these voyages, as if he doesn't want to be absent on the day of the catastrophe." Megías was King Alfonso's personal physician. The other Spanish passengers, "quieter and more reserved" than the other guests (according to Lady Grace) were Herrera, his colleague from military aviation Prince Alfonso de Orleans, an Asturian banker and big game hunter named González Herrero, and the writers Corpus Barga and Federico García Sánchiz. Herrera, the Prince, and Megías busied themselves organizing fly hunts. Arriving at Lakehurst from Brazil, Lady Grace observed that this had been the first trip when all the passengers had disembarked "in a spirit of complete security and confidence." In Madrid, although the voyage received more press attention than any aviation story since Ramón Franco's transatlantic hydroplane flight of 1926, official circles remained unconvinced. Franco himself noted that no practical result would emerge from this trip because the return leg was through the United States and not along the South Atlantic route, while Herrera's friend Joaquín de La Llave noted that so long as the passenger/crew ratio remained unfavorable (16 to 41) nothing practical would result.[26]

Herrera and Hypermechanics

In his *Memoirs,* Herrera recounts having been introduced to the geometry of *n* dimensions while on war duty in Africa. (The geometry of *n* dimensions, as developed by Gauss and Riemann, provided a metric for describing the properties of curved, or non-Euclidean, space which later gave Einstein the point of departure for conceptualizing the four dimensional space-time continuum of special relativity.) This was to lead to a lifetime of cosmological speculation, which, because of Herrera's conception of the nature of gravitation, was to bring him into a somewhat ambivalent relationship with Einstein and the theory of relativity. In his writings on these topics, there is a distinctive counterpoint between his admiration for Einstein's theories and his reluctance to abandon his own, which was firmly rooted in classical concepts of the mechanics of ether, the imponderable substance that was believed to occupy all of space. In the special theory of relativity, space did not require a special property like ether to account for the transmission of light.

Although the contradictions embedded in his cosmological writings are unbridgeable, they are better understood in the light of Herrera's own concept of the nature of science. For Herrera, there were three types of scientific inquiry. The first, which he called *direct,* was something like inductive research, drawing general principles from the observation of data. This was the most basic and valuable kind of science. The second type he called *inverse;* it was that science which we might think of as deductive and which investigates abstract principles or axioms. The third, the style of inquiry to which he himself was drawn, he called *transverse,* that which extended the findings of the first two into a purely speculative realm. In mechanics, for example, direct study concentrates on the dynamics of forces and masses in various systems; the indirect, on the nature of space, time, and movement; while the transverse "departs from tangible reality to investigate the laws which would control mechanical phenomena in a space of more than three dimensions."

In biology, direct study was descriptive; inverse was theoretical (for example, the origin of species and of life); transverse was the deduction of forms of life in every conceivable universe. Direct study was that which contributed to the development and progress of science on the greatest scale. Inverse study created the theoretical base of science, while the transverse, "departing from reality, cannot contribute more than to populate the domain of fantasy with beings and theories." In some cases, however, transverse science produces valuable results. For example, "the geometry of space, a transverse explanation of plane geometry, and above all, that marvelous edifice of relativistic Mechanics with which the genius of Einstein has replaced classical Mechanics, elevating it, deepening its bases and broadening it transversely by applying to physical reality theories which, like the space-time continuum, non-Euclidean geometries, absolute differential calculus, etc., could only have once been considered transverse excrescences, lacking any real application, of other classically conceived sciences of extent and quantity."[27] These words preceded Herrera's speech of reception in the Academy of Sciences in 1933, a sober and interesting disquisition on the interrelationship of science and aeronautics.

Herrera, like Kindelán (and, one may presume, the entire generation of early aeronauts), had been an avid reader of Jules Verne in his youth and, in his mature years, he adorned the walls of his apartment in Madrid with his own illustrations of Verne's novels.[28] From the peculiar perspective of aerotechnics, he was well aware that today's fantasy could be tomorrow's reality. If science could be regarded as a continuum from the known to the unknown and the unknowable, he felt comfortable on the "traverse" that led there. In this context, Herrera could struggle to come to grips with relativity, while at the same time developing an extremely speculative cosmology based on outmoded physical principles.

Herrera begins his 1916 formulation of the "Relationship between Hypergeometry and Celestial Mechanics" by noting that gravitational forces observed in space do not appear to obey Newtonian laws. Furthermore the observed anomalies of celestial mechanics (he had in mind the bending of light rays in a gravitational field) suggest that the metric of space might well be non-Euclidean or curved, rather than Euclidean and straight. He then explains gravitation by asserting that the space of our universe (which he assumed was filled with ether) must rotate, engendering centrifugal force in all bodies which it contains. The fourth dimension, in his view, was not time, but another direction, simultaneously perpendicular to all directions of three-dimensional space, that is, a "vortex" in which our universe rotates. (A fifth dimension would involve the placement of this four-dimensional universe within a five-dimensional one, and so forth.) From these considerations he deduced that our universe was a closed, spherical hyperellipsoid with a limited volume, and that the centrifugal force produced by its rotation "would create the transversal deformation of space, originating the apparent attraction between all bodies and the bending of geodesic lines of space and of the direction of a light ray passing through a gravitational field," among other phenomena.[29]

Although not so identified, such notions were of Cartesian inspiration, in that Descartes explained gravitation by the action exerted on the ether (or "second element") by the vortices of celestial bodies, causing centrifugal force of unequal distribution. Celestial massses were pushed toward the center of the vortex.

It is probable that Herrera did not become aware of General Relativity, Einstein's theory of gravitation which likewise pictured a curved non-Euclidean space and accounted for the bending of light rays, until the results of the 1919 eclipse observations confirming Einstein's predictions concerning the deflection of stellar light passing through the sun's gravitational field had been publicized. After at least a year of familiarity with the theory, he presented his views at the Oporto meeting of the Spanish Association for the Advancement of Science in June 1921. It was obvious that Herrera, to say the least, found Einstein's theory congenial to his own ideas: "The principal progress of the Theory of Relativity, and the origin of its successes is, besides the energetic concept of mass, the four-dimensional conceptualization of the physical universe as a continuum, according to time, of spaces deformed by the presence of the masses contained within them."[30] He added, in a brief reference to his previous articles, that the modification of the Newtonian law of gravitation and the bending of light in gravitational fields could also be explained without recurring to Einstein's theory, by simply admitting the rotation and deformability of our three-dimensional physical space with an extension of a higher order. Still, on a cosmological level, he could not disagree with the General Theory.

He could not, however, completely accept the Special Theory, at least not some of its philosophical ramifications, as he understood them. Special Relativity is based on a number of observations concerning the kinematics of light. It postulates that the velocity

of light is constant and independent of that of the body emitting
it; it therefore has the same value in all systems of reference. In
relativistic kinematics, moreover, events viewed as occurring simultaneously in one frame of reference may not so appear when
observed from another. In Einstein's famous example of a train
moving along an embankment, both distance travelled and time
elapsed will be measured differently by observers in each system.

Herrera and other Spanish engineers trained in the tradition
of nineteenth-century electromagnetism were unable to disentangle the kinematics of light from its dynamics, which depended
upon its interaction with the ether. Therefore, this aspect of Einstein's theories, and this one alone, struck Herrera as being contrary to intuition. All human knowledge, he asserted, had an intuitive
basis; if one of its principles be destroyed then we cannot be sure
that the rest is true. Counterintuitive science, such as non-Euclidean geometry, had been purely speculative until the appearance
of the theory of relativity. Therefore, resistance to relativity was
of a different order than resistance to other scientific innovations
had been historically. The struggle had always been among various
modes of relating specific phenomena to intuition, but relativity
had challenged the probity of intuition itself.[31] (It is difficult for
us to perceive now why Cartesian vortices should be any more
"intuitive" than the constancy of the velocity of light—c.) All the
other consequences of relativity were, for Herrera, comprehen-
sible intuitively, so long as one admitted the existence of geometric
dimensions exterior to our own space and time. It may be that
there was a simple philosophical problem for Herrera, based on
his religious convictions. Relativistic cosmology was in large part
definable by a number of numerical constants, one of which was
c. "It is an unsustainable error to suppose ourselves in possession
of numbers which limit and regulate creation. These figures can
only signify qualities peculiar to our own physical space-time, a
minute element of the total Universe."[32] The acceptance of a Cartesian universe, potentially infinite through the continual super-
position of additional vortices, was a way to retain a universe
traditionally conceptualized in Catholic theology as infinite, while
at the same time admitting that Einstein had provided the most
accurate description of the tetradimensional subset which was, in
itself, closed and finite. Only in this way could Herrera bridge the
gap between classical and modern cosmologies. (That Herrera's

concern was broader than the issues raised by relativity alone can be appreciated from an article written during the same period addressing Catholic fears that Ostwald's energeticism appeared to deny the orthodox distinction between matter and spirit.[33]) In the final analysis, Herrera indicates, our intuition itself will have to change in order to accommodate the constancy of c.

Einstein's visit to Madrid in March 1923 caused a wave of excitement to reverberate through the entire scientific community. Herrera, as vice-president of the Mathematical Society, thought the membership could best prepare itself for the scheduled meeting with the visitor by holding two preliminary meetings, before his arrival, to sort out and discuss any scientific or philosophical problems which could then be presented to Einstein in a systematic way. These meetings, with questions submitted in writing in advance, were held on February 20 and 22. At the subsequent meeting with Einstein on March 5 there was an inconclusive interchange between the visitor and the engineer Vicente Burgaleta on whether it was possible to conceive of a system of signals whose velocity of propagation was superior to that of light.[34] Burgaleta and Herrera were at the same time pursuing the same issue in a polemic concerning a "relativistic paradox" in the pages of *Madrid Científico*. The paradox, which had originally been published in *Nature*, concerned two rigid triangles of great length moving toward each other at half the speed of light. The point of their intersection would then appear to move toward an observer at twice the speed of light. The paradox was answered by Sir Arthur Eddington to the effect that many points move faster than the speed of light, but they are not signals. Herrera, unconvinced, exchanged a series of letters with Eddington, which were likewise inconclusive.[35]

During the meeting of the Mathematical Society there was an exchange between Einstein and Herrera. The substance is unrecorded but Alejandro Gómez Spencer recalled that the two men "volleyed integrals." Einstein accepted Herrera's invitation to visit the Aerodynamic Laboratory but then could not find the time to go, as he stated in a note of apology.[36]

The Hyper-Club

The reader of these memoirs cannot help but be impressed by Herrera's sense of humor, his taste for the ironic and the absurd, and his love of good jokes. In 1920 he sought to formalize an outlet for the cultivation of the absurd by founding a club, ostensibly devoted to the pursuit of "transverse" science but whose aims were really humorous. He closed one his *El Sol* articles on hyperspace by noting the current popularity of the subject:

> There is even talk of the organization in Madrid of a "Hyper-Club," a society designed to promote contacts among those who believe in these theories and to promote their study.
>
> Perhaps the competent authority should prohibit the formation of this club and order its members to submit to a curative program to equilibrate their mental faculties in some establishment in the vicinity of Madrid. But we believe that such an edict would be unjust. Although the members of the Hyper-Club (if it should be established) will not thereby achieve any great benefit for humanity, at least they would remove themselves from the suicidal action of the law of social self-destruction which weighs upon humankind, and which with enthusiasm and dispatch worthier of a better cause, the majority of mortals strive to execute, devoting to it all the activity which can possibly be developed within the happily few dimensions of this world in which we suffer the inconvenience to live.[37]

The Club was actually established at the headquarters of the Aero-Club of Madrid at the civil airfield of Getafe. The "Hyper-Members"—those whom Herrera had hinted were likely candidates for the asylum at Ciempozuelos, a psychiatric establishment in the vicinity of Madrid—were fellow flyers and aeronauts: Juan de la Cierva and his test pilot Alejandro Gómez Spencer, the pilot José Rodríguez Díaz de Lecea, and the secretary of the Aero-Club Mariano Moreno-Caracciolo, among others. Herrera wrote some bylaws, one of which held that the president (Herrera) was obliged to address the members with the formal *usted,* while they were to use the personal *tu* when addressing the chair. Indeed, the criterion for all the Club's activities was lack of common sense, and each member had to present a project in accord with this ideal. A Basque aviator named Legórburu presented his verse translation of Laplace's *Celestial Mechanics.* Lecea, a future air minister under Franco, devised a method of hunting bustards by flying above them and batting them down with the wings of his plane; when this "sport" was publicized, it brought the wrath of the British

SPCA down upon him. Gómez Spencer contrived a mathematical formula for ascertaining the work schedule of nocturnal guards, the *serenos* who opened apartment doors in Madrid and other cities; it was inversely proportional to latitude (thus, serenos working at the north or south poles would have six months of vacation yearly).[38]

It is interesting, in view of the great number of humorous anecdotes that Herrera records in his memoirs, that he mentions neither the Hyper-Club nor his close friendship with two of its members, Moreno-Caracciolo and Joaquín de La Llave. La Llave (b. 1882) was president of the Aero-Club in the mid-1920s and, like Herrera, a military engineer, balloonist, and airplane pilot. The three were inseparable friends throughout the 1920s, as is obvious both from newspaper and eyewitness accounts. In February 1921 they represented the Madrid engineering establishment at a banquet for Tullio Levi-Civita, the Italian mathematician who had come to Madrid to lecture on relativity. Tomás Rodríguez Bachiller, then a graduate student in mathematics, recounted how he translated the lectures into Castilian and then met after each presentation with those "three chums" (*tres amigotes*) to correct the translations.[39]

The Hyper-Club, then, was a group which included Herrera's closest colleagues and friends in the small world of aeronautical engineering, together with acquaintances—chiefly test pilots—who shared their daily acitivities, if not all their intellectual interests. These persons, plus a number of other air force colleagues such as Kindelán, who did not share in these activities on the fringes of science, together with mathematicians of the Sociedad Matemática, of which Herrera was vice-president and an active member, formed a distinctive social circle which provided much of the texture of Herrera's daily life in Madrid between 1920 and 1936.

Juan de la Cierva, according to Gómez Spencer, was too preoccupied with his invention, the autogyro, to contribute actively to the pursuits of the Hyper-Club. The autogyro was a conventional propeller-driven plane with short wings, fitted with freely-turning horizontally oriented rotary blades which allowed the aircraft to take off vertically and at low velocities. The plane was repeatedly tested in the 1920s at Getafe and Cuatro Vientos, with Gómez Spencer and Lecea as the primary test pilots, under the technical supervision of Herrera who both directed tests of autogyro models in his wind tunnel and officially certified the results of test flights. In early tests, as the rotors gained velocity in a clockwise direction, the plane would tip over to the right, often breaking the blades or the plane's right wheel. This phenomenon provided Herrera with one of his favorite running jokes, which became funnier with each variation that Herrera introduced into the telling of the joke, which was based on the rightward political orientation of La Cierva's family (his father Juan was a reknowned Conservative politician and minister). Interviewed in *La Nación* in 1928, some seven years after the tests took place, Herrera embroidered his comments on La Cierva's recent work with the now familiar set-piece:

> In the first tests La Cierva ascertained that the machine invariably inclined to the right. This fault, which had been observed earlier in heliocopters, was the basis of a deep preoccupation for the inventor and also of a humorous commentary embroidered with the fact that he is the son of Juan La Cierva, whose political convictions are well-known. Connecting this to the predisposition of the machine to incline "to the right," I found the failure a logical one, and with honest wit I advised my friend to seek the compensatory collaboration of Pablo Iglesias, the socialist leader.[40]

If Herrera infrequently recorded his humorous observations in print (with the exception of his memoirs), the drawings with which he accompanied his technical prose were often conceived in a playful or witty vein, particularly those accompanying his popular serialized articles on aerodynamics which appeared in *L'Aérophile* in the 1940s.

The Invention of the Space Suit

The development of enclosed gondolas brought about a renaissance in free ballooning in the 1930s aimed at the scientific exploration of the stratosphere. Auguste Piccard (1884–1962), the Swiss inventor and explorer, made an ascent to 15,781 meters (51,775 feet) in 1931 and another to 16,000 m. the following year, in a balloon with a spherical aluminum gondola containing its own atmosphere. The American *Explorer* I and II ascents of 1933–35 were even more spectacular, and the *Explorer* II, in which the aeronauts rode in an enclosed gondola equipped with oxygen

inhalers, reached an altitude of 22,612 m. (74,185 ft.). Here was
an enterprise to stir Herrera's blood! By 1934 he was far advanced
on his own version of stratospheric exploration. From the aviation
perspective, he felt that the region of 20–25 km. altitude was an
interesting object of exploration, because it was a region where
airplane velocities might someday reach 1000 km/hr and also permitted the observation of stars in daytime. He proposed to ascend
to 20 km in a hydrogen balloon with a diameter of 36 m. and a
capacity of 24,430 m³ (almost twice as large as Piccard's balloon
but vastly smaller than the gigantic *Explorers;* according to his own
computations a balloon diameter of 30 m. was sufficient to reach
the target altitude of 20 km.).[41]

In Herrera's view the crucial technical question in stratospheric
exploration was the choice between a closed gondola or a space
suit. The former had the double inconvenience of weighing a lot
and of making it hard to parachute out in case of emergency. In
addition, Piccard had found it difficult to carry out scientific tests
on the atmosphere from the inside. The individual suit, on the
other hand, required the solution of various problems related to
the movement of the joints because of the differential interior and
exterior atmospheric pressures.

Although the suit which Herrera devised, and described in his
memoirs, was popularly confused with a diving suit, which it su-
perfically resembled,[42] contrary principles underlay the two gar-
ments. The diving suit has to support increasingly greater pressures
from the exterior, whereas the space suit maintains a higher internal pressure, making normal movement difficult. Herrera's solution to this problem was to install accordion pleats at each joint.
His solution to other problems anticipated the future Apollo suit
in a number of other ways. His silver lamé cape to resist solar
heat became, in the American space suit, an outer covering of
aluminized nylon. The internal atmosphere was handled by an
oxygen inhaler supplied by two 6 kg bottles, while carbon dioxide
was absorbed by potash cartridges contained within the suit (the
American astronauts used lithium hydroxide).[43]

The suit was tested by Herrera in the Aerodynamic Laboratory,
the balloon was built at Guadalajara, and the scientific instrumentation for the ascent, planned for January 1935, was prepared
at the National Institute of Physics and Chemistry under the direction of Blas Cabrera, to meet the requirements of the research

Figure 3. Herrera's sketch of how he envisioned conducting his experiments in his balloon ascension into the stratosphere.

program designed by the Spanish Geographical Society and the military aeronautics division of the army. The scientific goals were, first, to explore the atmosphere (cosmic, electric and solar rays, magnetic charges, and so forth), second, the investigation of phenomena of aeronautical significance (density, pressure, temperature and chemical composition of the air, speed and direction of winds, observation of stars), and, third, to test the space suit. Figure 3 is Herrera's representation of himself performing scientific observations in the open gondola. The instrumentation was to have included a recording meteorograph, an aspirator-psychrometer (a thermometer shielded from the influence of solar radiation), a statoscope or vertimeter (which indicates whether the balloon is rising or falling), a mercury barometer, cameras with photographic plates sensitive to infrared light (two automatic cameras, one of them an ordinary wide-angle apparatus and another for infrared light, located on the vertex of the balloon, pointed upward to photograph stars), a Geiger counter and other instruments to measure cosmic radiation, a pump to store air for future analysis, a radiotelephone and batteries to power it and the electric instruments, as well as to provide heat.

On January 13, 1935, the ascent was postponed "in conformity with a request of the Academy of Sciences."[44] It was eventually rescheduled for October 1936. by which time it had become a casualty of the Civil War. All that survives of the space suit is the silver cape, still in the possession of his family.

The Civil War

The Civil War began on July 18, 1936, when Herrera was lecturing on aerodynamics at the International University of Santander. (There he drew in the autograph book of Solita Salinas, daughter of the poet Jaime, this volume's frontispiece illustration of himself clad in his space suit.) Of the pioneering generation of Spanish aviators, notably those of the first promotion, he was the only one to remain loyal to his oath to serve the Republic.[45] He served in his customary role of director of technical services of the air force; a lieutenant colonel when the war broke out, he was promoted to general on August 16, 1936. In the Republican air force only Herrera and the commanding officer, Ignacio Hidalgo de Cisneros, held the rank of general.

The *Memoirs* are largely silent regarding his daily activities during the war. The detail paid to aerial bombardments is more a reflection of the interests he cultivated in Paris in the early years of his exile when he wrote extensively on the subject. The loss in combat of his son Emilio, which embittered the rest of his life, may be a sufficient explanation of his silence. As he makes clear, he exchanged correspondence with his old friend Kindelán, then chief of the Nationalist air force, in an attempt to ascertain whether "Piquiqui" died in action or had been captured and shot. The exchange of letters was published after the death of both men and sheds light on the relationship between them. Earlier in the *Memoirs* Herrera describes his legal difficulties when, as comptroller of the Air Force, he was found in disobedience of a budgetary constraint imposed by the Treasury Minister José Calvo Sotelo (1893–1936). Herrera had represented materiel ordered as already received and paid for, a ruse agreed upon with his superior

Kindelán as the only way to keep the Air Force adequately supplied under the circumstances. Kindelán never took responsibility for his role in this episode, which left Herrera in a kind of administrative limbo until 1936. Nevertheless, in the wartime exchange of letters, Kindelán shows nothing but affection for his former comrade-in-arms and then enemy:

Zaragoza
December 8, 1938

Dear Emilio:

   I want to inform you of the truth of what happened, principally so that you and Irene might be relieved that poor Piquiqui did not suffer in his death. I was in Zaragoza on the occasion of the offensive against Belchite and was given documentation concerning three planes which had fallen behind our lines. In this material I saw, with the grief that you can imagine, your son's pilot license. I ordered an immediate identification by a physician, and an officer and some soldiers buried him, marked the site with a cross and located the exact burial site on a map. I kept some documents and personal effects, which I gave to your brother-in-law Rafael when I saw him, together with the map of the burial site. Thus, your son died bravely, in combat, and instantaneously, it seems, inasmuch as the plane had not burned. You do not know how sorry Lola and I felt, and still feel. There is no need to say more. There is so much that we should discuss, and that so sad, that it is better to leave it alone. Only know that you have been and continue to be one of the bitternesses of this war. Although life has in its final stage carried us into enemy camps, I cannot forget the fraternal affection that has united us always and which I still profess.

Alfredo[46]

On his trip to Chile in December Herrera replied to Kindelán, still unconvinced (some Italian prisoners claimed to have seen Piquiqui alive, and other information indicated that he had been shot). But Kindelán's letter consoled him and he had thought several times before to write him, "to express to you my hope and my wish that, even though fate has situated us in enemy camps, the day must arrive when once again we will fight together in the two wars which I believe to be inevitable: one, of decent persons against those who are not; and the other, of Spaniards against foreigners."[47] Kindelán, showing a streak of independence similar to Herrera's own then complained to Nationalist military justice that aviation must have full autonomy over the treatment of aviation prisoners and indicated that he had used Herrera as a conduit to secure the same treatment for Nationalist flyers from Prieto, the Republican Defense Minister.[48]

The comparison of Kindelán's political behavior with that of Herrera is instructive. Kindelán was, like Herrera, loyal to Alfonso XIII, but, unlike him, was an ideological monarchist who believed that supporting Franco was the best way to ensure the restoration of the monarchy. He joined the 1936 rebellion as head of Franco's air force, but thereafter displayed an uncompromising streak, which was indeed reminiscent of his Loyalist colleague. He openly opposed the promotion of Franco's brother Ramón, an aviation hero who was a political opportunist of proven disloyalty to the monarchy, having air-dropped pro-Republican leaflets over the Royal Palace during an abortive Republican rising in 1930. Later, in the 1940s, when it became clear that Franco had no immediate intention of restoring the Bourbons, Kindelán conspired actively against the regime, was removed as Captain-General of Barcelona, briefly assigned to an educational post and twice imprisoned. He ended his days in fruitless politicking for the monarchy, in Madrid, but in some ways as much an exile as Herrera was in Paris. (In the same period, Herrera wrote to the pretender Don Juan that the restoration of the monarchy was only acceptable if it was the result of a plebiscite.[49])

In the early 1930s, Herrera published a number of articles in *Acción Española,* a revanchist monarchist journal of the traditional right directed by Ramiro de Maeztu. It may be supposed that Herrera's participation, mainly on scientific subjects, was owing to his friendship with Maeztu; on the other hand his monarchist sympathies were well-known. Only one of his articles, on the errors of communism, had political content.[50] But that article was written from Herrera's idiosyncratic perspective and it is difficult to read into it any sympathy for a reactionary political program. In it, he portrays himself as a scientist disinterested in political activity. Addressing the theory, not the practice of Marxism, he finds that the dictatorship of the proletariat offends mathematics; according to probability theory, the capacity of an entire class to govern effectively would be about the same as that of one of its members, chosen dictator by lot. Similarly, the abolition of religion offends physics (Voltaire attempted to refute belief with mechanical principles now known to be false); and the abolition of the family offends biology (the familial instinct of animals).

Herrera remained loyal because he had a sharply different view of the relationship of the military to civil authority than did his more traditionalist colleagues. He was one of only a small group of Spanish officers who, before the war, had interacted regularly with professional colleagues in western democracies who held a similar professional ethic. Such a stance could only have been reinforced by Herrera's position in Spanish science, shaped by the conditions of "civil discourse" which I have described. Herrera's attitude toward the new physics helps to locate him in the intellectual history of modern Spain. He was both uncomfortable with it and fascinated by it. He never abandoned his Cartesian cosmology at the same time as he openly admitted the veracity of the Einsteinian universe. The open discourse between an old science which many persons who shared Herrera's conservative social views refused to abandon and the new one, which the left hailed as "revolutionary," took place within himself. This tension between the traditional and the modern was not uncommon among Spanish scientists of Herrera's generation because it was a faithful image, internalized, of broader tensions inherent in the process of modernization. Other Spanish supporters of Einstein—José M. Plans, Esteban Terradas, Enrique de Rafael—members of the Mathematical Society and conservative Catholics all—felt similar tensions. But Herrera was one of the few who drew the connection between the civil discourse which underlay the scientific surge of the early twentieth century with analogous principles obtaining in political democracies. He stood for openness; the Nationalists for closure. High on Franco's agenda was an end to civil discourse in science and a return to the "Catholic unity of the sciences" which had prevailed before the Enlightenment (according to the statutes of the Francoist Council of Higher Research in 1939–40). Herrera could no more have countenanced that than he could the breaking of his soldier's oath.

Years of Exile

Because of his first-hand experience with fascist bombardment of Spanish cities, particularly Barcelona, during the Civil War, Herrera arrived in Paris a recognized expert on the effects of aerial attacks upon civilian populations. His very first article as an exile, published in *L'Aérophile* in April 1939, was an essay on the psychology of bombardment, in which he argued that the Spanish experience disproved the enemy strategy which presumed that the victims of aerial bombardments would lose hope and press their leaders to surrender. "The partisans of totalitarian aerial attacks suppose that the civil population's fear grows in direct proportion to the intensity of the attack, but they did not take other psychological factors into consideration." Contrary to fascist military theory, the population's fear diminished once the attack began, and the citizens of both Madrid and Barcelona were observed carrying on normally in the face of continuous day and night bombardments. Hatred of the enemy, moreover, grew in proportion to the intensity of the attacks, having the effect, for example, of even converting some "Fifth Columnists" in those cities into enemies of Franco.[51] Several months later, Herrera dealt with the technical issue of passive defense against bombardments. During the continuous attacks on Spanish cities, he noted, republican aeronautical engineers had studied the intensity of explosion waves and their effects in the air and on terrain and buildings, in order to lessen their danger to the civilian population. Here experience suggested that persons in the upper floors of buildings were safer from harm than those on lower ones, because large bombs fell through to lower floors if they hit the roof of a building, while if they landed in the street they likewise caused greater damage to lower floors.[52]

L'Aérophile provided much of his income through 1943. In its pages, he published a serialized popular treatise on aerodynamics, illustrated with dozens of his own drawings, many of them fanciful or surrealistic, filled with his irreverent humor. In one, a physician is diagnosing a sick airplane wing in a hospital bed. Another presents Archimedes discovering the principle of floating bodies, in his bathtub in Syracuse; another depicts the exchange of energy in the Universe as a roulette game. Much of his art was inspired by science fiction: there is a Martian landscape inspired by H. G. Wells; a strange world, Logarithmland, in which the size of everything increases as one moves northward; and illustrations of airships described by Wells and Verne.[53] Meanwhile, the emphasis of his technical articles shifted from bombardments to mega-aviation, a term that Herrera used to characterize large airplanes capable of transporting huge tonnages. Here he was interested in calculating the stress limits of conventional metals used to build planes and the superiority over these of duralumin (he was, during this period, also employed as a consultant by a French aluminum manufacturer). If his findings were not heeded, he warned, using another Greek neologism, the result would be necro-aviation![54]

Herrera had been following advances in atomic physics and, in the dramatic circumstances described in his *Memoirs,* predicted that a uranium bomb would end the war, long before the atomic bomb was actually used. His article was published in *Le Génie Civil* on July 15, 1945, less than a month before Hiroshima. He vastly overestimated the amount of fuel that would be needed to complete the chain reaction, but that was because, as he pointed out in his analysis of the bombs dropped on Japan, he had no clue from the literature available to him, that the explosive actually used was not simple uranium, but the isotope U-235, plutonium. Herrera achieved a certain notoriety in France owing to this prediction, and he continued to comment on the rapidly unfolding developments in atomic weaponry. Articles followed on the Bikini tests of July 1946 and on the hydrogen bomb.[55]

Herrera combined this new interest with his expertise in aerial bombardments to produce a series of essays on defense against atomic attacks, including a civil defense manual that was an effective popularization of atomic energy. He thought that world government was the only plausible "defense" against atom bombs. He drew the president of the world speaking with regional leaders on a bank of two-way televisions, communicating, interestingly, in Esperanto. Years before, Herrera had been an activist in the promotion of this artificial *lingua franca* and in 1924 had represented Spain at an international congress on its scientific use, along with Torres Quevedo and the meteorologist Vicente Inglada.[56]

Herrera's continual conflicts with the French aeronautical establishment are detailed in his *Memoirs.* By 1950 he began to view his situation in Paris as desperate and accordingly, on July 20, he wrote to Albert Einstein, enclosing a copy of Einstein's note of regret of 1923 to jog his memory and adding, "Perhaps you have had some reference about my projected stratospheric ascent in a free balloon with a special scaphander." He then asked Einstein's help in acquiring a position in the scientific section of UNESCO (inasmuch as Spain did not then belong to UNESCO and, he might have added, in view of his difficult position as a political exile). Einstein obligingly wrote to Jaime Torres Bodet, the director general, recommending Herrera as "undoubtedly an able man." Torres replied that he had forwarded Einstein's recommendation to the head of UNESCO's natural sciences department for further action.[57]

Herrera was apparently found an acceptable candidate by the division director Pierre Auger, but by May of the following year the appointment was still up in the air. "It seems that there are new obstacles," Herrera explained to Einstein, "on account of the increasing influence of General Franco in UNESCO which has invited him to participate in its meetings." Franco's influence was felt in French science, he continued, through Maurice Roy, the aeronautical engineer who had been invited several times by the regime to lecture in Madrid. While employed by the French Office for Aviation Research (ONERA), Herrera had been assigned to evaluate Roy's volume on jet propulsion, *Thermodynamique des systems propulsifs a réaction* (Paris, 1947), and had produced a highly critical report. Since 1919 Herrera had been a proponent of jet-propelled engines, which he viewed as offering numerous advantages over conventional motors (they would be lighter, function more simply, not be susceptible to gyroscopic effects, and, of course, produce flight at higher speeds and altitudes).[58] His expertise in this area was well established. In this case, he found that the Detonation Jet (Stato-Reactor), an engine designed by Roy, who stated it would fly at 4600 km/hr, was useless. "A very simple calculus [calculation]," he wrote to Einstein, "can prove that the drag of this engine [w]ould be very much bigger than its pull, and I have shown my calculus to the Defense Ministry in order to avoid useless expenses in constructing and testing this inoperative engine." The result, as Herrera here recounts, was that he was fired from ONERA when Roy became its director, both because he was opposed to Franco and critical of Roy. He begged Einstein to study his calculations and submit an impartial opinion.[59]

Herrera soon had second thoughts and wrote again to say he should never have troubled Einstein with his problems with Roy's engine, assuring him that "I see that you are quite right in refusing to give lessons about such elementary things." Roy, he says, has made it impossible for him to publish anything in French scientific or technical journals; and the editor of a Swiss journal (*Interavia*) said he would publish Herrera's articles "but only if they don't refer to M. Roy's work and always without my signature, because he doesn't want to have any trouble with the almighty Roy." The French communists had offered to help him but he had refused. "I am not a communist nor a politician of any kind and I desire to struggle only [on] scientific ground." He closed with a statement of his political credo:

> I love social justice, freedom and peace and believe that everybody must fight for these ideals as strongly as possible. I have seen the admirable work that you have done in this sense by mean[s] of your declarations to the worldwide press.[60] Surely, nobody better than you has merited the Peace Prize.
>
> I am quite alone, without any help, but absolutely decided to break all my lances against the enemies of these ideals of humanity, [like] Franco and his friends, in order to unmask them and cut off their claws, following the example of my countryman Don Quixote till the last. Probably, although I believe that I am right, I shall finish beaten down, as the "Caballero de la Triste Figura" did. French *chauvinisme* and Franco's influence in France are giants much more dangerous than the windmills of La Mancha.[61]

Herrera was, in fact, hired by UNESCO, and he spent several years in Geneva editing documents dealing with atomic energy matters. He resigned in 1955 to protest Spain's admittance to the international organization.[62]

Possibly there followed another exchange of letters, which do not survive, in which Herrera attempted to explain his 1916 paper on hypermechanics, which Einstein could not follow. This is the sense of the last letter by Herrera preserved in the Einstein papers, dated February 23, 1952:

I am infinitely sorry on account of my senile dullness and also
my very bad English that make me unable to indicate such simple
(and, I believe, logical) things as:

1) Our three-dimensional hyperspace is situated on a four-
dimensional one and so on till infinity.

2) All these spaces rotate, as everything in the Universe.
That is all.

The rest of my paper is the result of applying the calculus of
n-dimensional Mechanics to those two principles.

I began this calculus 40 years ago, in 1913, and it was
published in several [journals, such] as *Memorial de Ingenieros, El
Debate, Madrid Científico, Ibérica, Anales de la Sociedad Española de
Física y Química* (Spanish), and *Le Ciel* (French). The Spanish
scientific [community] was interested in this study, of which I
made several lectures in Madrid University and in the Academy
of Sciences, because it gives one explanation of gravitation,
although it did [lead] to some "absurdities" such as: "the space of
our Universe is spherically curved with a limited volume =
$2\pi^2 r^3$," "the masses [cause] the bending of light beams," etc. (in
the year 1913 your Relativity Theory was unknown in Spain).
Lastly, I have improved the calculus, but I have been unable to
explain it to you.

I don't want to importune you any more. I beg your pardon
and remain always your most grateful and humble admirer.

I cite this letter in full because it demonstrates that Herrera was
more than content to regard his theory as a precursor of General
Relativity, which he accepted as a true account of gravitational
phenomena (in *our* universe, to be sure), even though he continued to develop his own model as a kind of "transverse" exercise.
His final statement, published in 1963, both placed his theory in
an explicitly Cartesian framework (which he had not done in previous versions) and compared its results to Einstein's universe.[63]
Here he continues to develop a mechanical model of a Cartesian
universe, based on rotating vortices, claiming that Descartes's cosmology was a deductive one, derived from intuitive principle,
while that of Einstein is inductive and based on observed facts.
Here, as in his 1920 presentation, there is an odd melange of
statements, some affirming the explanatory power of Special Relativity by alluding to its experimental successes (such as equiva-
lence of matter and energy, which underlay atomic energy), and

others indicating that he was still unable to resolve his doubts concerning the physical meaning of the velocity of light.

Throughout the 1960s the physicist Julio Palacios (1891–1970), whom Herrera had, years before, employed as an instructor at the School of Aerotechnics, waged a campaign against relativity in the Spanish press and in scientific articles and monographs. In his popular writings, Palacios concentrated primarily on demonstrating the absurdity of the Special Theory's conceptualization of simultaneity. Einstein had used the example of a moving train and a station to show that because the speed of light is not infinite, time in the moving frame is not the same as that in the stationary one. Palacios, like many before him, misconstrued Einstein's point, as Herrera pointed out in a letter written to his nephew Juan Aguilera in 1966, the year before his death:

> I have been, and continue to be, a good friend of Professor Palacios, to whom I gave the chair of physics at the School of Aeronautics which I directed because I believed him to be the most qualified man in Spain in this discipline, with the exception of Blas Cabrera who, owing to his age and position, could not accept this post. But the admiration which I felt for Professor Palacios is not compatible with his present attempt to ridicule and destroy Einstein's theory of relativity which he has undertaken in the Spanish press.
>
> He has invented a personage called Don Ingénuo who, leaving Madrid in a train with the velocity v, with his watch synchronized with that of the station, would have to see his watch slowed down with respect to the other stations he would pass (according to the idea which he has of the theory of relativity), at the same time that the stationmasters would see that their watches had slowed down with relation to that of Don Ingénuo. Since this is impossible, Einstein's theory is wrong.
>
> In order that [Palacios] with this article in which he demonstrates that he hasn't understood relativity . . . might not continue to put Spanish science in ridicule abroad, I have written him a number of letters trying to disabuse him of his error, but without success. He sent his calculations to scholars and Academies of Science across the world, but no one answers him. He says that a conspiracy of science has been established against him, but what has really happened is that scientists and Academies don't want to waste time discussing things which are arch-established.

I told him that I also had these doubts which, with my colleagues of the Mathematical Society, I expressed to Einstein himself when he was in Madrid and he did not resolve them perfectly. Referring to Special Relativity (which is that which Palacios opposes in particular), I reminded him that its first principle is that, in each system, things happen in the same way, whether the system is in repose or in uniform rectilineal motion. Thus, meters are meters, hours are hours, and one is born, lives and dies as if the system was quiet, even though it may move with the speed of light.

What relativity says is that, for a system B which moves with velocity v with relation to system A (and reciprocally), time and space in the observed system are divided by $\sqrt{1 - \frac{x^2}{c^2}}$ (with c the the velocity of light), *relative to the observer,* so that, for Don Ingénuo, time and the length of the track will have been extended. If, for example, the velocity v of the train was 180,000 km/second, that is, three-fifths of c, the hours of the stations and the kilometers of the track would be drawn out to 5/4 of those which the kilometer posts and clocks would show. If the trip had lasted one hour on Don Ingénuo's watch, one hour would also have elapsed on the station clocks, but the hour of the stations, *relatively for Don Ingénuo,* would [have the value of] five-fourths of an hour, so that the hour recorded by the station clocks would always be the same as that recorded by Don Ingénuo's watch. This is analagous to distances observed in an airplane from a height of 1000 m above the ground, which seem, to the aviator, much smaller than they are.

In order to convince him I proposed the case that, in the stations, lineal clocks were used, that is, a horizontal tape on which the hours are marked which would be running and would mark the hour on an index fixed over the door of the station, where the stationmaster would read the hour. But for the traveller on the train, Don Ingénuo, the tape would have stretched out and its speed would have increased in equal proportion. Therefore the hour recorded would be the same. . . .

These articles of Professor Palacios are discrediting our science to the point where Spain is mentioned as being totally uncultivated in these matters. In a number of the American *Atomic Journal,* Professor Hans Bethe . . . published an article saying that the flight to Russia of Klaus Fuchs, an atomic scientist who had worked on the atomic bomb, was a serious matter, because there are fine scientists in Russia, as well as great laboratories and factories where Fuchs' knowledge could be of great value. But if he had gone to Spain instead of Russia, the matter would be of scant importance *because there is no one there who understands these matters.*

It is significant that Herrera's final statement on twentieth-century science was a defense of Special Relativity, that theory which, because of its "anti-intuitive" nature, had caused him such difficulties.

The final phase of Herrera's career as a science writer centered on the discovery of sub-atomic particles, a phenomenon which excited his "transverse" mentality, and artificial satellites, a problem which showed his talents as a practical aeronautical technician. The discovery of the positron (positively charged electron) suggested the existence of anti-protons from which anti-matter could be formed. Herrera noted that the explosion of a bomb containing only two grams of hydrogen and anti-hydrogen could produce enough radiation to destroy all humanity.[64] The original draft of this article had been submitted to an agency of UNESCO which refused its publication on the grounds that the existence of "negative protons" was impossible. A decade later, Herrera wrote to his nephew observing that "Now, in atomic energy centers like that of Geneva, we have seen tubes of 40 cm in diameter through which circulate negative protons, which cannot exist according to UNESCO."[65]

A study of published specifications of the American "Mouse" satellite and the aerodynamic problems relating to its successful launch, which Herrera wrote in 1956, was followed by his own analysis of the prerequisites for a similar launching in France. Consistent with his own experience—he had now witnessed all aeronautical advances from the balloon to space vehicles—Herrera suggested that the French launch a balloon satellite weighing 50 kg (10 kg less than Sputnik I). This would be relatively economical (about twice the cost of a V-2 rocket) and, although it could not carry the instrument package envisioned for the Mouse, it would have the ability, which the former lacked, of being easily observable from the earth, making it possible to study its orbit easily.[66]

Soon after the Civil War ended, the Franco regime conducted a comprehensive purge of Spanish academia, separating many politically suspect professors from their university chairs and declaring vacant seats held by Loyalists in the various academies. Accordingly, on May 10, 1941 Herrera was officially removed from his seat in the Academy of Exact Sciences, where he had occupied chair number 15, once held by José de Echegaray (1832–1916), mathematician and Nobel laureate in literature. The seat remained unoccupied until José Antonio de Artigas was elected in 1955. When a copy of his inaugural discourse reached Herrera in Paris, it elicited the following response:

> Aside from my interest in learning about your new scientific work, I was also interested to see how you were able to get around the statutory pitfall of having to begin your speech with a few words of praise about your predecessor, and I can appreciate the ingenious ruse with which you overcame this difficulty by means of a leap backwards, thereby dispensing with me, nullified as a scientific personality by the Caudillo, and with the distinguished scientific personality of General Aranaz, my illustrious predecessor, as well (without apparent motive for this omission), letting all your well-deserved eulogies fall on the exalted figure of Don José Echegaray, the predecessor of General Aranaz. Thus, the statutory obstacle was surmounted, the Caudillo satisfied, and your speech perfect.
>
> But I have to tell you that . . . the medal number 15 that the Academy gave you is a "false" medal, made expressly for you with that number. The real one, the one that the reknowned Echegaray displayed on his breast, is the one I have. . . .
>
> When death (and not the Caudillo) disposes of me, and that "Academy" has recovered its dignity and its freedom to elect and retain its members, the true medal number 15, the one Echegaray wore, will be restored to the Academy by my heirs, and then, if you are re-elected to fill my vacancy, you can wear it on your breast. Before that, no.[67]

Herrera's memoirs terminate in 1956, a full decade before his death. In 1959 he reached the age of eighty, the eighth "milestone" in his personal chronology, which divided his life into nine-year periods. From May 1960 to February 1962 he served as Prime Minister of the Republican government in exile, a largely symbolic post which nevertheless carried humanitarian responsibilities for the large numbers of exiles and also directed political opposition to Franco. The most noteworthy accomplishment of his tenure was the signing in February 1961 of a pact with the National Independence Movement of Portugal, headed by General Humberto Delgado, to coordinate the programs and policies of the two anti-fascist organizations.[68]

This Edition

The manuscript of the *Memoirs* was made available to me by General Herrera's daughter-in-law Carmen Soler de Herrera and her sons Emilio and Fernando, all of whom aided me to their utmost in the preparation of this edition, as did my friend Juan Aguilera, Herrera's nephew. The manuscript was completely unedited, having been typed after Herrera's death. I have completed the names of as many persons mentioned as possible, to aid in their identification. Some minor changes and clarifications are indicated in brackets.

Notes

1. On the history of the Aerostatic Service, see Antonio Carner, *Biografía de Pedro Vives Vich* (Igualada, 1955), pp. 35–47.
2. Herrera, *Ciencia y Aeronáutica* (Madrid, 1933), pp. 52–53.
3. *Balloon Flight and Atmospheric Electricity* (Washington, D.C., 1923). Technical Memorandum No. 271 of the National Advisory Committee for Aeronautics.
4. Charles H. Gibbs-Smith, *The Rebirth of European Aviation, 1902–1908* (London, 1974), p. 311.
5. Alfredo Kindelán, *La verdad de mis relaciones con Franco* (Barcelona, 1981), p. 152.
6. *La Nación* (Buenos Aires), October 25, 1928.
7. On the Laboratory and wind tunnel, see Joaquín de La Llave, "El Laboratorio Aerodinámico de Cuatro Vientos," *Ibérica*, 15 (1921): 52–55; Herrera, "Aviación," in *Enciclopedia Universal Ilustrada, Apéndice* I (1930): 1088–91, with photographs of airplane and dirigible models in the tunnel; Olivié's balance is represented in *ibid.*, p. 1091 (Fig. 39) and in Herrera, *Aerotecnia* (Madrid, 1936; facsimile ed., 1979), p. 468. See the description of the tunnel in *ibid.*, pp. 464–69.
8. Herrera, "La participación española en el IV Congreso Internacional de Navegación Aérea," *Ibérica*, 28 (1927): 380–81. Herrera notes that Tullio Levi-Civita, whom he had met in Madrid in 1921, was a participant in the Rome Congress.
9. Interview with Tomás Rodríguez Bachiller, Madrid, April 10, 1980.
10. *La Nación*, November 20, 1928. The date of 1919 given for the "España" flight is a misprint. Torres Quevedo and Kindelán built their first dirigible in 1905, but testing began at Guadalajara in 1908.
11. Herrera, *La travesía aérea del Atlántico* (Madrid, 1918); Raffe Emer-

son, "Atlantic Liner Airships," *American Review of Reviews*, 78 (1928): 622–23; *La Nación*, November 20, 1928.

12. *New York Times*, August 7 and November 24, 1921.

13. *La Nación*, October 21, 1928.

14. *El Sol* (Madrid), October 12, 1928; *La Nacion*, October 16, 17.

15. Emerson, "Atlantic Liner Airships," p. 624. The Spanish government had already committed itself to expend 30 million pesetas on the airdock (Royal Decree of February 12, 1927); Herrera, "El accidente del 'Graf Zeppelin' y la Linea Area Sevilla-Buenos Aires," *Ibérica*, 31 (1929): 396.

16. Douglas H. Robinson, *Giants in the Sky: A History of the Rigid Airship* (Seattle, 1973), p. 267.

17. *La Nación*, October 27, 1928.

18. *New York Times*, October 18, 1928. On the other hand, Rosendahl published a glowing popular account of his trip on the *Graf*, in which the squall was not mentioned at all; "Inside the Graf Zeppelin," *Scientific American*, 140 (1929): 201–5.

19. "Una turbonada en el viaje transatlantico del Graf Zeppelin," *Ibérica*, 31 (1929): 280–83.

20. *New York Times*, October 19, 1928; *La Nación*, October 17, 20, 25.

21. *El Sol*, October 12, 1928.

22. *La Nación*, November 16, 17, 20, 1928.

23. *La Nación*, October 16, 20, 1928.

24. *El Sol*, November 3, 1928.

25. *La Nación*, May 25, June 1, 3, 1930.

26. *La Nación*, May 23, 1930.

27. *Ciencia y aeronáutica*, pp. 11–16.

28. Kindelán in particular speaks eloquently on the impact, inconceivable today, of Verne on his generation; *La verdad de mis relaciones con Franco*, pp. 43–44.

29. "Relación de la hipergeometría con la mecánica celeste," *Memorial de Ingenieros de Ejército*, 71 (1916): 371–83; and summary of his views, which practically did not change thereafter, in "El universo y la hiperdinámica," *Anales de la Sociedad Española de Física y Química*. 32 (1934): 121.

30. *Algunas consideraciones sobre la teoría de la relatividad de Einstein* (Madrid, 1922), p. 22.

31. "La intuición y la ciencia," *Madrid Científico*, 30 (1923): 17–19.

32. *Algunas consideraciones*, p. 24.

33. "La energética y la crisis de la materia y del espíritu," *El Sol*, January 21, 1921.

34. On the meeting with Einstein, see M. Lucini, "El profesor Einstein," *Madrid Científico*, 30 (1923): 65–66.

35. *Madrid Científico*, 30 (1923): 33–35.

36. "Se peloteaban integrales"; interview with Alejandro Gómez Spencer, Madrid, February 20, 1980. A copy of Einstein's note to Herrera, dated March 11, 1923 and written on the stationery of the Royal Academy of Exact Sciences, is preserved in the Einstein Papers, Princeton University.

37. "La cuarta dimension: El hiperespacio," *El Sol*, October 22, 1920.

38. My information on the Hyper-Club comes from two interviews with Alejandro Gómez Spencer in Madrid: one on February 18, 1980, by José García Diego, who provided me with a protocol, and another by myself two days later. Salvador de Madariaga, *Españoles de mi tiempo* (Barcelona, 1974), p. 263, reports on Legórburu, but other details about the Club, and Herrera's career generally, are inexact or erroneous. There is a photograph of Lecea with a bustard caught by his method in *Alas*, 1 (1922), 57; and M. Moreno-Caracciolo refers to his troubles with the British SPCA in *Madrid Científico*, 31 (1924), 147. See also, José Warleta, *Autogiro: Juan de la Cierva y su obra* (Madrid, 1977), pp. 53–54.

39. Tomás Rodríguez Bachiller, interview, Madrid, April 10, 1980. On La Llave, see the biographical sketch in *Alas*, 4 (1925): 130.

40. *La Nación*, November 16, 1928. See also, Warleta, *Autogiro*, p. 35, following a version recounted by Moreno-Caracciolo in 1930 in which Juan de Usabiaga, one of the few socialist engineers, was the reference point.

41. "¿A cuarenta mil metros?," *Madrid Científico*, 40 (1933): 375.

42. Herrera used the word *escafandra* to describe the suit. At that time the word was understood as meaning diving suit, and the English-language press described it as such. See, e.g., *The London Times*, of February 22, 1934, reporting Herrera's planned ascent in a "diving suit."

43. On Herrera's space suit, see *Proyecto de exploración a la estratósfera en globo libre* (Madrid, 1930); "Vers la Stratonautique," *L'Aérophile*, 42 (1934): 182–83; "Le bombardement stratosphérique," *ibid.*, 49 (1941): 173, 178; and "Le scaphandre de l'espace," *Ingenieurs et Techniciens*, no. 189 (July-August 1965): 44–46. On the Apollo suit, which was designed with no knowledge of Herrera's prototype, see Walter M. Schirra, Jr., "Our Cozy Cocoon," in M. Scott Carpenter, *et. al.*, *We Seven* (New York, 1962), pp. 143–55.

44. *New York Times*, January 14, 1935.

45. Juan Antonio Ansaldo's account of Herrera's decision to remain loyal is erroneous. See *¿Para qué?* (Buenos Aires, 1951), p. 259, where Herrera is quoted as saying that the rebellion surprised him at Cuatro Vientos and that his loyalty was to his subordinates, not, it is implied, to the political system. Like many of his generation of Spanish military

men, Ansaldo could not comprehend Herrera's conception of fidelity to the military oath, untainted by ideology.

46. Kindelán, *La verdad de mis relaciones con Franco*, p. 104.

47. Herrera to Kindelán, December 23, 1936; *ibid.*, p. 104.

48. *Ibid.*, pp. 102–103.

49. A truncated facsimile of a letter to this effect from Herrera to (ostensibly) Don Juan is reproduced in Victor Salmador, *Don Juan de Borbón* (Barcelona, 1976), p. 267.

50. "Los errores del comunismo," *Acción Espanola*, 8 (1933): 652–55. Herrera's first article in this journal, "El vuelo sin motor" (I: 76–80), is signed Emilio Herrera y Aguilera, the name of Herrera's son. But the author is obviously Herrera, and is so identified in the index.

51. "De l'efficacité des attaques aériennes sur le moral des populations civiles," *L'Aérophile*, 47 (1939): 76–77.

52. "La défense passive contre les bombardements," *L'Aérophile*, 47 (1939): 175–77.

53. *L'Aérophile*, 49 (1941): 27, 28, 137, 141, 232; 50 (1942): 209; 51 (1943): 138.

54. "Jusqu'ou la mégaviation?," *L'Aérophile*, 50 (1942): 194–96.

55. "L'Utilisation de l'énergie atomique: La bombe à uranium," *Le Génie Civil*, 122 (1945): 108–9; "La bombe atomique," *ibid.*, 173–77; "Que se passera-t-il le 1er juillet," *L'Aérophile*, 53 (1946): 122–23, 138; "Les expériences atomiques de Bikini," *Le Génie Civil*, 123 (1946): 273–75; "Les bombes a hydrogène," *ibid.*, 127 (1950): 189–192.

56. "Defense contre la bombe atomique," *L'Aérophile*, 53 (1945): 10–11; *Comment echapper a la mort atomique* (Paris, 1952), with Lt. Col. Callard; and "El esperanto y la ciencia," *Madrid Científico*, 32 (1925): 177–80.

57. Herrera to Einstein, July 20, 1950; Einstein to Torres Bodet, July 24; Torres Bodet to Einstein, August 2. Einstein Papers, Princeton University. Herrera's letter, as well as the three cited below, is written in English.

58. See Herrera's paper, *Los propulsores de reacción en aeronáutica* (Madrid, 1920), a communication read at the First National Congress of Engineering, Madrid, 1919.

59. Herrera to Einstein, May 10, 1951. Einstein Papers, Princeton.

60. Herrera may have had in mind statements (some authorized, some not) attributed to Einstein regarding the propriety of American relations with Franco Spain.

61. Herrera to Einstein, June 11, 1951. Einstein Papers, Princeton.

62. "El General Don Emilio Herrera" (Editorial), *Ibérica* (New York), October 15, 1967, p. 12.

63. "L'Univers de Descartes," *Le Génie Civil*, 140 (1963): 280–83, and following.

64. "La découverte et les possibilités de l'antiproton: La bombe photonique," *Le Génie Civil*, 133 (1956): 7–10.

65. Herrera to Juan Aguilera, June 1966.

66. "Les satellites artificiels,"*Le Génie Civil*, 133 (1956): 184–91; "Les possibilités de lancement d'un satellite artificiel français," *ibid.*, pp. 350–55.

67. Herrera to José Antonio de Artigas, September 24, 1955. This letter was circulated among all academicians, including Julio Rey Pastor whose copy I consulted with the permission of Dr. Ernesto Garcia Camarero.

68. José Maria del Valle, *Las instituciones de la Republica española en exilio* (Paris, 1976), pp. 338–40.

Publications of Emilio Herrera

Herrera was a prolific writer. This preliminary bibliography, compiled in collaboration with Juan Aguilera Sánchez, represents only a portion of his published work.

Abbreviations

Ar	*L'Aérophile* (París)
GC	*Le Génie Civil* (París)
Ib	*Ibérica* (Tortosa)
MC	*Madrid Científico* (Madrid)

1911

Apuntes de navegación aeronáutica. Madrid: Memorial de Ingenieros del Ejército.

1916

"El problema de la aeronáutica y sus soluciones," *Ib*, 5: 200–202.
"Señales para aviadores," *Ib*, 5: 407.
"Comparación entre globos y aeroplanos," *Ib*, 6: 104–6.
"Aeroplanes gigantes," *Ib*, 6: 235–36.
"Relación de la hipergeometría con la mecánica celeste," *Memorial de Ingenieros del Ejército*, 33: 371–83.

1917

"Relación de la hipergeometría con la mecánica celeste," *Memorial de Ingenieros del Ejército*, 34: 221–35.

1918

"La travesía aérea del Atlántico," *Ib*, 10: 152–54.
La travesía aérea del Atlántico. Madrid.

1919

"La aeronáutica después de la guerra," *MC*, 26: 224–27 [interview with Mariano Moreno-Caracciolo].

1920

"¿Compraremos la luz por kilos?" *El Sol* (Madrid), January 16.
"No todo ese peso es luz," *El Sol*, February 12.
"Todos conformes," *El Sol*, February 20.
"Et facta est lux,"*El Sol*, March 19. [Polemic with R. Yzaguirre, M. Correa, and Sir Arthur Eddington over the weight of light.]
"La cuarta dimensión," *El Sol*, October 15.
"La cuarta dimensión: El hiperespacio," *El Sol*, October 20.
"Sobre la cuarta dimensión," *El Sol*, November 12.
"Mas sobre la cuarta dimensión," *El Sol*, December 3.
"Los propulsores de reacción en aeronáutica," *España Automóvil y Aeronáutica*, 14: 69–71, 81–82, 92.
Los propulsores de reacción en aeronáutica. Madrid: Memorial de Ingenieros del Ejército.
"España en al Federación Aeronáutica Internacional," *Ib*, 14: 285–86.

1921

"La comunicación aérea entre España y América del Sur," *Ib*, 15: 364–67 and *España Automóvil y Aeronáutica*, 15: 83–86.
"La energética y la crisis de la materia y del espíritu," *El Sol*, January 21.

1922

"La navegación aérea entre España y América del Sur," *Ib*, 17: 236–39, 267–70
"La isla Penedo de San Pedro debe ser cedida a Portugal," *El Sol*, May 2.
"La isla Penedo de San Pedro ha sido cedida a Portugal," *El Sol*, June 20.
Algunas consideraciones sobre la teoría de la relatividad de Einstein. Madrid: Memorial de Ingenieros del Ejército.

1923

"La intuición y la ciencia," *MC*, 30: 17–19.

"Una paradoja relativista," *MC*, 30: 33–35 [exchange with Sir Arthur Eddington over a problem of special relativity].

"Intuición, ciencia y conocimiento," *MC*, 30: 102–3.

Balloon Flight and Atmospheric Electricity, Technical Memorandum No. 271 of the National Advisory Committee for Aeronautics (Washington, D.C.).

1925

"El esperanto y la ciencia," *MC*, 32: 177–80.

1926

"Una ojeada el Universo," *Ib*, 25: 235–38 and *MC*, 33: 133–36.

"La ruta del Oriente," *Ib*, 25: 344–46.

"Pasatiempos matemáticos: La paradoja de Bertrand," *MC*, 33: 3–6.

"La aeronáutica y la Academia," *MC*, 33: 85–87.

"La velocidad comercial en la Aviación," *MC*, 33: 121–22.

"El combustible sin peso," *MC*, 33: 293–94.

"El asalto aéreo al Polo Norte," *MC*, 33: 325–27.

1927

"Participación española en el IV Congreso Internacional de Navegacion Aérea," *Ib*, 28: 380–81.

"La pérdida del avion gigante," *MC*, 34: 9.

"Los motores de explosivo," *MC*, 34: 129–30.

"La conquista del espacio," *MC*, 34: 369–72, and *Ib*, 29 (1928), 19–21.

1928

"El progreso técnico de la Aeronáutica durante 1927,: *MC*, 35: 129–30.

"La orientación astronómica sin instrmentos," *MC*, 35: 145–47.

"De haber tenido en mitad del trayecto informes meteorológicos, habriamos evitado las averias," *La Nación* (Buenos Aires), October 18 [on *Graf Zeppelin*].

"Deseo que la linea de dirigibles Sevilla-Buenos Aires se inaugure junto con la Exposición Ibero-Americana," *La Nación*, October 27 [diary on board the *Graf Zeppelin*].

"Una turbonada en el viaje transatlántico del Graf Zeppelin," *Ib*, 31: 280–83.

"El accidente del Graf Zeppelin y la linea aérea Sevilla-Buenos Aires," *Ib*, 31: 396–97.

"El pilotaje ciego de los aviones," *Ib*, 31: 85–87, and *MC*, 36: 4–5.
"El problema meteorológico de la linea aérea Sevilla-Buenos Aires," *MC*,
36: 129–31.

1930

"Primer viaje a Sudamérica del Graf Zeppelin y doble viaje transatlántico
del R–100," *Ib*, 33: 184–90.
"Causas probables de la catástrofe del R–101," *Ib*, 33: 344–46.
"Los aeródromos flotantes del Atlántico," *MC*, 37: 177–78.
"El nuevo record mundial de distancia," *MC*, 37: 284.
[Untitled article on Seville-Buenos Aires dirigible service], *La Nación*,
June 3.
"Aviación," *Enciclopedia Universal Ilustrada, Apéndice* (Madrid: Espasa-Calpe),
I: 1074–38.
Proyecto de exploración a la estratosfera en globo libre. Madrid [date uncer-
tain].

1931

"A 16 Km. de altura en globo libre," *MC*, 38: 308–9.
"La aeronáutica del mañana," *MC*, 38: 369–71.
"El vuelo sin motor," *Acción Española*, 1: 76–80.
"Iniciación al estudio del movimiento de un hilo pesado y flexible, fijo
por un punto," *Actas*, Asociación Espanola para el Progreso de las
Ciencias, Congreso de Lisboa, Sección I.

1932

"La Escuela Superior Aerotécnica," *MC*, 39: 313–14.
"Alrededor del desarme," *MC*, 39: 321–22.
"Una red internacional de rutas aéreas," *MC*, 39: 337–39.
"La Tierra y el Aire," *MC*, 39: 355–56.

1933

"La Aeronáutica mundial," *MC*, 40: 129–39.
"La máquina que piensa," *MC*, 40: 145–47.
"Barberan y Collar," *MC*, 40: 197–99.
"La crociera del decennale," *MC*, 40: 244–47.
"Los últimos 'records' mundiales," *MC*, 40: 277–79.
"La exploración de la estratosfera," *MC*, 40: 309–11.
"Del pilón Wright a la catapulta Heinkel," *MC*, 40: 341–43.
"¿A cuarenta mil metros?" *MC*, 40: 374–75.

Ciencia y Aeronáutica. Madrid: Academia de Ciencias, Exactas, Físicas y
   Naturales.
"Los errores del comunismo," *Acción Española,* 8: 652–55.

1934

"El vuelo sin motor," *MC,* 41: 21–23.
"Sin alas ni timones," *MC,* 41: 51–53.
"La Ingeniería Aeronáutica," *MC,* 41: 89–91.
"El universo y el UNIVERSO," *MC,* 41: 113–14.
"¿Autogiros o Helicópteros?" *MC,* 41: 132–33.
"Sevilla, aeropuerto terminal de Europa," *MC,* 41: 148–49.
"Los accidentes," *MC,* 41: 166–68.
"La ingeniería aeronautica para x.x.x.," *MC,* 41: 185–86.
"La Aeronáutica rusa y la catástrofe del 'Sirius,'" *MC,* 41: 213–14.
"Un progreso en la navegación con dirigibles," *MC,* 41: 245–46.
"El motor auxiliar en los planeadores," *MC,* 41: 277–78.
"La exploración de la estratosfera y sus aplicaciones militares," *MC,* 41:
   289–91.
"¿Settle? ¿Prokofieff? ¿Fedosechenko?," *MC,* 41: 309–11.
"Microaeronáutica," *MC,* 41: 341–42.
"Los problemas actuales de la aviación," *MC,* 41: 373–74.
"Aviación," *Enciclopedia Universal Ilustrada, Suplemento de 1934,* pp. 129–
   47.
Review of Luis Rodés, *El firmamento, Acción Española,* 10: 675–80.
Review of Rodés, *Un siglo de progreso en la medición de distancias celestes,
   Acción Española,* 11: 386–88.
"El universo y la hiperdinámica," *Anales de la Sociedad Española de Física
   y Química,* 32: 109–27.
"Vers la Stratonautique," *Ar,* 42: 182–83.

1935

"El vestuario estratonáutico," *MC,* 42: 21–23.
"La Hipermecánica y el Apocalípsis," *MC,* 42: 37–42.
"Los accidentes en los dirigibles," *MC,* 42: 55–56.
"Causas de accidentes en los dirigibles," *MC,* 42: 85–86.
"La partida en punto fijo," *MC,* 42: 118–20.
"Ese es el camino," *MC,* 42: 149–51.
"España y la CINA," *MC,* 42: 181–82.
"Se desgarra el globo 'Biggest in the World,'" *MC,* 42: 245–47.
"El confort en las lineas aéreas," *MC,* 42: 279–80.
"La prensa soviética y mi proyectada ascensión estratoférica," *MC,* 42:
   309–11.

"Aportaciones españolas al desarrollo de la aeronáutica," *MC*, 42: 343–44.

"La ascensión estratoférica del globo Explorer II," *MC*, 42: 374–75.

"Aviación," *Enciclopedia Universal Ilustrada, Suplemento de 1935*, pp. 80–91.

1936

Aerotecnia. Madrid: Gráficas Ruíz Ferry.

1939

"De l'efficacité des attaques aériennes sur le moral des populations civiles," *Ar*, 47: 77–78.

"La défense contre les bombardements," *Ar*, 47: 175–78.

"Les chemins de la locomotion aérienne," *Ar*, 47: 201–3.

"La vulnérabilité aérienne," *Ar*, 47: 262.

1940

"Mathématiques pures," *Ar*, 48: 98–99.

"Qu'est-ce que l'air?" *Ar*, 48: 132–34.

"Qu'est-ce qu'un tourbillon?" *Ar*, 48: 146–49.

"Qu'est-ce qu la résistance de l'air?" *Ar*, 48: 170–74.

"Qu'est-ce que la portance?" *Ar*, 48: 194–99.

1941

"Qu'est-ce qu'une aile," *Ar*, 49: 2–8.

"Qu'est-ce qu'une polaire," *Ar*, 49: 26–33.

"Qu'est-ce que l'induction aérodynamique?" *Ar*, 49: 46–51.

"Qu'est-ce que le nombre de Reynolds?" *Ar*, 49: 66–71.

"Qu'est-ce qu'une hélice?" *Ar*, 49: 88–94.

"Qu'est-ce qu'un moulinet?" *Ar*, 49: 112–17.

"Qu'est-ce qu'un aéronef?" *Ar*, 49: 136–41.

"Qu'est-ce qu'une cellule portante?" *Ar*, 49: 160–65.

"Le bombardement stratosphérique: Le probleme mathématique," *Ar*, 49: 171–73, 178.

"Qu'est-ce que la commande?" *Ar*, 49: 184–91.

"La musique de l'avion et les métaux légers," *Ar*, 49: 194–96.

"Qu'est-ce que la stabilité?" *Ar*, 49: 208–14.

"Qu'est-ce que le groupe motopropulseur?" *Ar*, 49: 232–37.

"L'investigation des phénomenes ultra-rapides en aéronautique," *Ar*, 49: 243–45.

"Le poids minimum dans la construction des avions et des maquettes volantes," *Ar*, 49: 122–23.

1942

"Le répartition de la fatigue dans les alliages légers," *Ar*, 50: 106–7.
"Qu'est-ce que la train d'atterrissage?" *Ar*, 50: 116–21.
"Qu'est-ce que l'envol?" *Ar*, 50: 134–36.
"Qu'est-ce que le vol normal?" *Ar*, 50: 157–60, 169–70.
"Ce que le record de vitesse doit aux métaux légers," *Ar*, 50: 176–77.
"Qu'est-ce qu'une performance?" *Ar*, 50: 190–92, 209–12.
"Jusqu'ou la mégaviation?" *Ar*, 50: 194–95.
"Les possiblités actuelles des longs courriers aériens," *Ar*, 50: 214–15.
"Qu'est-ce qu'un virage?" *Ar*, 50: 229–32, 250–54.
"Les marches de la grande escalade," *Ar*, 50: 236–38.
"Les marches de la grande escalade, ou: Le trafic en altitude," *Ar*, 50: 256–57.
"Qu'est-ce que le vol par vent?" *Ar*, 50: 271–74, 288–91.
"Magénsium ou aluminium?" *Ar*, 50: 276–77.

1943

"La légèreté dans les voilures tournantes," *Ar*, 51: 2–3.
"Qu'est-ce que la descente," *Ar*, 51: 18–21, 39–41.
"Que doit-on espérer des aérodynes a voilure tournante?" *Ar*, 51: 22–24.
"A bas les chaines!," *Ar*, 51: 42–44 [polemic with G. Hamel on mega-aviation].
"Qu'est-ce que l'atterrissage?" *Ar*, 51: 59–61, 78–81.
"Léon Rith, cet inconnu," *Ar*, 51: 70–71.
"Qu'est-ce que le vol sans moteur?" *Ar*, 51: 98–101, 118–20.
"Contrepoint aérotechnique," *Ar*, 51: 102–3 [continuation of polemic with Hamel].
"Qu'est-ce que l'hydroaviation?" *Ar*, 51: 137–39, 159–62.
"Les revêments travaillants en acier et en duralumin," *Ar*, 51: 142–43.
"Qu'est-ce que l'acrobatie?" *Ar*, 51: 175–78, 197–98, 216–18.
"L'armistice est signé," *Ar*, 51: 182–83 [end of polemic with Hamel].
"Mégavion transatlantique," *Ar*, 51: 204–5.
"Qu'est-ce qu'un aérodyne?" *Ar*, 51: 236, and 52 (1944), 8–9, 23, 36–37, 50, 53.
"Sur les Cartes orthométriques à double projection," *Comptes rendus de l'Académie des Sciencies*, 217: 275–76.

1944

"Qu'est-ce qu'un autogyre?" *Ar*, 52: 62–63, 75–76.

1945

"L'utilisation de l'énergie atomique: La bombe à uranium," *GC*, 122: 108–9.

"La bombe atomique," *GC*, 122: 173–77.

"L'age atomique," *Ar*, 53 (September), 4–5, 18.

"Ce que la guerre a fait pour l'aviation," *Ar*, 53 (October), 18–19; (November), 2–3.

"Défense contra la bombe atomique," *Ar*, 53 (November), 10–11.

1946

"Espace, temps, aviation," *Ar*, 53: 30–32.

"Armes de guerre et aviation de paix: Rêve ou realité?" *Ar*, 53: 105.

"Que se passera-t-il le 1er juillet?" *Ar*, 53: 122–23, 138.

"La strato-aérodynamique," *Ar*, 53: 208–9.

"La barrèire du son," *Ar*, 54: 254–55.

"Les expériences atomiques de Bikini," *GC*, 123: 273–75.

1947

"Comment colent et fonctionnent les aérodynes a voilure tournante," *Ar*, 54: 32–34, 68–70.

"L'Hélicopètre a réaction a-t-il un avenir?" *Ar*, 54: 206–7, 209.

"A propòs de l'hélicoptère a réaction," *Ar*, 55: 57.

1950

"Flexi-calculateur Herrera pour intégrales et fonctions elliptiques," *GC*, 127: 174–75.

"Flexi-calculateur pour intégrales et fonctions elliptiques, son application au calcul de la 'courbe de l'claireur,'" *Comptes Rendus de l'Académie des Sciences*, 230: 1134–36.

"Les bombes a hydrogène," *GC*, 127: 189–92.

1952

"Le double coup de canon de la vitesse transsonique," *GC*, 129: 435.

Comment echapper a la mort atomique. Paris: C.M.P. [with Lt. Col. Callard].

1953

"Abaque à points alignés pour le calcul de la vitesse dans une soufflerie par la formule de Saint Venant," *GC*, 130: 71–72 [with Gabriel Viguier].

1956

"La découverte et les possibilités de l'antiproton: La bombe photonique," *GC*, 133: 7–10.
"Les satellites artificiels," *GC*, 133: 184–91.
"Les possibilités de lancement d'un satellite artificiel français," *GC*, 133: 349–55.
"Le neutrino, dernier corpuscule atomique connu," *GC*, 133: 393–98.

1957

"Vers la vitesse de libération d'un projectile par la trajectoire AC_n," *GC*, 134: 374–78.

1958

"Le probléme de la trajectoire des fusées intercontinentales," *GC*, 135: 1–7.

1959

"Les conditions de lancement d'un projectile vers la lune," *GC*, 136: 1–9.
"Les satellites artificiels et la résistance de l'air," *GC*, 136: 304–7.
"Le point de chute de Lunik II sur la lune," *GC*, 136: 421–22.

1961

"Le probléme des trois corps et l'astronomique," *GC*, 138: 34–37.
"Les primers hommes de l'espace," *GC*, 138: 303–4.
"L'anneau artificiel lancé par un satellite autour de la terre," *GC*, 138.

1962

"Remarques sur la catastrophe du Boeing 707 'Chateau de Sully,'" *GC*, 139: 366–67.

1963

"La vitesse de la lumière par rapport au corps en mouvement," *GC*, 140: 262–64.
"L'Univers de Descartes,: *GC*, 140: 280–82, 308–11, 327–29, 352–55, 477–78.

1965

"Le scaphandre de l'espace," *Ingenieurs et Techniciens*, #189 (July-August): 44–46.

Index